FROM MYCENAE TO OLYMPUS

TRACING THE EVOLUTION OF GREEK RELIGION

M.L. RUSCSAK

Olympian Echoes: A Comprehensive Study of Ancient Greek Religion

Trient Press
3375 S Rainbow Blvd
#81710, SMB 13135
Las Vegas,NV 89180

Ordering Information:
Quantity sales. Special discounts are available on quantity purchases by corporations, associations, and others. For details, contact the publisher at the address above.
Orders by U.S. trade bookstores and wholesalers. Please contact Trient Press: Tel: (775) 996-3844; or visit www.trientpress.com.

Printed in the United States of America

Publisher's Cataloging-in-Publication data
Ruscsak, M.L.
A title of a book : From Mycenae to Olympus: Tracing the Evolution of Greek Religion

ISBN
Hard Cover   979-8-88990-135-8

Paper Back   979-8-88990-136-5

Ebook   979-8-88990-137-2

Other books of the "Olympian Echoes: A Comprehensive Study of Ancient Greek Religion" Series

Book 1 : From Mycenae to Olympus: Tracing the Evolution of Greek Religion

Book 2 : Of Sky, Sea, and Grove: The Pantheon of Major and Minor Deities in Greek

Book 3: Sacred Celebrations and Prophetic Voices: The Vibrant Heart of Greek

Book 4: The Divine Palette: The Influence of Greek Religion on Art and Literature

Book 5: Shadows of Olympus: The Decline, Transformation, and Unfading Impact of Greek Religion

From Mycenae to Olympus: Tracing the Evolution of Greek Religion

Part 1 - Introduction

Part 2 - Origins and Evolution

Forward

In the study of 'The Sacred Journey: Exploring Ancient Spiritual Traditions and their Influence on Modern Religions', we set forth on an epic expedition, retracing the indelible imprints of ancient spiritual practices on our contemporary religious tapestry. At this juncture, the book 'From Mycenae to Olympus: Tracing the Evolution of Greek Religion' serves as a critical portal into the Hellenic realm, initiating an exploration into the complexities of Greek religious practices and their lasting impacts.

'From Mycenae to Olympus' sets the stage for this exploration. It uncovers the intricate weavings of history, culture, and spirituality that define the Greek religious landscape, from the early Mycenaean civilization to the towering deities of Mount Olympus. This exploration, however, is not an end in itself. The book forms a pivotal layer of a broader academic investigation and will be enriched and expanded upon in companion textbooks, lectures, and stimulating class discussions throughout this course.

The course, in its entirety, is a symphony of diverse sources and methodologies. Ranging from sacred texts and archaeological artefacts to historical accounts and philosophical discourses, each medium contributes a unique note to the composition. By cultivating a critical approach towards these sources, students are empowered to discern patterns, identify shared motifs, and highlight distinctive elements in the religious tapestry.

This journey, while academically rigorous, is also one of introspection and self-discovery. Engaging with the plurality of religious experiences necessitates wrestling with interpretive challenges, understanding cultural contexts, and accounting for historical contingencies. The resultant discourse, vibrant with counterarguments and dissenting views, fosters not just academic growth, but a holistic maturation of thought and perspective.

Embarking on this enlightening journey will demand intellectual perseverance, but it assures a wealth of knowledge and insight. Through the lens of our spiritual heritage, we can better comprehend the multifaceted forces shaping our world today, fostering a more profound sense of our place within the grand narrative of history.

As we set forth on this sacred journey, I encourage you to approach it with an open mind and an inquisitive spirit. Every participant will bring their unique viewpoint, enriching our collective understanding. Let this be a voyage of not just intellectual exploration, but also of personal growth and revelation. Together, we will decode the enigmas of the past, address the questions of the present, and perhaps, glimpse the potentialities of the future.

Welcome to 'The Sacred Journey: Exploring Ancient Spiritual Traditions and their Influence on Modern Religions'. Guided by 'From Mycenae to Olympus' and the layered depths of our collective inquiry, may this shared exploration challenge, inspire, and transform you.

Chapter 1: Introduction to Ancient Greek Religion

Ancient Greek religion was characterized by a polytheistic belief system, wherein multiple gods and goddesses held sway over various aspects of the natural and human realms. This multifaceted theological structure played a pivotal role in shaping the religious and cultural fabric of ancient Greek society. The concept of polytheism allowed for a diverse pantheon of deities, each with their own distinct personalities, powers, and responsibilities.

The significance of polytheism in ancient Greek religion extended beyond mere belief; it permeated all facets of life, including politics, ethics, and arts. The pantheon of gods and goddesses represented an array of human emotions, virtues, and vices, making them relatable and providing a moral compass for individuals and communities.

The Pantheon of Gods and Goddesses

At the heart of ancient Greek religion were the Olympian gods and goddesses, who resided atop Mount Olympus. Among them were Zeus, the mighty king of the gods; Athena, the wise goddess of wisdom and warfare; Apollo, the radiant god of music and poetry; and Aphrodite, the alluring goddess of love and beauty. Each deity played a crucial role in the cosmos, shaping natural phenomena, human destinies, and mortal endeavors.

These divine figures were far from mere abstractions; they were anthropomorphic, embodying human traits and emotions, which lent them an approachability not found in other religious systems. Their relationships with mortals were both benevolent and capricious, and their stories depicted the complexities of the human condition.

Mythology as a Window to Belief

Greek mythology served as the bedrock of religious beliefs, providing narratives that explained the creation of the world, the origins of gods, and the destinies of heroes and mortals alike. These myths not only entertained but also served as a medium to transmit moral lessons and cultural values.

The stories of heroes such as Hercules and Odysseus demonstrated qualities such as bravery, cunning, and loyalty, inspiring ancient Greeks to emulate these virtues in their own lives. Additionally, myths like the tale of Prometheus showcased the complexities of divine-human interactions and raised questions about fate, free will, and the balance between divine authority and human agency.

By analyzing and interpreting these myths, we gain insights into the worldview of the ancient Greeks and their perceptions of the divine and the human realms. Furthermore, exploring the symbolic and allegorical elements of these narratives enriches our understanding of the multifaceted religious tapestry that influenced ancient Greek society.

Ancient Greek Religious Practices

Ancient Greek religious practices encompassed a wide array of rituals, ceremonies, and observances that connected mortals with the divine. Sacrifices, offerings, and prayers were key components of these rituals, aimed at appeasing the gods, seeking their favor, or expressing gratitude. These acts of devotion were conducted in temples, sanctuaries, and sacred groves, where the physical and spiritual worlds intertwined.

Religious festivals played a significant role in ancient Greek life, with events such as the Olympic Games, the Panathenaea, and the Dionysia serving as occasions for communal celebration and reverence. These festivals not only honored specific deities but also fostered a sense of unity and identity among the city-states and their citizens.

Moreover, oracles and divination practices were integral to seeking guidance from the gods. Sites like the Oracle of Delphi held immense influence, and their prophetic pronouncements often shaped major political decisions and personal choices.

Through a comprehensive examination of these religious practices, we can grasp the profound impact of ancient Greek religion on the daily lives and collective consciousness of its adherents. Understanding these rituals and their underlying beliefs allows us to appreciate the enduring cultural legacy of ancient Greece and its relevance in the study of human history and spirituality.

Understanding Polytheism and its Significance

In the tapestry of ancient Greek religion, the foundational principle that underpinned the entire belief system was polytheism. Derived from the Greek words "poly" (meaning "many") and "theos" (meaning "god"), polytheism refers to the veneration and worship of multiple gods and goddesses. This concept stood in stark contrast to monotheistic religious systems, where a single deity reigns supreme.

Polytheism offered a unique lens through which the ancient Greeks perceived and interacted with the divine. Unlike a monotheistic god, who might be seen as omnipotent and omniscient, each deity in the Greek pantheon possessed specific powers and dominions. These gods were both anthropomorphic and transcendent, embodying human-like traits while wielding cosmic authority.

The significance of polytheism extended beyond theological beliefs; it was interwoven with the fabric of ancient Greek society and culture. Gods and goddesses were not distant and aloof figures but relatable beings whose actions, emotions, and relationships mirrored human experiences. Their myths and stories, passed down through generations, served as allegorical tales that shed light on human nature, moral dilemmas, and the complexities of life.

Through their worship of various deities, the ancient Greeks sought to navigate the multifaceted tapestry of existence. Each god offered blessings, protection, or guidance in specific domains, ranging from war and wisdom to love and fertility. Citizens turned to Athena for wisdom in state affairs, invoked Poseidon for safe voyages, and implored Aphrodite for matters of the heart.

The polytheistic framework also afforded a sense of interconnectedness with the natural world. Gods and goddesses were associated with natural elements, such as the sea, the sun, and the harvest, underscoring the ancient Greeks' profound reverence for nature and its divine manifestations.

Moreover, polytheism fostered a communal and inclusive religious experience. Citizens from different city-states could find common ground in the shared veneration of certain deities during religious festivals and ceremonies. The pantheon united the diverse Greek communities, creating a sense of identity and cohesion.

By embracing polytheism, the ancient Greeks cultivated a rich tapestry of religious expression that found its way into every aspect of their lives. The intricate interplay of gods, myths, and rituals shaped their art, literature, ethics, politics, and spirituality. This multifaceted belief system resonated with the ancient Greeks, guiding them through the complexities of existence and offering profound insights into the human condition.

As we embark on a comprehensive exploration of ancient Greek religion, it is vital to grasp the fundamental significance of polytheism as the guiding principle of this intricate tapestry. Through this understanding, we can delve deeper into the multifaceted world of the gods and goddesses, their interactions with mortals, and the enduring cultural legacy that still echoes in the modern world.

Class Exercises for Critical Thinking and Discussion

Reflect on the key differences between polytheistic and monotheistic religious systems. How might these differences have influenced the respective cultures' worldviews and societal structures?

Explore examples of anthropomorphism in the representation of gods and goddesses in ancient Greek art and literature. How does the humanization of divine beings enhance their relatability and significance in religious practices?

Consider the role of nature and natural elements in the Greek pantheon. How might the association of gods with specific natural phenomena have contributed to the ancient Greeks' reverence for the environment?

Discuss the concept of syncretism in the context of ancient Greek religion. How did the assimilation of foreign deities and beliefs shape the evolving pantheon and religious practices?

Analyze the ways in which myths served as narratives of moral lessons and cultural values for ancient Greeks. Provide examples of myths that exemplify particular virtues or philosophical concepts.

Problems

Investigate how specific deities were worshipped in different city-states, and identify any regional variations in their attributes and cult practices.

Research the ways in which ancient Greek religion influenced the architectural design and artistic representations of temples and sanctuaries.

Definition and characteristics of polytheism in the context of ancient Greek religion

Polytheism, an integral facet of ancient Greek religion, is a theological construct centered on the belief in and veneration of multiple gods and goddesses. Rooted in the Greek words "poly" (meaning "many") and "theos" (meaning "god"), polytheism stands in stark contrast to monotheistic systems, where a singular divine entity reigns supreme.

At its core, polytheism embodies a diverse pantheon of deities, each vested with distinct attributes, personalities, and dominions. These gods and goddesses preside over various aspects of the natural world, human affairs, and cosmic forces, forging an intricate celestial hierarchy. The pluralistic nature of the Greek pantheon allows for a multifaceted representation of divine beings, reflecting the intricate tapestry of human experiences.

One of the defining characteristics of ancient Greek polytheism is anthropomorphism. The gods and goddesses are portrayed in human-like forms, endowed with emotions, desires, and flaws. This anthropomorphic quality imbues these divine beings with relatability and familiarity to mortals, bridging the gap between the human and divine realms. Consequently, the gods' actions and interactions with mortals within the myths serve as allegorical tales that resonate with the complexities of the human condition.

Furthermore, Greek polytheism lacks a strict, centralized dogma or doctrinal framework. While the Olympian deities occupy a central position in the pantheon, there exist numerous local deities, lesser gods, and nature spirits that hold significance in various regions and communities. This decentralized structure allows for a diverse array of religious expressions, rituals, and cult practices across different city-states and regions.

The gods' influence permeates every aspect of ancient Greek life. Their patronage extends to diverse domains, including war, wisdom, love, agriculture, and craftsmanship. As such, individuals and communities turn to specific deities for guidance, protection, and blessings, seeking favor in different aspects of their lives.

Moreover, ancient Greek polytheism exhibits a dynamic and interactive relationship between mortals and gods. Through rituals, sacrifices, and festivals, adherents engage in reciprocal exchanges with the divine, offering devotion in exchange for divine favor and protection. Temples, sanctuaries, and sacred spaces serve as conduits for this communion, allowing individuals to express reverence and seek divine guidance.

Counterarguments to polytheism often stem from the perceived challenges in reconciling the multiplicity of gods and their varying attributes. Critics may question the coherence of a system that encompasses gods with diverse, sometimes conflicting, roles and personalities. Additionally, the perceived anthropomorphism of the divine may raise debates about the gods' transcendence and the implications of human-like traits in divine beings.

However, proponents of polytheism argue that its diversity and flexibility allowed for a rich tapestry of religious expression and cultural dynamism. The decentralized nature of the pantheon accommodated local beliefs and fostered a sense of community identity within individual city-states. Moreover, the gods' multifaceted nature captured the multifarious dimensions of human life, offering solace, guidance, and inspiration in various aspects of existence.

Understanding the definition and characteristics of polytheism within the context of ancient Greek religion is essential for exploring the complex religious beliefs, practices, and interactions between mortals and the divine. This foundational knowledge forms the basis for a comprehensive exploration of the pantheon of gods and goddesses, the myths that elucidate their nature, and the religious practices that shaped the lives of the ancient Greeks.

Class Exercises for Critical Thinking and Discussion

Reflect on the unique characteristics of Greek polytheism and compare them to those of other ancient polytheistic religions. What common themes and differences emerge across various polytheistic belief systems?

Discuss the significance of anthropomorphism in the representation of gods and goddesses in ancient Greek religion. How might this characteristic have influenced the Greeks' perception of the divine and their religious practices?

Explore the implications of a decentralized religious system in ancient Greek society. How did the absence of a central religious authority contribute to the diversity and adaptability of Greek religious beliefs and practices?

Engage in a debate about the challenges and benefits of polytheism versus monotheism. What are the strengths and limitations of each theological framework in understanding the complexities of human spirituality and the divine?

Problems

Investigate the regional variations in cult practices and deities across different ancient Greek city-states. Analyze how the local cults contributed to the cultural identity of specific communities.

Compare and contrast the portrayal of gods and goddesses in ancient Greek art and literature. How do these representations reflect the religious significance and cultural values attributed to divine beings?

Comparing and contrasting polytheism with other religious systems

In the vast tapestry of human religious beliefs, polytheism stands as one of the most ancient and prevalent forms of theological expression. While monotheism, atheism, and other religious systems also hold significance across human history, understanding the unique characteristics of polytheism and comparing them to these alternative frameworks sheds light on the diverse ways in which human societies have sought to comprehend the divine and the cosmos.

Polytheism: The Multifaceted Divinity

At the heart of ancient Greek religion lies the theological construct of polytheism, a system that embraces a pantheon of multiple gods and goddesses, each possessing distinct domains and attributes. Among the various civilizations that employed polytheism, the ancient Greek religion stands as a prime exemplar, offering a rich tapestry of divine beings, myths, and religious practices.

✧ The Diverse Pantheon of Gods and Goddesses

Within the Greek pantheon, a vibrant assembly of gods and goddesses claimed their celestial roles, each presiding over specific aspects of the natural world, human existence, and cosmic forces. At the helm of this multifaceted divinity stood Zeus, the formidable king of the gods, whose dominion extended over thunder, sky, and governance. Athena, the wise and strategic goddess, held sway over wisdom, warfare, and the arts, while Poseidon governed the seas and tides with his tempestuous might. Additionally, gods such as Aphrodite embodied love and beauty, Hermes symbolized communication and travel, and Demeter governed fertility and agriculture.

The gods, though powerful and immortal, did not embody the characteristics of omnipotence or omniscience typically attributed to a singular, all-encompassing deity. Instead, they personified distinct aspects of the cosmos and human life, collectively forming a pantheon that mirrored the complexities of existence.

✧ Anthropomorphism: Bridging the Divine and the Human

A defining characteristic of the Greek pantheon was its anthropomorphic portrayal of gods and goddesses. Divine beings were depicted in human-like forms, often adorned with emotions, virtues, and vices. This anthropomorphic quality served to humanize the gods, making them accessible and relatable to mortals. The gods' emotions and actions mirrored those of humans, blurring the boundaries between the divine and human spheres.

For instance, in the myth of Demeter and Persephone, the grief-stricken mother goddess Demeter experiences the anguish of losing her daughter, Persephone, to the Underworld. This emotional resonance allowed ancient Greeks to connect with the gods on a personal and emotional level, fostering a sense of empathy and understanding of their divine attributes.

✧ The Rich Tapestry of Divine Myths

The multifaceted divinity of the Greek pantheon is woven into a rich tapestry of myths, narratives that delve into the interactions between gods and mortals. These myths serve as allegorical tales, presenting moral lessons, cultural values, and philosophical insights.

In the tale of Prometheus, the Titan god who defied Zeus to grant humanity the gift of fire, ancient Greeks grappled with the concepts of divine authority and the consequences of human ambition. The myth of Pandora's box explored the complexities of human curiosity and the unpredictable outcomes of choices.

Exercises for Critical Thinking and Discussion

Analyze the characteristics and roles of a specific deity from the Greek pantheon and consider the impact of this god or goddess on human life and culture.

Compare the portrayal of gods and goddesses in Greek mythology with those in other polytheistic belief systems, such as the deities of Norse mythology or Hinduism. How do these depictions reflect the cultures' values and worldviews?

Engage in a discussion about the potential benefits and challenges of anthropomorphism in religious representations. How might this characteristic influence the perception of the divine and its role in human life?

Problems

Research the architectural features and artistic representations of temples dedicated to specific gods or goddesses in ancient Greece. How did the design and artwork of these sacred spaces reflect the characteristics and domains of the deities they honored?

Explore the concept of divine patronage and the worship of gods in specific city-states. How did the choice of a city's patron deity influence its cultural identity and religious practices?

The multifaceted divinity of ancient Greek polytheism underscores the intricate interplay between the human and the divine. Through anthropomorphic portrayals and mythological narratives, the gods became figures of relatability, influencing the moral and philosophical dimensions of ancient Greek society. By immersing ourselves in this rich tapestry of religious beliefs and divine interactions, we gain insights into the profound questions of existence and human nature that have captivated human societies throughout history.

Monotheism: The Singular Divine Authority

In stark contrast to the multifaceted divinity of polytheism, monotheism emerges as a distinct religious system centered on the belief in a singular, all-encompassing divine entity. Within the broader spectrum of monotheistic traditions, prominent religions such as Judaism, Christianity, and Islam hold the monotheistic God as the supreme being, representing the source and sustainer of the universe.

❖　The Omnipotent Creator and Sustainer

The monotheistic God, often described as omnipotent, possesses boundless power, having created and governing the entire cosmos. In monotheism, the divine is not limited to specific attributes or domains, but rather, it encompasses all aspects of existence. This concept of an all-powerful deity presents an ultimate unifying force, serving as the foundation of creation itself.

❖　The Omniscient and Transcendent Nature

Furthermore, the monotheistic God is attributed with omniscience, possessing infinite knowledge of all that exists. In this divine omniscience, the singular deity is aware of the past, present, and future, offering adherents a profound sense of divine providence and guidance.

Moreover, the monotheistic God is perceived as transcendent, existing beyond the material realm and beyond human comprehension. This transcendence underscores the incomprehensible nature of the divine, leading to a sense of awe and reverence among believers.

❖　The Source of Moral Authority

Central to the monotheistic worldview is the concept of the divine as the ultimate moral authority. Unlike the pantheon of gods in polytheism, who may embody specific virtues and vices, the monotheistic God serves as the source of absolute morality. Divine commandments, sacred scriptures, and prophetic revelations provide adherents with ethical guidance and a moral framework for their lives.

For instance, in the Abrahamic tradition of Judaism, the Ten Commandments, revealed to Moses on Mount Sinai, form the cornerstone of ethical conduct and social order. Similarly, in Christianity, the teachings of Jesus Christ, as recorded in the New Testament, offer moral guidance and principles for leading a virtuous life.

✦ Divine Revelations and Sacred Scriptures

In monotheistic religions, divine revelations and sacred scriptures serve as the means through which adherents access the divine will and ethical guidance. These scriptures contain religious texts that are considered authoritative and carry profound significance in the faith's doctrinal beliefs and practices.

For example, the Quran in Islam is believed to be the word of God as revealed to the Prophet Muhammad. It serves as a comprehensive guide for personal conduct, governance, and spiritual enlightenment. Similarly, the Bible, comprising the Old and New Testaments, holds immense importance for Christians, containing narratives of divine interventions, moral teachings, and prophecies.

Exercises for Critical Thinking and Discussion

Engage in a debate on the concept of divine omniscience in monotheistic traditions. How does the belief in an all-knowing deity impact human free will and moral responsibility?

Investigate the role of religious prophets in monotheistic faiths. Compare and contrast the significance of prophetic revelations in shaping religious doctrines and practices.

Discuss the potential challenges and benefits of a singular, all-encompassing divine entity in monotheism. How might this theological framework impact religious unity and diversity of thought?

Problems

Explore historical instances of theological debates within monotheistic religions. Analyze how different interpretations of sacred scriptures have led to diverse sects and denominations.

Research the impact of monotheistic beliefs on the arts, architecture, and cultural expressions of civilizations that embraced these religious systems.

In the embrace of a singular, all-encompassing divine entity, monotheism diverges from the multifaceted divinity of polytheism. The concept of an omnipotent, omniscient, and transcendent God underpins monotheistic beliefs, shaping moral authority, ethical frameworks, and the spiritual lives of its adherents. Understanding the nuances of monotheistic systems allows for a comprehensive appreciation of the diversity and complexity of human religious expression throughout history.
Atheism: Absence of a Divine Belief System

While polytheism and monotheism focus on belief in divine entities, atheism represents the absence of belief in gods or the divine altogether. Atheism encompasses a broad spectrum, from the explicit denial of the existence of gods to a more agnostic perspective that holds no firm belief in a divine presence.

Agnosticism: The Unknowability of the Divine

Amidst the panorama of religious beliefs, agnosticism emerges as a nuanced and contemplative stance concerning the existence of gods or a divine reality. Positioned within the spectrum of religious thought, agnostics adopt an epistemological perspective, asserting that the ultimate nature of the divine lies beyond the grasp of human knowledge. They abstain from definitive affirmations or denials regarding the existence of the supernatural, recognizing the inherent limitations of human understanding in comprehending such ineffable realms.

✧ Embracing Humility: Acknowledging the Boundaries of Human Understanding

Agnosticism embodies a humble recognition of the limitations of human cognition when confronted with the enigmatic concept of the divine. Adherents of this philosophical standpoint accept that the nature of the supernatural realm and its possible manifestations transcend the grasp of human senses, empirical observations, and rational inquiries. In doing so, agnostics refrain from asserting claims based on insufficient evidence or limited human perspectives.

✧ Theological Agnosticism and Existential Agnosticism

Within the framework of agnosticism, two distinct subcategories emerge, namely theological agnosticism and existential agnosticism.

✧ Theological Agnosticism

Theological agnostics adopt a specific stance concerning the existence of gods or a divine being. They maintain that the question of God's existence lies beyond empirical demonstration or conclusive disproof. While theological agnostics do not outright deny the possibility of the divine, they also refrain from endorsing specific religious dogmas that claim definitive knowledge about the nature of the supernatural.

✧ Existential Agnosticism

Existential agnosticism extends beyond the question of the divine to encompass broader existential inquiries. Existential agnostics ponder fundamental questions about the nature of existence, the purpose of life, and the potential afterlife. They acknowledge the uncertainty surrounding such existential inquiries and refrain from embracing rigid dogmas or ideologies that claim to possess absolute answers.

✧ An Intellectual Journey: A Philosophical Approach to the Divine

For agnostics, the journey towards understanding the nature of the divine involves a deep intellectual exploration, contemplation, and humility. This introspective pursuit encourages a critical evaluation of various religious and philosophical perspectives while recognizing the intricacies of human cognition in the face of transcendental questions.

✧ Agnosticism and Ethics

Agnosticism's agnostic perspective on the divine raises questions concerning ethics and morality. In the absence of a definitive religious framework, adherents might turn to secular humanism or philosophical ethics to derive guiding principles for ethical conduct and decision-making. The absence of absolute divine commandments necessitates a reflective engagement with ethical dilemmas and the pursuit of moral principles based on reason, compassion, and empathy.

Exercises for Critical Thinking and Discussion

Engage in a philosophical debate about the strengths and limitations of agnosticism as a stance on the divine. Discuss how agnosticism encourages intellectual humility and open-mindedness in religious inquiry.

Explore the historical development of agnosticism as a philosophical concept. Analyze the contributions of prominent thinkers to the evolution of agnostic thought.

Discuss the potential implications of agnosticism on individual spirituality and the quest for meaning and purpose in life.

Problems

Investigate instances in which agnosticism influenced art, literature, and intellectual movements throughout history. How has agnosticism shaped cultural and intellectual expressions?

Analyze the significance of agnosticism in modern ethical debates, such as those concerning bioethics or environmental ethics.

Agnosticism offers a thought-provoking and introspective stance on the divine, inviting critical engagement with the nature of human knowledge and the complexities of existence. By recognizing the boundaries of human understanding, agnostics engage in a philosophical exploration of the supernatural and embrace intellectual humility in the face of the ineffable. This nuanced perspective encourages students to contemplate fundamental questions about the nature of reality, the divine, and the diverse ways in which human societies grapple with the enigmas of existence.

Comparative Insights: Common Themes and Divergent Notions

Exploring the diverse religious systems allows us to discern common themes and divergent notions across different cultures and historical periods. At the heart of all religious systems lies the human quest for understanding the cosmos, morality, and the purpose of existence. The anthropomorphic portrayal of gods in polytheism reflects humanity's need for relatable divine figures that embody virtues and human traits. Similarly, the search for divine revelation and ethical guidance is evident in both monotheistic religions and some polytheistic traditions.

However, the distinctions between these religious systems are equally profound. While polytheism allows for diverse divine personalities and interactive relationships between gods and humans, monotheism emphasizes the unity and omnipresence of a singular deity. Atheism and agnosticism, in turn, offer perspectives that question or suspend belief in the divine, with varying degrees of certainty about its existence.

Exercises for Critical Thinking and Discussion

Engage in a debate about the merits and limitations of polytheism, monotheism, atheism, and agnosticism as frameworks for understanding the cosmos and human existence. Consider the implications of each system on ethics, society, and culture.

Investigate historical instances of syncretism, where polytheistic and monotheistic beliefs coexisted or blended. Analyze the motivations behind syncretic practices and their impact on religious identities.

Compare the concept of anthropomorphism in different religious traditions. How do the portrayals of gods in polytheism and deities in monotheism differ, and what cultural significance do these representations hold?

Problems

Research the history and impact of monotheistic religions on ancient Greek society. How did the emergence of monotheism influence the religious landscape and cultural dynamics in the Hellenistic period?

Examine the role of skepticism and rationalism in shaping agnostic perspectives on the divine. How have prominent philosophers throughout history contributed to agnostic thought?

By exploring the nuances and complexities of polytheism, monotheism, atheism, and agnosticism, we deepen our understanding of the diverse ways in which human societies have sought meaning, ethics, and spiritual connections. This comparative analysis invites critical thinking, encouraging students to contemplate the profound questions of existence and the varying expressions of religious beliefs across time and cultures.

The Pantheon of Gods and Goddesses

At the heart of ancient Greek religion lies a magnificent and diverse pantheon of gods and goddesses. This intricate assembly of divine beings serves as the foundation of polytheistic beliefs, each deity presiding over specific domains, phenomena, and aspects of human life. The study of the Greek pantheon offers a fascinating exploration into the multifaceted nature of divinity, reflecting the complexities of human existence and the natural world.

An Array of Divine Personalities

The Greek pantheon boasts a diverse array of gods and goddesses, each imbued with distinct personalities and attributes. Among the mighty Olympian gods, Zeus reigns supreme as the king of the gods and the deity of thunder and sky. The wise Athena personifies intellect and strategic warfare, while Apollo embodies music, prophecy, and the arts. Aphrodite, the goddess of love and beauty, evokes sentiments of passion and desire. Meanwhile, gods like Poseidon and Hades govern the seas and the Underworld, respectively, symbolizing the enigmatic forces of nature and the afterlife.

Anthropomorphism: The Divine in Human Form

A defining feature of the Greek pantheon is the anthropomorphic representation of the gods and goddesses. Unlike abstract or animalistic deities, Greek gods are depicted in human-like forms, adorned with emotions, virtues, and flaws. This anthropomorphic quality allows for an intimate and relatable connection between the divine and mortal realms. As a result, the gods' actions and interactions in mythological narratives often parallel human experiences, echoing universal themes of love, jealousy, ambition, and sacrifice.

For instance, the rivalry between the goddesses Hera and Aphrodite for the title of fairest goddess in the myth of the Judgement of Paris reflects the human desire for recognition and validation. Similarly, the love affair between Zeus and the mortal woman Alcmene in the tale of Hercules explores themes of divine intervention and the consequences of mortal-immortal relationships.

Divine Myths: Narratives of the Divine Drama

The Greek pantheon comes to life through an intricate tapestry of myths, captivating narratives that shed light on the gods' personalities, powers, and interactions with mortals. These myths serve as allegorical tales, conveying moral lessons, cultural values, and philosophical insights.

The myth of Demeter and Persephone, for instance, reflects the cycle of seasons and the significance of agriculture in ancient Greek life. The tale of Prometheus stealing fire from the gods to give to humanity touches on themes of rebellion, the balance of power, and the consequences of crossing divine boundaries.

The Divine and Human Interaction

One of the distinguishing features of the Greek pantheon is the interactive relationship between gods and mortals. Unlike distant and aloof deities, Greek gods actively engage with humans, both shaping and intervening in mortal affairs. Mortals seek the gods' favor through rituals, sacrifices, and prayers, hoping to receive blessings and protection in return.

The Greek concept of "xenia" exemplifies the importance of hospitality and the divine-human bond. Guests and hosts exchanged mutual respect and protection, seeking to please the gods through virtuous conduct. Violating the principles of "xenia" could incur the wrath of the gods, as seen in the tragic tale of King Tantalus, whose acts of hubris led to divine punishment.

Exercises for Critical Thinking and Discussion

Analyze the roles and attributes of a specific god or goddess from the Greek pantheon and consider the significance of their domains in ancient Greek society.

Engage in a debate about the nature of anthropomorphism in religious representations. How does the portrayal of gods in human-like forms influence religious practices and cultural identity?

Discuss the moral lessons conveyed through divine myths and their relevance to contemporary ethical dilemmas.

Problems

Research the architectural features and artistic representations of temples dedicated to specific gods or goddesses in ancient Greece. How did the design and artwork of these sacred spaces reflect the characteristics and domains of the deities they honored?

Explore historical instances of divine intervention in the mortal realm as depicted in Greek myths. Discuss the cultural significance of these interactions and their impact on religious beliefs.

The pantheon of gods and goddesses in ancient Greek religion embodies a rich tapestry of divine personalities and mythical narratives. By delving into the multifaceted nature of the Greek pantheon, students gain profound insights into the complexities of human existence, the interplay between the divine and human spheres, and the enduring cultural and philosophical significance of these ancient beliefs. The study of the Greek pantheon opens doors to critical thinking and engaging discussions about the diversity of religious expressions and their impact on human societies across the ages.

Chapter 2 :An in-depth exploration of the major deities in Greek mythology and their domains

Within the pantheon of ancient Greek religion, a captivating array of major deities emerges, each personifying distinct domains and facets of human existence. These gods and goddesses, steeped in rich mythology and cultural significance, not only held influence over natural phenomena but also shaped the moral and social fabric of ancient Greek society.

Titan	Children	Greek God	Children	Demigods
Cronus	Zeus, Hades, Poseidon	Zeus	Athena, Apollo, Artemis, Hermes, and more	Hercules, Perseus, Theseus, etc. (see Demi-Gods)
Rhea	Zeus, Hades, Poseidon	Hades	Melinoe	-
Oceanus	Oceanids	Poseidon	Triton, Polyphemus, and more	-
Tethys	Oceanids	Hestia	-	-
Hyperion	Helios, Selene, Eos	Hera	Hebe	-
Mnemosyne	Muses	Demeter	Persephone	-
Themis	Horae, Moirai	Ares	Eros	-
Coeus	Leto	Athena	-	-
Crius	Astraeus, Pallas	Hermes	Pan	-
Iapetus	Atlas, Prometheus, Epimetheus	Dionysus	-	-

The Titans: Primordial Deities of Ancient Greek Mythology

In the intricate web of ancient Greek mythology, the Titans emerge as the awe-inspiring primordial deities, existing before the era of the Olympian gods. The origins of these powerful beings are rooted in the cosmogonic narrative, which chronicles the creation and formation of the universe.

The Divine Genealogy: Offspring of Gaia and Uranus

According to Greek cosmogony, the Titans were born from the divine union of two foundational entities: Gaia, the embodiment of the Earth, and Uranus, the personification of the Sky. From this sacred union, the Titans emerged as the celestial offspring, representing the very essence of the natural world and the celestial heavens.

The Lineage of the Titans

The lineage of the Titans traces back to the union of Gaia and Uranus. Among the most notable Titans were:

✧ Cronus (Kronos): The Cyclical Ruler of Time and the Divine Struggle

In the intricate tapestry of Greek mythology, Cronus, also known as Kronos, emerges as one of the most illustrious and enigmatic figures among the Titans. As the leader of the divine siblings, Cronus held a prominent position in the cosmic order, representing the concept of time and the cyclical nature of existence. His deeds and actions would reverberate throughout the annals of mythological history, culminating in a daring and pivotal act that set the stage for a divine struggle for power.

✧ The Timeless Ruler: Symbolizing the Cyclical Nature of Life

Cronus was intrinsically tied to the passage of time, embodying the cyclical rhythms that governed the natural world and the mortal realm. Often depicted with a scythe, a symbol of harvest and the cutting of crops, Cronus encapsulated the cyclical nature of life, with each harvest marking the continuous cycle of birth, growth, death, and rebirth. This timeless and eternal aspect of Cronus connected him to the very fabric of existence, establishing him as a deity with cosmic significance.

✧ The Divine Castration: Overthrowing Uranus

The most infamous tale of Cronus revolves around his audacious and treacherous act against his father, Uranus, the Sky. Motivated by a prophecy that foretold his eventual overthrow by one of his own children, Uranus faced an imminent threat to his dominion. In a bold and decisive move, Cronus took it upon himself to challenge his father's authority.

Armed with a sickle fashioned by his mother, Gaia, Cronus ambushed Uranus and castrated him, severing his connection to the divine heavens. This ruthless act of patricide and castration set into motion a tumultuous chain of events, leading to the rise of the Titans to power and the establishment of a new divine order.

✦ The Divine Struggle: The Titanomachy

The audacious act of castration had profound repercussions, as Uranus's severed genitalia fell into the sea, giving birth to the goddess Aphrodite. The divine struggle initiated by Cronus's actions would continue in the form of the Titanomachy, a cataclysmic war between the Titans and the younger generation of gods, the Olympians.

Fueled by his fear of prophecy and driven by a desire to maintain control, Cronus swallowed each of his offspring as they were born, attempting to prevent the prophecy from coming to fruition. However, the cunning of his wife, Rhea, would save their youngest son, Zeus, who would later orchestrate the downfall of the Titans.

Problems

Delve into the concept of time in ancient Greek philosophy and its relation to the symbolism of Cronus. How did philosophers like Plato and Aristotle perceive time in the context of the cyclical nature of the universe?

Analyze the psychological implications of the divine struggle within the Titanomachy. How might the fear of prophecy and the struggle for power impact the psyche of mythical figures like Cronus?

Conclusion

Cronus, the cyclical ruler of time and leader of the Titans, stood at the center of a divine struggle that shaped the course of Greek mythology. His representation of time as both an eternal force and a cyclical phenomenon underscores the ancient Greeks' perception of existence and its enduring patterns. The audacious act of castration and the subsequent Titanomachy illustrate the timeless themes of power, prophecy, and the cyclical nature of the cosmos, themes that continue to resonate in the human psyche across cultures and millennia.

✦ Rhea: The Maternal Figure and Divine Consort

In the intricate pantheon of Greek mythology, Rhea, the sister and consort of Cronus, stands as a prominent and significant figure. Revered for her role as the embodiment of motherhood and fertility, Rhea played a pivotal part in the destiny of the Olympian gods, leaving an indelible mark on the divine order and the course of ancient Greek religion.

❖   The Maternal Figure: Nurturing and Fertility

Rhea's paramount aspect lay in her identity as the maternal figure of the gods. As the daughter of Gaia and Uranus, she inherited the nurturing qualities of the Earth and the generative powers of the heavens. Rhea's association with motherhood and fertility solidified her position as a central deity in ancient Greek religious beliefs, as she was venerated for her ability to nurture and sustain life.

❖   The Mother of the Olympians: Shaping Destiny

Among Rhea's most profound roles was her position as the mother of the Olympian gods. Fated to marry her brother, Cronus, Rhea bore him several children, including Zeus, Hera, Poseidon, Hades, Demeter, and Hestia. These divine offspring would go on to become the dominant generation of gods in Greek mythology, overthrowing the Titans in the Titanomachy and ascending to power on Mount Olympus.

Rhea's significance as a mother was not merely confined to her act of giving birth. In a desperate bid to save her youngest son, Zeus, from the fate of his siblings, whom Cronus swallowed in fear of prophecy, Rhea displayed cunning and resourcefulness. She secretly entrusted Zeus to the care of the nymphs on Mount Ida in Crete, presenting a stone wrapped in swaddling clothes to deceive Cronus.

❖   The Stone of Deception: A Symbol of Sacrifice

The act of replacing Zeus with a stone is a poignant symbol of sacrifice and maternal devotion. Rhea's cunning deception exemplifies the lengths to which a mother would go to protect her child. This selfless act allowed Zeus to grow in secrecy, far from the grasp of his father's tyranny, and to eventually challenge Cronus's reign, leading to the Titanomachy and the establishment of the Olympian pantheon.

Problems

Explore the archetypal representation of motherhood in various mythologies and religions, comparing Rhea's characteristics with other maternal figures, such as Isis in Egyptian mythology or Demeter in Greek mythology.

Investigate the role of goddesses as protectors and nurturers in different ancient cultures and analyze how these roles intersect with broader societal expectations and norms.

Conclusion

Rhea, the maternal figure and consort of Cronus, epitomizes the enduring archetype of motherhood and fertility in ancient Greek mythology. Her pivotal role as the mother of the Olympian gods, and her cunning deception to save Zeus from his father's grasp, highlights the significance of maternal love and sacrifice in shaping the divine order. Rhea's multifaceted character serves as a source of reflection and contemplation on the complexities of motherhood and its portrayal in both mythological narratives and human experiences.

✧   Oceanus: The Personification of the Ever-Flowing Ocean

In the grand tapestry of ancient Greek mythology, Oceanus emerges as a figure of profound significance, symbolizing the boundless and eternal expanse of the ocean. As a primordial deity, Oceanus held a pivotal role in shaping the cosmos, personifying the vast body of water that encircled the world and connecting the realms of the divine and the mortal.

✧   The Primordial Waters: A Cosmic Symbol

Oceanus, the offspring of Gaia and Uranus, stands as one of the Titans, the divine beings who predated the rise of the Olympian gods. His realm, the ocean, serves as a potent symbol of the primeval chaos and the limitless potential from which all existence emerged. In Greek cosmogony, the ocean is both the source of life and a representation of the unknown and the mysterious depths of the universe.

✧   The Majestic Figure: Seated on a Seashell

Described as majestic and powerful, Oceanus is often depicted as a regal figure, seated on a magnificent seashell, floating atop the endless waters. This iconic imagery highlights his dominion over the vast oceanic expanse and evokes a sense of serenity and mystery associated with the seas. Oceanus's connection with seashells, a symbol of the ocean's bounty, underscores his role as the embodiment of the life-giving and nurturing qualities of water.

✧   Oceanus in Myth and Symbolism

In Greek mythology, Oceanus played a vital role in the narratives of creation and the birth of divine beings. As the river that encircled the earth, he served as a boundary between the known world and the unexplored realms beyond. The concept of this vast river surrounding the world is echoed in various mythological traditions across cultures, exemplifying the universal significance of water as a life-giving force.

✧ Exploring Oceanic Spirituality and Ecospirituality

Oceanus's association with the primal waters and the ocean's enduring power finds resonance in modern spiritual practices, such as ecospirituality. The reverence for the natural world and the recognition of its intrinsic value are mirrored in the veneration of Oceanus as the personification of the ocean. This ecological approach to spirituality emphasizes the interconnectedness of all living beings and the need for ecological stewardship.

Problems

Research and analyze the representation of water deities in various cultures and mythologies. Compare and contrast Oceanus with other water deities, such as Tiamat in Babylonian mythology or Varuna in Hindu mythology.

Investigate the significance of water as a symbol in ancient Greek religion and its connection to various rituals and practices in ancient Greek society.

Conclusion

Oceanus, the personification of the ever-flowing ocean, holds a profound place in ancient Greek mythology. As a primordial deity symbolizing the boundless and life-giving waters, Oceanus represents the interconnectedness of all existence and the mysterious depths of the cosmos. His majestic presence and association with water as a symbol of life and creation continue to resonate with modern ecospiritual perspectives, underscoring the enduring relevance of ancient mythological concepts in shaping our understanding of the natural world.

✧ Tethys: The Nurturer of Fresh Waters

In the intricate fabric of ancient Greek mythology, Tethys emerges as a significant figure, personifying the nourishing and life-sustaining qualities of fresh water, with a particular emphasis on rivers and springs. As a primordial deity and the wife of Oceanus, Tethys played a vital role in shaping the natural world and connecting the mortal realm with the divine.

✧ The Essence of Fresh Waters: Rivers and Springs

Tethys's dominion over fresh waters sets her apart from her husband, Oceanus, who represented the vast and unending expanse of the ocean. Instead, her realm encompassed the myriad rivers and springs that crisscrossed the land, quenching the thirst of living beings and irrigating the fertile earth. In this aspect, Tethys became a symbol of the life-giving properties of water, sustaining both human and natural communities.

✧　　　The Maternal Figure: Nurturer and Protector

As the embodiment of the nurturing qualities of fresh waters, Tethys assumed a maternal role in ancient Greek mythology. Her presence as a protective and caring deity was deeply intertwined with the survival and well-being of all living beings that relied on freshwater sources for sustenance. Her benevolence extended to the flora and fauna that thrived along riverbanks and around springs, fostering a harmonious and interconnected relationship between humans and nature.

✧　　　Tethys in Myth and Ritual

In Greek mythology, Tethys's significance extended beyond her role as a deity of freshwater. She was also acknowledged as the mother of the Oceanids, nymphs who personified the various bodies of water. This association further emphasized her maternal qualities, as she presided over a multitude of freshwater realms, each with its unique characteristics and attributes.

Rituals and offerings dedicated to Tethys often sought her blessings for bountiful harvests and the continuous flow of freshwater sources. Communities living along rivers and relying on springs for irrigation and drinking water venerated her, recognizing the profound impact of water on their daily lives.

✧　　　Relevance in Contemporary Ecospirituality

Tethys's embodiment of the nurturing and life-sustaining properties of freshwater finds relevance in modern ecospiritual perspectives. The veneration of water as a precious and essential resource mirrors the ancient reverence for Tethys and her role in maintaining ecological balance. Contemporary rituals and practices centered around water conservation and the protection of freshwater sources echo the enduring influence of this primordial deity.

Problems

Investigate the role of freshwater deities in other mythological traditions and cultures. Compare and contrast Tethys with deities associated with rivers and springs in different pantheons.

Explore the historical significance of rivers and springs in ancient Greek society and their impact on agriculture, trade, and cultural practices.

Conclusion

Tethys, the nurturing and life-sustaining deity of fresh waters, holds a significant place in ancient Greek mythology. Her association with rivers and springs highlights the vital role of freshwater in sustaining life and fostering harmony between humans and nature. As a maternal figure and protector, Tethys exemplifies the interconnectedness of all living beings with the natural world. In modern times, her representation finds resonance in ecospiritual perspectives, underscoring the enduring relevance of ancient mythological concepts in shaping our understanding of environmental stewardship and the importance of freshwater conservation.

✧ Hyperion: The Luminous God of the Sun

In the annals of ancient Greek mythology, Hyperion ascends as a prominent deity closely associated with the celestial luminary, the Sun. Revered for his embodiment of radiant brilliance and celestial splendor, Hyperion assumed the role of the god of light, illuminating the heavens and inspiring awe among mortals and immortals alike.

✧ The Radiant Brilliance of the Sun

Hyperion's preeminence as a solar deity originates from his intimate connection with the Sun, the celestial body that graces the heavens with its radiant light. As the god of light, Hyperion heralded the dawn, signaling the commencement of a new day as the Sun ascended the sky, casting its warm rays upon the world below. His divine essence radiated the essence of celestial luminosity, and ancient Greeks perceived him as a symbol of hope, enlightenment, and the cyclical nature of time.

✧ Hyperion in Cosmic Context

Beyond his association with the Sun, Hyperion also symbolized the celestial grandeur and cosmic order of the heavens. His divine presence was intertwined with the broader cosmological framework, aligning with the cosmic principles of light and darkness, day and night. In this cosmic context, Hyperion represented the eternal dance between celestial forces that governed the heavens and shaped the earthly realm.

✧ Solar Symbolism and Ancient Rituals

The worship of Hyperion and the reverence for the Sun held significant importance in ancient Greek religious practices. Sun-worship was prevalent in various cultures, as the Sun's life-giving properties were essential for agricultural fertility, navigation, and seasonal cycles. Rituals and festivals dedicated to Hyperion often sought to invoke his benevolence, requesting abundant harvests, protection from darkness, and the perpetuation of life through the Sun's nourishing rays.

✧   Hyperion in Mythology and Art

While Hyperion's presence in Greek mythology is not as extensive as some other deities, he is referenced in ancient literary works and art. His lineage as a Titan, the son of Gaia and Uranus, places him within the primordial hierarchy of divine beings that preceded the Olympian gods. His depiction in ancient art often portrays him as a radiant figure with celestial attributes, embodying the magnificence of the Sun's light.

✧   Relevance in Modern Perspectives

In contemporary contexts, the symbolism of Hyperion as a solar deity continues to hold significance in various spiritual and philosophical frameworks. Concepts of enlightenment, illumination, and the cyclical nature of life find resonance in the archetypal figure of Hyperion. In neo-pagan and new age beliefs, the Sun is often revered as a symbol of spiritual awakening, guiding individuals on their personal journeys of self-discovery and transformation.

Problems

Investigate the significance of solar deities in other ancient civilizations and explore the common themes and symbols associated with them.

Analyze the representation of the Sun in art and literature from different historical periods, noting the variations in its symbolism and cultural interpretations.

Conclusion

Hyperion, the illustrious god of the Sun, occupies a distinguished place in ancient Greek mythology, representing the radiant brilliance of the celestial luminary. As a solar deity, Hyperion embodies the essence of light and its significance in the cosmic order. His portrayal in ancient art and rituals showcases the reverence for the Sun's life-giving properties and its impact on agricultural fertility and seasonal cycles. In contemporary contexts, the symbolism of Hyperion endures, evoking themes of enlightenment, cosmic order, and spiritual awakening, resonating with diverse spiritual and philosophical perspectives.

✧   Mnemosyne: The Divine Embodiment of Memory and Oral Tradition

In the vast pantheon of ancient Greek mythology, Mnemosyne assumes a significant role as the personification of memory and remembrance. Revered as one of the Titans, the primordial deities that predate the Olympian gods, Mnemosyne's divine essence emanates from her intimate connection to the profound human faculty of memory. As the goddess of memory, she stands as a pivotal figure associated with oral tradition, storytelling, and the preservation of cultural heritage.

✧   Memory as the Foundation of Human Consciousness

Mnemosyne's significance extends to the very fabric of human consciousness. Memory, in its multifaceted forms, constitutes a fundamental aspect of human cognition, enabling individuals to retain, recall, and reconstruct past experiences, knowledge, and emotions. In ancient Greek thought, memory was regarded as a potent mental faculty that underpinned learning, wisdom, and the continuity of cultural heritage across generations.

✧   The Art of Oral Tradition and Storytelling

Mnemosyne's divine realm intertwines with the art of oral tradition and storytelling. In the absence of widespread literacy during ancient times, oral storytelling served as the primary means of transmitting knowledge, history, myths, and cultural values from one generation to another. Skilled storytellers, or bards, would recite epic tales, heroic deeds, and sacred myths, passing down the collective wisdom of the past to ensure the preservation of cultural identity.

✧   Mnemosyne and the Muses

The nine Muses, the daughters of Mnemosyne, epitomized the creative inspirations and artistic endeavors that emanate from the realm of memory. Each Muse represented various artistic domains, such as poetry, music, dance, and history. The Muses, in their collaborative roles, fostered the creative and intellectual endeavors of humanity, bestowing their gifts upon poets, musicians, and scholars alike.

✧   The Relevance of Mnemosyne in Contemporary Contexts

In contemporary perspectives, the significance of Mnemosyne and memory remains pertinent in fields such as psychology, neurology, and cultural studies. Memory, as a subject of scientific inquiry, continues to intrigue scholars seeking to unravel its intricacies and cognitive processes. Additionally, in the digital age, debates arise concerning the potential impact of technology on human memory, as individuals increasingly rely on external devices for information storage and retrieval.

Problems

Investigate the role of oral tradition and storytelling in preserving cultural heritage in other ancient civilizations, such as Mesopotamia, Egypt, or the indigenous cultures of the Americas.

Explore the relationship between memory and identity formation in the context of cultural assimilation and diaspora.

Conclusion

Mnemosyne, the venerable goddess of memory and remembrance, epitomizes the profound significance of memory in the human experience. Linked to the art of oral tradition and storytelling, Mnemosyne and her daughters, the Muses, played a pivotal role in preserving cultural heritage and fostering creativity across generations. The relevance of memory extends beyond ancient Greek mythology, encompassing diverse disciplines such as psychology, neurology, and contemporary debates on the impact of technology on human cognition. As students delve into the realm of Mnemosyne, they gain insights into the power of memory as a foundational aspect of human consciousness and cultural continuity.

✧   Themis: The Divine Embodiment of Order, Law, and Justice

In the intricate tapestry of ancient Greek mythology, Themis commands a paramount position as the embodiment of divine order, law, and justice. Revered as one of the primordial deities, the Titans, Themis represents an immutable and cosmic force that upholds the intricate balance of the universe. As the personification of natural and moral order, Themis plays a pivotal role in shaping the fabric of existence and guiding human affairs towards equity and righteousness.

✧   The Cosmic Harmony of Themis

Themis presides over the cosmic harmony that governs the heavens and the earthly realm. Her domain encompasses the celestial laws that regulate the movements of celestial bodies, the changing seasons, and the ebb and flow of natural phenomena. The constancy of these cosmic laws reflects the inherent wisdom and balance in the grand design of the universe.

✧   The Moral Order and Divine Justice

Beyond the celestial realm, Themis is venerated for her role in establishing and maintaining the moral order that governs human conduct. As the guardian of divine justice, she embodies the principles of fairness, accountability, and ethical rectitude. Her impartiality in meting out judgments ensures that wrongdoings are duly punished, and virtuous deeds are justly rewarded.

✧   Themis and Oracle at Delphi

The oracle at Delphi, one of the most renowned sanctuaries in ancient Greece, holds a significant connection to Themis. The sanctuary served as a sacred conduit through which Themis transmitted her divine wisdom and prophecies. Consulted by kings, leaders, and individuals seeking guidance, the oracle played a critical role in shaping political decisions and determining the outcome of significant events.

✧   Themis and the Birth of Law

Themis also symbolizes the origin of human law and legal systems. The establishment of just and equitable laws was attributed to her divine influence. Her connection to the concept of "Themistes" represents the collective traditions and customs that formed the foundation of ancient Greek legal practices.

✧   The Relevance of Themis in Modern Society

The principles embodied by Themis, such as justice, fairness, and the rule of law, continue to resonate in contemporary legal systems and societies worldwide. The concept of justice as an objective and impartial arbiter remains a fundamental pillar in ensuring the integrity and stability of judicial systems.

Problems

Analyze the portrayal of justice and law in different cultural and religious traditions, such as the concept of "Dharma" in Hinduism or "Ma'at" in ancient Egyptian beliefs.

Investigate the representation of Themis or similar deities in other ancient civilizations and explore the similarities and differences in their roles as embodiments of order and justice.

Conclusion

Themis, the divine embodiment of order, law, and justice, stands as a guiding force that shapes the cosmos and human affairs. Her role as a cosmic harmonizer and the guardian of moral order has enduring relevance, not only in ancient Greek mythology but also in the foundations of human legal systems and concepts of justice in modern society. The study of Themis and her significance stimulates critical reflection on the timeless principles of equity, impartiality, and ethical conduct that continue to shape human civilizations.

✧   Coeus: The Celestial Embodiment of Intellect and Rationality

In the rich tapestry of ancient Greek mythology, Coeus occupies a prominent position as a Titan associated with intellect and rationality. Revered as one of the primordial deities, the Titans, Coeus personifies the profound and inquisitive nature of the human mind. As the celestial embodiment of intellect, he plays a vital role in inspiring curiosity, questioning, and the pursuit of knowledge.

✧   The Titan of Intellectual Inquiry

Coeus's domain centers on the realm of intellectual inquiry and the relentless quest for understanding. He represents the innate human curiosity that drives individuals to explore the mysteries of the cosmos, unravel the complexities of nature, and seek insights into the human condition. As the embodiment of rationality, Coeus encourages the use of reason, logic, and critical thinking to discern truth and enlightenment.

✧   Coeus and the Pursuit of Wisdom

The pursuit of wisdom and knowledge was closely linked to Coeus's influence. In Greek culture, wisdom, often associated with the goddess Athena, held significant value and was regarded as a virtue to be admired and sought after. Coeus's connection to wisdom resonates with the idea that intellectual exploration leads to a deeper understanding of oneself and the world.

✧   The Relevance of Coeus in Modern Education

The principles embodied by Coeus have profound implications in the realm of education. Encouraging the questioning and inquisitive nature of students fosters a dynamic learning environment that stimulates critical thinking and the cultivation of well-informed perspectives. Emphasizing rationality and the application of logical reasoning equips individuals with the tools to make informed decisions and solve complex problems.

✧   Coeus and Philosophical Traditions

Coeus's association with intellect aligns with the traditions of ancient Greek philosophy, which birthed renowned thinkers such as Socrates, Plato, and Aristotle. These philosophers sought to explore the fundamental questions of existence, morality, and knowledge. Coeus's influence can be seen as a precursor to the philosophical inquiries that have shaped Western intellectual thought.

Problems

Analyze the depiction of rationality and intellectual pursuit in different mythological traditions and explore how these deities or figures influenced human endeavors in different societies.

Compare Coeus's attributes with those of other deities associated with knowledge and wisdom in various cultural and religious contexts.

Conclusion

Coeus, the celestial embodiment of intellect and rationality, exemplifies the profound curiosity and inquisitiveness inherent in human nature. As a patron of intellectual inquiry, Coeus encourages the pursuit of wisdom and knowledge, fostering critical thinking and rationality. His influence extends beyond ancient Greek mythology, resonating with the principles that underpin education and philosophical traditions in various societies. The study of Coeus and his attributes ignites a deeper understanding of the human thirst for knowledge and the timeless value of intellectual exploration.

The Titanomachy: The Epic Clash of the Titans and Olympians

The ascent of the Olympian gods marked a pivotal turning point in ancient Greek mythology. The Titans, led by Cronus, initially ruled over the cosmos. However, fearing a prophecy that one of his children would overthrow him, Cronus devoured his offspring. Zeus, the youngest and most cunning of the children, escaped this fate, and with the help of his mother Rhea and the assistance of the Cyclopes and Hecatoncheires, he eventually dethroned Cronus and the Titans in a tumultuous battle known as the Titanomachy.

The Reign of the Olympians and the Legacy of the Titans

The victory of the Olympians established Zeus as the king of the gods and ruler of Mount Olympus. The Olympian pantheon, which included deities like Athena, Apollo, Hera, and Poseidon, became the dominant divine order in ancient Greek religion.

Though overthrown, the Titans continued to hold a place in Greek mythology, serving as figures who represented the forces of nature and primordial aspects of the cosmos. They were often depicted in myths and epics, symbolizing the enduring influence of the ancient cosmic powers in the Greek worldview.

The legacy of the Titans and their Titanomachy remained a significant aspect of Greek cultural expressions, inspiring artistic representations, poetic narratives, and philosophical reflections on the nature of divine authority, rebellion, and the cyclical nature of time.

Exercises for Critical Thinking and Discussion

Analyze the significance of Cronus' act of castrating Uranus and its metaphorical implications in ancient Greek mythology. What symbolic meanings might this act hold?

Discuss the attributes and domains associated with various Titans in Greek mythology. How did their roles in shaping natural phenomena and cosmic forces influence ancient Greek religious beliefs?

Explore the theme of divine succession and the shift in power from the Titans to the Olympians. How does this mythological motif resonate in other cultural and religious traditions?

Problems

Research other mythologies and cultures that feature divine struggles for power or similar themes of succession and overthrow of elder deities.

Investigate the influence of the Titanomachy and the characters of the Titans on later literary works, such as the works of ancient Greek playwrights or later epic poems.

The captivating saga of the Titans and their Titanomachy showcases the rich complexity of ancient Greek mythology. As the primordial deities who shaped the cosmos, the Titans left an indelible mark on the cultural consciousness of the ancient Greeks. Their conflict with the Olympians exemplifies the eternal struggle for power and the rise of new divine orders throughout human history, making their enduring legacy one of fascination and philosophical contemplation.

✧ Zeus: The King of the Gods

At the pinnacle of the Greek pantheon reigns Zeus, the sovereign deity and preeminent ruler among the gods. With an unparalleled domain that stretches over the heavens and the skies, Zeus commands the elemental forces, notably thunder and lightning, which he wields through his emblematic thunderbolt. His supreme authority extends not only over the divine realm but also governs the lives and destinies of mortal beings.

✧ The Thunderous Majesty: Control of the Skies

Zeus's dominion over the skies epitomizes his celestial prowess. As the god of thunder, he orchestrates the rumbling storms that sweep across the heavens, unleashing bolts of lightning that illuminate both the earthly and the divine realms. The awe-inspiring spectacle of thunderstorms serves as a potent reminder of Zeus's majestic power and his capacity to disrupt or preserve the natural order.

✧ The God of Governance and Law

Among his many roles, Zeus emerges as the divine arbiter of governance and law. As the head of the divine assembly, he presides over the Council of the Gods, deliberating on matters that pertain to both gods and mortals. His wise judgments, symbolized by his scepter, maintain harmony and balance among the celestial beings and establish a moral compass for the mortal world.

✧ "Xenia": The Sacred Duty of Hospitality

Central to Zeus's divine persona is his role as the protector of "xenia," a sacred concept encompassing hospitality and guest-friendship. In ancient Greek society, the sacred bond between host and guest was a pivotal aspect of social cohesion and ethical conduct. Adhering to the principles of "xenia" ensured that both travelers and hosts were treated with respect and kindness, for it was believed that Zeus himself would oversee the observance of this duty.

✧   The Thunderbolt: Destruction and Order

The thunderbolt, an emblem of Zeus's divine might, represents both destructive force and the preservation of cosmic order. In the face of transgressions or challenges to divine law, Zeus could wield the thunderbolt to mete out punishment, serving as a reminder of the consequences that awaited those who dared defy the divine will. Simultaneously, the thunderbolt symbolizes the maintenance of universal harmony and the continuity of the natural world.

✧   Zeus and Mortal Interactions

Zeus's influence extends beyond the divine realm, as he frequently interacts with mortals in mythological narratives. These interactions range from acts of benevolence, such as offering guidance to heroes, to tests of character that explore moral virtues and human folly. The tale of King Midas, granted the golden touch by Zeus as both a gift and a curse, illustrates the complexities of divine intervention in the lives of mortals.

Problems

Investigate the cultural and historical significance of Zeus's worship in specific regions of ancient Greece. How did local traditions and festivals celebrate his role as the king of the gods?

Research the parallels and differences between Zeus and other supreme deities in various polytheistic belief systems around the world. How do these deities reflect the diverse cultural and geographical contexts in which they emerge?

The study of Zeus, the paramount god of the Greek pantheon, unveils a multifaceted exploration of power, governance, and the intricate relationship between the divine and the mortal spheres. As the king of the gods, Zeus's influence reverberates through myth and religious practices, shaping the moral and social fabric of ancient Greek civilization. His embodiment of both destructive and preservative forces highlights the nuanced nature of divinity, inviting students to critically contemplate the complexities of religious beliefs and the enduring legacy of Zeus's role in shaping ancient Greek culture and thought.

✧   **Hera: The Queen of the Gods**

Among the esteemed inhabitants of the Greek pantheon, Hera assumes a commanding role as the queen of the gods and the embodiment of marriage and family.

As the consort of Zeus, her divine union with the king of the gods represents the sacred bond that sustains the cosmic order and the divine hierarchy.

✧ The Goddess of Marriage and Family

Hera's paramount domain is that of marriage and family life. As the goddess of marriage, she presides over the sacred institution of matrimony, bestowing her blessings upon unions and ensuring the fidelity of husbands and wives. In the ancient Greek context, marriage was not merely a secular contract but held profound religious significance, and Hera's presence was invoked to safeguard the sanctity and stability of these unions.

✧ The Protector of Women

Hera's role as the protector of women extends beyond her jurisdiction over marital bonds. She watches over women in their various roles, including motherhood and family caretaking. As the goddess of childbirth, Hera oversees the safety of mothers during labor and the well-being of newborns, embodying the nurturing and protective aspects of motherhood.

✧ Vengeance and Discord in the Divine Realm

Despite her divine stature, Hera's character is not devoid of human-like emotions. Her position as Zeus's wife occasionally plunges her into fits of jealousy and anger, stemming from her husband's numerous extramarital affairs. In response to Zeus's infidelities, Hera manifests her wrath, often inflicting punishment upon Zeus's lovers and illegitimate offspring. The myths of Io and Hercules offer striking examples of Hera's retribution and the discord it sowed among both divine and mortal beings.

✧ Hera's Influence in Myth and Religion

Hera's influence extends to various mythological narratives and religious practices. Temples and festivals dedicated to her veneration existed in several regions of ancient Greece, notably in Argos and Samos. The worship of Hera was significant in the Greek city-state of Argos, where her cult was deeply intertwined with the city's identity and governance.

✧   The Complexities of Hera's Persona

Hera's portrayal in Greek mythology encapsulates a nuanced blend of divine grandeur and human-like emotions. As the queen of the gods, she represents the idealized aspects of marriage and womanhood, while her jealous tendencies highlight the complexities of divine personalities. In exploring Hera's myths, students can delve into discussions about the representation of gender roles, the nature of divine emotions, and the interplay between gods and mortals.

Problems

Research the influence of Hera's worship in different city-states of ancient Greece. How did the perception of Hera and her divine attributes vary across these regions?

Explore the depiction of Hera in ancient Greek art and iconography. How did artists symbolically represent her roles as the goddess of marriage, family, and divine retribution?

The study of Hera, the queen of the gods, unravels an intriguing tapestry of divine authority, marital bonds, and complex human emotions within the Greek pantheon. Her role as the protector of women and the enforcer of divine justice invites students to critically examine the intersection of gender, power, and emotions in religious narratives. The multifaceted nature of Hera's persona reflects the intricacies of ancient Greek beliefs and cultural values, inviting scholars to engage in stimulating discussions about the multifaceted nature of divine beings and their impact on ancient Greek society.

✧   Athena: The Goddess of Wisdom and Warfare

Athena, an eminent deity within the Greek pantheon, embodies a multifaceted domain that encompasses wisdom, strategic warfare, and the arts. As a revered patron of knowledge and martial prowess, Athena's influence permeated various aspects of ancient Greek life, leaving an indelible mark on culture, philosophy, and the intricacies of war.

✧   The Divine Embodiment of Wisdom

At the heart of Athena's persona resides her unparalleled wisdom, which surpasses the boundaries of mere intelligence. She stands as the embodiment of rationality, strategic thinking, and prudent counsel. Her patronage of wisdom extends to the pursuit of knowledge in various fields, including philosophy, mathematics, and the arts, making her an esteemed muse for scholars and artists alike.

✧   The Martial Strategist

Athena's role as a goddess of warfare highlights her tactical brilliance and martial acumen. Unlike the impulsive and violent Ares, she represents the disciplined aspect of warfare, focusing on strategic planning, courage, and just warfare. Athenian soldiers invoked her guidance and protection on the battlefield, seeking her wisdom to ensure victory while minimizing casualties.

✧   The Guardian of Cities

Athena's sphere of influence extends to the realm of cities and the establishment of civilized society. As the patron goddess of Athens, she played a pivotal role in the city-state's governance and identity. Her wisdom guided the Athenians in matters of law, justice, and the cultivation of civic virtues, fostering a harmonious and culturally rich society.

✧   The Arts and Cultural Expression

In addition to her association with wisdom and warfare, Athena reigns as the patroness of the arts and cultural expression. She inspired artisans, poets, and musicians, encouraging creative endeavors and celebrating the harmonious integration of beauty and reason. The Parthenon, a magnificent temple in Athens dedicated to her worship, stands as a testament to her cultural significance and enduring legacy.

✧   Athena in Mythological Narratives

Numerous myths and stories showcase Athena's involvement in the lives of gods and mortals. Her rivalry with Poseidon for the patronage of Athens, culminating in the contest to offer the city the most valuable gift, illustrates her role as a protector and benefactor of cities. The tale of Arachne, a talented mortal weaver who challenged Athena to a weaving competition, exemplifies the goddess's pursuit of excellence and her capacity for both reward and punishment.

Problems

Research the influence of Athena's worship in other regions of ancient Greece beyond Athens. How did local traditions and beliefs shape her significance in different city-states?

Investigate the depiction of Athena in various literary works, including poetry, plays, and philosophical treatises. How do different authors present and interpret her wisdom and attributes?

The exploration of Athena, the goddess of wisdom and warfare, illuminates the intricate interplay between intellect, military strategy, and cultural expression within ancient Greek civilization. Her patronage of cities and the arts, combined with her role as a martial strategist, showcases the multidimensionality of her persona and her enduring influence on ancient Greek thought and society. Athena's legacy invites students to critically ponder the complexities of divine attributes and their impact on human endeavors, encouraging profound discussions about the integration of wisdom, valor, and creativity in both ancient and contemporary contexts.

✧ Poseidon: The God of the Sea

Poseidon, a formidable deity within the Greek pantheon, holds dominion over the vast expanse of the seas and the elemental forces that shape maritime activities, fishing endeavors, and seafaring voyages. As the esteemed brother of Zeus and a prominent Olympian god, Poseidon's influence permeates both the divine and mortal realms, reflecting the duality of the seas as both life-giving and treacherous.

The God of the Seas and Maritime Activities

Poseidon's principal domain is that of the seas and oceans. As the god of the waters, he presides over the vast realm of the oceans, the tides, and the waves. Mariners and sailors invoke his protection and favor before embarking on perilous journeys across the unpredictable waters. His influence extends to maritime activities, blessing fishing expeditions and facilitating safe sea passages for traders and explorers.

A Mighty Olympian God

Among the illustrious Olympian gods, Poseidon holds a prestigious position, seated alongside his brother Zeus and the divine assembly. His association with the seas endows him with great power and authority, as the vastness of the oceans mirrors the immensity of his divine influence. His divine presence is invoked in various rituals and ceremonies, seeking his favor and guidance for abundant catches and safe voyages.

The Benevolent and Volatile Seas

Poseidon's nature is a study in contrasts, reflecting the dual aspects of the seas themselves. On one hand, the waters provide sustenance, fertile fishing grounds, and trade routes that bolster the prosperity of coastal communities. On the other, the seas can unleash devastating storms and tempests, endangering ships and lives. Poseidon's personality, like the oceans, exhibits both benevolence and volatility.

Control over Elemental Forces

Beyond his dominion over the seas, Poseidon's influence extends to the earth itself. As the god of earthquakes, he wields power over the elemental forces that shape the land. The rumblings of earthquakes serve as a reminder of his mighty presence, emphasizing the interconnectedness of the gods with natural phenomena.

Poseidon in Mythology and Beyond

Numerous myths and narratives feature Poseidon's involvement in the lives of gods and mortals. The story of Theseus and the Minotaur illustrates Poseidon's involvement in the fate of mortal heroes, while the myth of the contest for the patronage of Athens exemplifies the rivalry and tensions among the Olympian gods.

Problems

Research the depiction of Poseidon in religious practices and iconography in regions beyond ancient Greece. How did other cultures interpret and incorporate his influence into their belief systems?

Investigate the connection between Poseidon and other deities associated with water and the seas in different ancient mythologies. How do these deities reflect the diverse cultural and geographical contexts in which they emerged?

The exploration of Poseidon, the master of the seas and elemental forces, unveils the multifaceted aspects of his divine persona, spanning benevolence and volatility, and the intricate interplay between gods and the natural world. His influence on maritime activities and the symbolic significance of earthquakes invites students to critically contemplate the interdependence of ancient Greek society with the seas and elemental forces. Poseidon's complex nature challenges students to engage in profound discussions about the dynamics of divine personalities and their role in shaping both human endeavors and the forces of nature.

✧ Apollo: The God of Music, Prophecy, and Healing

Apollo, a revered and versatile deity within the Greek pantheon, commands a vast domain encompassing music, prophecy, healing, and the illuminating power of the sun. As a prominent Olympian god, Apollo's influence permeates diverse spheres, ranging from artistic expressions to the guidance of kings and cities through his renowned oracle at Delphi.

The God of Music and the Arts

Apollo's foremost domain is that of music and the arts. As the god of music, he is often depicted with a lyre, the instrument he masterfully plays to create celestial melodies. His influence extends to poetry and the pursuit of aesthetic beauty, fostering a harmonious balance between artistic creativity and order. Apollo serves as a patron deity to musicians, poets, and artists, inspiring their endeavors and elevating cultural expressions.

The Oracle at Delphi: The Voice of Prophecy

One of the most significant aspects of Apollo's persona is his role as the god of prophecy. The oracle at Delphi, a sacred sanctuary in ancient Greece, served as the conduit through which Apollo communicated divine prophecies to mortals. Kings, rulers, and individuals sought counsel and guidance from the oracle, making it a revered institution that played a vital role in political decisions and personal matters.

The Sun and the Illumination of Knowledge

As the god of light and the sun, Apollo symbolizes the illumination of truth and knowledge. The sun's rays are seen as the manifestation of his divine presence, bringing light to both the physical world and the realm of intellect. Apollo's association with knowledge emphasizes the pursuit of wisdom and enlightenment, transcending mere physical light to the realm of intellectual and spiritual enlightenment.

Healing and Medicine

Apollo's diverse influence also extends to healing and medicine. He is venerated as a god of healing, with his temples serving as centers for medicinal practices and divine intervention in curing ailments. The concept of "hygieia," denoting cleanliness and hygiene, traces its origin to Apollo's role as a deity concerned with the well-being of both body and mind.

Apollo in Mythology and Beyond

Numerous myths and narratives feature Apollo's interactions with gods and mortals, reflecting his various roles and attributes. The myth of Apollo and Daphne illustrates his pursuit of beauty and unattainable love, while his connection with the founding of Delphi showcases his prophetic authority and influence on ancient Greek religious practices.

Problems

Research the influence of Apollo's worship in regions beyond Greece, such as ancient Rome and other Hellenistic civilizations. How did his attributes and associations differ in these cultural contexts?

Investigate the significance of Apollo's temples and sanctuaries in ancient Greek cities. How did these religious centers contribute to the social and political fabric of urban life?

The exploration of Apollo, the god of music, prophecy, and healing, offers an insight into the rich tapestry of ancient Greek religious beliefs and cultural expressions. His multifaceted attributes as a patron of the arts, a prophetic authority, and a healer challenge students to grapple with the intersections of knowledge, aesthetics, and divine authority. Apollo's enduring influence on art, medicine, and the pursuit of wisdom invites students to engage in meaningful discussions about the interplay between human creativity and the guidance of divine forces in both ancient and contemporary contexts.

✧ Aphrodite: The Goddess of Love and Beauty

Aphrodite, a captivating and revered goddess within the Greek pantheon, reigns supreme as the embodiment of love and beauty. Her divine sphere encompasses a profound spectrum of emotions, from physical desire to profound spiritual connections. As the goddess of love, she holds sway over matters of attraction, romance, and emotional bonds, captivating both gods and mortals alike through her irresistible allure.

Love in All its Forms

Aphrodite's primary domain is that of love, encompassing a vast array of expressions and experiences. From passionate desire to tender affection, her influence spans the spectrum of human emotions and connections. Aphrodite's presence is invoked in various rituals and offerings seeking blessings in matters of love, relationships, and fertility.

Beauty and Aesthetics

In addition to her dominion over love, Aphrodite embodies exquisite beauty and aesthetics. Her divine allure transcends physical attractiveness, symbolizing the inherent power of beauty to inspire desire, admiration, and artistic creativity. As the patroness of beauty, she influences concepts of aesthetic perfection in art, architecture, and the natural world.

The Interplay of Love and Turmoil

Aphrodite's captivating charm extends beyond the divine realm, as she often intervenes in the lives of mortals, weaving threads of love and turmoil among them. Her stories of love affairs with both gods and humans depict the complex interplay of passion, jealousy, and desire. The Trojan War, precipitated by the judgment of Paris and the dispute over Aphrodite's gift of Helen of Troy, exemplifies the goddess's influence in mortal affairs.

The Temple of Aphrodite

Throughout ancient Greece, Aphrodite's worship was celebrated in various temples and sanctuaries. The Temple of Aphrodite at Knidos, adorned with striking sculptures, epitomizes the embodiment of her divine grace and beauty. Worshipers sought her favor and guidance, seeking to evoke her presence and blessings in matters of love, fertility, and harmonious relationships.

Aphrodite in the Modern Context

Aphrodite's significance endures in contemporary contexts, resonating in various fields, from art and literature to modern notions of romance and beauty. The celebration of love and beauty in modern society can be traced back to the enduring allure of this divine goddess.

Problems

Research the representation of Aphrodite in ancient Greek religious artifacts and iconography. How do different forms of artistic expression convey her divine attributes and the significance of beauty in her worship?

Investigate the perception of Aphrodite in various contemporary spiritual and religious traditions, such as modern Wicca and neo-paganism. How is her image and influence reinterpreted in these belief systems?

The exploration of Aphrodite, the goddess of love and beauty, offers students an opportunity to delve into the profound human emotions and connections that lie at the heart of ancient Greek religious beliefs. Her divine allure and multifaceted attributes encourage critical analysis of the interplay between love, beauty, and artistic expression in ancient and modern contexts. Aphrodite's enduring impact on human emotions and cultural expressions invites students to explore the universal themes of desire, romance, and the significance of beauty in shaping human experiences.

✧ **Hermes: The Messenger of the Gods**

Hermes, a multifaceted and dynamic deity within the Greek pantheon, assumes the role of the divine messenger, bridging the gap between the immortal gods and mortal humans. As the patron of travelers and merchants, he oversees matters of communication, trade, and agility, exemplifying the swift pace at which information and goods traverse the ancient world. Hermes' duality is apparent in his capacity for both benevolent guidance and playful mischief, rendering him a complex and enigmatic figure in Greek mythology.

The Divine Messenger and Communicator

Hermes' primary domain lies in his role as the divine messenger of the gods. With his winged sandals and a herald's staff, he traverses the boundaries of the divine and mortal realms, conveying the will and messages of the Olympian deities. He is the bearer of news, prophecies, and divine commands, facilitating communication between the gods and humanity. His presence in ancient religious rites symbolizes the importance of effective communication in both spiritual and temporal matters.

Patron of Travelers and Merchants

Beyond his messenger role, Hermes also assumes the role of the patron of travelers and merchants. The ancient world was interconnected through trade routes, and Hermes was invoked to safeguard journeys, secure successful trade, and protect those embarking on long voyages. As the divine protector of roads and boundaries, he ensured safe passage for travelers, emphasizing the significance of commerce and connection among ancient civilizations.

The Cunning Trickster

Hermes' dynamic character also includes a penchant for trickery and mischief, best exemplified in the stories of his youth. As a cunning infant, he outwitted his half-brother Apollo, stealing the latter's sacred cattle and inventing the lyre from a tortoise shell. Hermes' playful nature and skill in cunning acts cemented his status as a clever trickster in Greek mythology.

Hermes in Cultural Expressions

Hermes' influence extended beyond religious practices and found expression in various fields of ancient Greek culture. He was venerated in various festivals, including the Hermaea, which celebrated the coming-of-age of young men. Additionally, Hermes' association with communication inspired the development of ancient Greek oratory and rhetoric, highlighting the role of persuasive speech in shaping public discourse.

Hermes in Neo-Paganism and Modern Traditions

Hermes' dynamic character continues to resonate in modern spiritual practices, including neo-paganism and modern interpretations of ancient Greek religion. His portrayal as the guide to the spiritual realm and the divine messenger has inspired contemporary interpretations of communication with the divine.

Problems

Research the concept of "herms" in ancient Greek art and architecture. How do these sculpted pillars symbolize Hermes' significance in ancient religious practices and the protection of boundaries?

Investigate the prevalence of Hermes' worship in different ancient Greek city-states. How did local cults and festivals celebrate his various attributes and roles?

The exploration of Hermes, the swift messenger and patron of travelers, offers students a compelling narrative of divine communication and the interconnectedness of ancient civilizations. His multifaceted attributes as a protector of travelers, a cunning trickster, and the divine messenger invite critical thinking and discussions about the interplay of communication, trade, and cultural expressions in the ancient world. Moreover, Hermes' enduring influence in modern traditions encourages students to explore the continuity of ancient Greek religious beliefs and their impact on contemporary neo-pagan practices and spiritual expressions.

✧   **Demeter: The Goddess of Fertility and Agriculture**

Demeter, a revered and essential goddess within the Greek pantheon, presides over the vital domains of fertility, agriculture, and the cyclical nature of the seasons. As the nurturer of crops and the guardian of agriculture, she embodies the profound connection between human sustenance and the bountiful gifts of nature. Demeter's significance in ancient Greek society is intricately woven into the fabric of daily life, as the success of agriculture and the changing seasons profoundly impacted the survival and well-being of communities.

The Fertility Goddess

At the heart of Demeter's divine sphere lies her role as the fertility goddess. As the nurturer of the earth's fertility, she bestows her blessings upon the fields, ensuring abundant harvests and the growth of crops. Ancient Greek farmers invoked her favor, offering prayers and rituals to secure successful agricultural outcomes.

The Cycle of Seasons

The myth of Demeter and Persephone stands as a poignant representation of the connection between the goddess and the cycle of seasons. Persephone's abduction to the underworld by Hades brings about the sorrowful period of winter when Demeter mourns her daughter's absence. When Persephone returns to the world above, Demeter's joyous reunion with her daughter heralds the arrival of spring, symbolizing the renewal of life and the return of fertility to the land.

Demeter's Mysteries: Rituals of Fertility and Renewal

The Eleusinian Mysteries, dedicated to Demeter and Persephone, were among the most significant and secretive religious ceremonies in ancient Greece. These mysteries offered initiates an opportunity to connect with the divine aspects of Demeter's fertility and the promise of life's renewal. The sacred rituals of the Eleusinian Mysteries were considered transformative experiences, ensuring prosperity and a blessed afterlife.

Demeter and the Circle of Life

Demeter's influence extends beyond agricultural prosperity, as she embodies the cycle of life and death. Her association with both fertility and mourning illustrates the inseparable relationship between life's abundance and its inevitable transience. In this aspect, Demeter's influence permeates various aspects of ancient Greek cultural expressions, including funerary rites and commemorations of the deceased.

Demeter in Ecospirituality

The reverence for Demeter's connection with the natural world continues to resonate in modern times through the lens of ecospirituality. Environmental movements and contemporary spiritual practices often draw inspiration from Demeter's nurturing qualities and the sacredness of the earth's fertility.

Problems

Research the representation of Demeter in ancient Greek art and sculpture. How do artists portray her divine attributes and her role as the nurturer of crops?

Investigate the role of agricultural deities in other ancient civilizations and cultural traditions. How do these deities compare to Demeter in terms of their significance and attributes?

The exploration of Demeter, the goddess of fertility and agriculture, invites students to delve into the intricate relationship between ancient Greek religious beliefs, agricultural practices, and the cycles of nature. Her portrayal as the nurturer of crops and the guardian of the changing seasons provides a captivating lens through which to explore the profound interplay between human survival, ecological sustainability, and the enduring significance of the natural world. Additionally, Demeter's association with life's transience and the circle of life encourages discussions on the interconnectedness of birth, growth, and death within the context of ancient Greek religious expressions and modern ecospirituality.

Problems

Analyze the historical and cultural significance of ancient Greek festivals and rituals dedicated to specific deities. How did these religious practices shape the identity and cohesion of Greek city-states?

Research how specific major deities were represented in different forms of ancient Greek art, such as pottery, sculpture, and relief work. What symbolic elements and attributes were employed to signify their respective domains?

The exploration of the major deities in Greek mythology and their domains unveils a fascinating tapestry of divine personalities and their significance in ancient Greek religious, cultural, and philosophical contexts. By delving into the complexities of these divine beings and their interactions, students embark on a profound journey of understanding the interplay between the human and the divine and the enduring influence of ancient Greek beliefs on human thought and expression. Through critical analysis and discussion, students gain deeper insights into the complexities of religious systems and their impact on human societies throughout history.

Demigods of Zeus: Heroes and Legends

Greek mythology is a vast tapestry of divine beings, fantastical creatures, and heroic legends. Among the most captivating figures are the demigods, beings born of the union between a mortal and a deity. These hybrid individuals occupy a unique and revered position within Greek mythology, possessing both mortal and divine attributes. The term "demigod" itself stems from the fusion of "demi," meaning half, and "god," signifying their dual nature.

The allure of demigods lies in their exceptional qualities, bestowed upon them by their divine parentage. They inherit a blend of human vulnerability and the extraordinary powers of the divine realm. As such, demigods often find themselves embarking on extraordinary quests, their destinies entwined with heroic feats and epic adventures.

Zeus as the Father of Demigods

At the pinnacle of the divine hierarchy stands Zeus, the formidable god of thunder and lightning, and the ruler of Mount Olympus. Zeus assumes a central role in the narrative of demigods, for he is the most prolific deity when it comes to fathering these exceptional offspring. His amorous escapades with mortal women, goddesses, and even nymphs have resulted in a myriad of legendary demigods.

The affairs of Zeus with mortal women are often a source of intrigue and wonder. His interactions with these women and the subsequent birth of demigods play a pivotal role in shaping the mythical landscape of ancient Greece. The exploits and lineage of these demigods intertwine with Greek history, philosophy, and religious practices, making them indispensable to the fabric of Greek culture.

Importance and Significance of Demigods in Greek Culture

The significance of demigods in Greek culture extends beyond mere mythical tales. These extraordinary beings exemplify the interaction between the divine and mortal realms, blurring the boundaries between gods and humanity. Their unique status embodies the complexities of human existence, reflecting the struggle to navigate through the mortal world while possessing divine heritage.

Moreover, demigods serve as archetypal figures, representing the aspirations, virtues, and flaws of humanity. Their heroic feats inspire courage and determination, while their vulnerabilities serve as a reminder of the shared human experience. The tales of demigods resonate not only with the ancient Greeks but also with subsequent generations, becoming timeless symbols of heroism and the quest for greatness.

In "Demigods of Zeus: Heroes and Legends," we embark on a scholarly journey to explore the multifaceted world of demigods in Greek mythology. Through rigorous analysis and in-depth examination, we will unravel the tales of these extraordinary beings, their lineage, and the lasting impact of their adventures on Greek culture and beyond. Join us as we delve into the realm of heroes and legends, where the divine and mortal collide in epic tales of courage, love, and destiny.

Hercules (Heracles)

In the intricate tapestry of Greek mythology, few figures loom as large and awe-inspiring as Hercules, known in Greek as Heracles. Revered as the quintessential hero, Hercules embodies the union of mortal and divine, a demigod whose extraordinary strength and valor captivated the imaginations of ancient Greeks and continues to resonate across the ages.

Born from the union of the mighty Zeus and the mortal woman Alcmena, Hercules inherited a legacy fraught with both divine blessings and mortal challenges. His exceptional physical prowess, marked by his renowned Twelve Labors, earned him a place of honor among the pantheon of heroes in Greek culture.

The narrative of Hercules weaves together elements of heroism, tragedy, and divine destiny, illustrating the complexities of navigating the dual nature of human existence. His journey is a profound exploration of the human condition, where courage and frailty intermingle, shaping a tale that reflects the timeless quest for identity and redemption.

As we delve into the life and exploits of Hercules, we embark on a voyage that transcends the bounds of time, bridging ancient and modern realms. This demigod's legacy endures as an emblem of valor, resilience, and the enduring allure of heroic tradition in Greek mythology. Through his trials and triumphs, Hercules remains a beacon of inspiration and a testament to the enduring power of mythic storytelling in shaping the human psyche.

Birth and Parentage

Hercules, renowned as one of the most celebrated and iconic demigods in Greek mythology, owes his existence to a complex tale of divine interference and mortal lineage. Born to Alcmena, a mortal woman, and Zeus, the king of the gods, Hercules exemplifies the merging of human vulnerability and divine might. His conception, however, emerged amidst a web of divine intrigue.

Zeus, captivated by Alcmena's beauty, took the form of her husband, Amphitryon, and spent a night with her. That same night, Alcmena's true husband, Amphitryon, also lay with her, leading to a dual conception. Thus, Hercules and his twin brother Iphicles were conceived together, each possessing distinct parentage.

The intricate circumstances of Hercules' birth set the stage for his exceptional attributes, as he inherited the extraordinary strength and divine blood of Zeus. This unique combination endowed him with unparalleled physical prowess, a crucial element that would later define his heroic endeavors.

Twelve Labors of Hercules

Among the most illustrious feats associated with Hercules are the Twelve Labors, a series of daunting tasks imposed upon him as punishment for the madness induced by the goddess Hera, who held a longstanding animosity towards Zeus' illegitimate son. Each labor was designed to test Hercules' strength, courage, and resourcefulness to their limits.

The Twelve Labors encompassed a wide array of challenges, ranging from slaying the Nemean Lion, a fierce and impervious creature, to capturing the elusive Erymanthian Boar. Hercules also faced the formidable Hydra, a serpent-like creature with regenerative heads, and confronted the Ceryneian Hind, a divine deer sacred to Artemis.

These trials represented the epitome of heroism, showcasing Hercules' indomitable will and divine favor. Successfully completing the Twelve Labors established him as the quintessential hero, capturing the imagination of ancient Greeks and inspiring generations to come.

Divine and Mortal Aspects

Hercules' journey is a tapestry of both divine and mortal elements, reflecting the inherent struggle between his human nature and divine lineage. While his divine heritage bestowed him with immense strength and courage, it was tempered by the frailty and vulnerability of his mortal aspect.

Throughout his life, Hercules faced numerous challenges that tested his mortal side. His infamous fit of madness, which led him to kill his wife and children, serves as a poignant reminder of the consequences of his divine parentage, as Hera's wrathful jealousy sought to disrupt his mortal life.

Despite these trials, Hercules remained an exemplar of heroism, displaying humility and virtue in his quest for redemption. His divine heritage, though a source of great power, also brought about immense responsibilities, illustrating the complexities of navigating both the mortal and divine realms.

Impact and Legacy in Greek Mythology

The legacy of Hercules in Greek mythology is immeasurable, leaving an indelible mark on ancient cultural consciousness. His triumphs and struggles provided a framework for understanding the human condition, as he embodies the timeless struggle for identity, belonging, and the pursuit of greatness.

Hercules' heroism also inspired artistic expression, finding its way into numerous works of art, literature, and drama across the ages. His Labors and exploits have been a wellspring of inspiration for poets, playwrights, and artists, exemplifying the enduring power of myth to capture the human imagination.

Furthermore, Hercules' tale continues to reverberate in modern culture, with adaptations and reimaginings in contemporary media. From films and television to literature and comics, Hercules' legacy persists as a symbol of valor, strength, and resilience.

In conclusion, the myth of Hercules embodies the essence of Greek heroic tradition, blurring the boundaries between mortal and divine. His epic journey, from birth to ascension among the gods, encapsulates the human pursuit of glory and virtue. The multifaceted narrative of Hercules stands as a testament to the enduring allure of demigods in Greek mythology and the profound impact of mythic storytelling on human consciousness.

Perseus

In the labyrinthine world of ancient Greek mythology, few figures shine as brightly as Perseus, a renowned hero whose exploits captivated the imaginations of generations. Embarking on a series of extraordinary quests, Perseus' journey encompasses daring feats, divine intervention, and symbolic depth, making him a paradigm of heroism in the Greek pantheon.

This introduction delves into the captivating tale of Perseus, unveiling the layers of his myth, exploring the significance of his divine lineage, and unraveling the profound symbolism behind his heroic deeds. From the perilous encounter with the Gorgon Medusa to the rescue of the imprisoned princess Andromeda, Perseus' odyssey offers a glimpse into the timeless struggle between chaos and order, darkness and light.

As we embark on this literary odyssey, we shall venture beyond the realm of storytelling and delve into the deeper currents of human nature and the archetypal quest for virtue. Perseus' journey, infused with divine gifts and unwavering resolve, embodies the quintessential hero's path—a journey of self-discovery, moral triumph, and the eternal quest for meaning and purpose.

Drawing from a rich tapestry of myths and ancient sources, we shall unravel the multifaceted layers of Perseus' myth, pondering the timeless questions it poses and exploring the relevance of heroic ideals in contemporary thought and culture. Along this intellectual voyage, we shall engage in critical analysis, contemplating counterarguments, and immersing ourselves in the vibrant world of Greek mythology.

Through the lens of Perseus' mythical legacy, we shall navigate the realm of ancient Greek religion, investigating the interplay of gods and mortals, exploring the intricate web of symbolism, and uncovering the enduring allure of heroic narratives that have transcended time and culture.

Thus, join us on this scholarly odyssey as we set sail on the epic voyage of Perseus, discovering the depths of his heroic spirit, the essence of his humanity, and the profound wisdom enshrined in his timeless myth. Embrace the challenges and rewards that await, as together, we delve into the heart of Perseus' myth—a beacon of inspiration and a testament to the indomitable spirit of the human quest for heroism.

The Quest to Defeat Medusa

Perseus, renowned in Greek mythology as a formidable hero, embarked on a daring quest to slay the Gorgon Medusa, a monstrous creature with serpents for hair and a gaze that turned any who met it to stone. This perilous mission was initiated by King Polydectes, who sought to rid himself of Perseus and win the affection of his mother, Danaë. Perseus, determined and resourceful, accepted the challenge, venturing on a treacherous journey to confront the dreaded Gorgon.

Guided by divine aid from the Olympian gods, Perseus received gifts to aid him on his quest: the winged sandals of Hermes, the reflective shield of Athena, and a cap of invisibility from Hades. Armed with these extraordinary artifacts, Perseus approached the lair of the Gorgons, where he skillfully beheaded Medusa while using the shield to avoid her deadly gaze. In a feat of ingenuity, he stowed the severed head within a bag for safekeeping, harnessing its petrifying power to confront his adversaries.

Rescue of Andromeda

Perseus' journey did not end with the defeat of Medusa. On his return voyage, he encountered the beautiful princess Andromeda, chained to a rock as a sacrifice to a sea monster due to her mother's pride and vanity. Perseus, moved by her plight, intervened, and with the aid of Medusa's head, he turned the sea monster to stone, liberating Andromeda from her fate. This act of heroism exemplifies Perseus' chivalrous and compassionate nature, as he rescues the damsel in distress and restores order to the realm.

Divine Gifts and Heroic Exploits

Beyond the defeat of Medusa and the rescue of Andromeda, Perseus embarked on further heroic exploits. Utilizing the gifts bestowed upon him, he navigated through challenges and adversaries, demonstrating not only physical prowess but also wit and strategic acumen. His divine lineage, being a son of Zeus, imbued him with exceptional qualities, elevating him above ordinary mortals.

Perseus' heroic achievements continued as he confronted the monstrous sea serpent Cetus, a perilous creature threatening the land of Ethiopia. With the winged sandals' swiftness and the aid of his reflective shield, Perseus confronted and vanquished the beast, earning the admiration and gratitude of the Ethiopian kingdom.

Symbolism and Heroic Traits

Perseus' myth carries profound symbolic significance, transcending the realm of storytelling to convey deeper truths about human nature and the struggle for virtue. The beheading of Medusa symbolizes the hero's triumph over chaos and evil, representing the conquering of one's inner demons and the attainment of self-mastery.

Furthermore, Perseus' divine gifts and lineage symbolize the union of human potential with the divine, exemplifying the notion that true heroism arises from a harmonious integration of mortal and divine qualities. His resourcefulness, courage, and compassion showcase the multifaceted dimensions of heroism, extending beyond mere physical prowess to encompass moral integrity and benevolent action.

In essence, Perseus' myth encapsulates the essence of the hero's journey—an archetypal motif recurring across cultures and time periods. Through the lens of Perseus' transformative odyssey, we glean insights into the human psyche and the perennial yearning for heroic ideals. His tale remains a timeless testament to the enduring power of myth to inspire and instill the virtues of bravery, resilience, and moral excellence in the hearts of humankind.

Theseus

In the annals of ancient Greek mythology, Theseus stands as an emblematic hero whose journey weaves together elements of legend and history. From his mysterious birth to his legendary feats, Theseus' saga encompasses a tapestry of heroism, political significance, and enduring cultural impact. This section will delve into the multifaceted narrative of Theseus, exploring the intricacies of his birth and early life, his legendary triumph over the fearsome Minotaur, his establishment of Athens, and the historical and mythical significance of his tale.

Birth and Early Life

At the crossroads of myth and history, Theseus' origins remain shrouded in both mystery and divine intervention. Born to Aegeus, the King of Athens, and Aethra, a mortal princess, Theseus' parentage is marked by divine paternity and mortal heritage. His journey begins with a series of pivotal events, including the retrieval of his father's sword and sandals from beneath a massive boulder, placed there by Aegeus before his departure.

The revelation of his divine lineage and the heroic nature of his early deeds lay the groundwork for Theseus' destiny as a champion of Athens and a symbol of heroism in Greek mythology. We shall examine the symbolism behind these significant moments, pondering the intersection of fate and free will in shaping the hero's identity and purpose.

Slaying the Minotaur

One of the most iconic and dramatic episodes in Theseus' mythological odyssey is his daring expedition to Crete to confront the monstrous Minotaur. As Athens faced the cruel tribute of sending seven young men and seven maidens to the labyrinth each year, Theseus rose to the challenge, volunteering to be one of the chosen youths. Guided by Ariadne's thread, he navigated the labyrinth's intricate passages, eventually encountering the fearsome Minotaur.

The heroic encounter between Theseus and the Minotaur captures the essence of the hero's journey, embodying themes of courage, sacrifice, and the triumph of good over evil. We shall analyze the psychological and cultural significance of this tale, exploring how it reflects the broader human struggle against darkness and chaos.

Establishing Athens and Leadership

Theseus' journey did not end with the slaying of the Minotaur; rather, it marked the beginning of his transformative role as a leader. Upon his triumphant return to Athens, he sought to consolidate his father's realm and establish a harmonious city-state. From confronting internal challenges, such as the treacherous Cretan princess, Medea, to securing Athens' borders through diplomatic marriages and alliances, Theseus emerged as a statesman and a ruler.

Through historical and mythical lenses, we will examine the portrayal of Theseus' leadership and governance, delving into the complexities of ancient politics and the hero's capacity to unite disparate elements under his rule.

Historical and Mythical Significance

Beyond the realm of myth, Theseus bears historical significance as a figure intertwined with the development of Athens and its identity as a burgeoning city-state. He exemplifies the archetypal hero whose legend served to inspire generations, embodying virtues and ideals that were central to Greek culture.

This section will explore the varying interpretations of Theseus' character, his evolving portrayal in different historical periods, and the enduring legacy of his myth within the context of ancient Greek religion and society. We will critically analyze the different narratives surrounding Theseus, shedding light on the complexities of myth-making and the malleability of heroic personas over time.

In tracing the path of Theseus, we will journey beyond the boundaries of his myth, investigating the historical contexts that gave rise to his legend and examining the cultural resonance of his heroic deeds in diverse fields such as literature, art, and philosophy.

Thus, with a keen eye on scholarship and an appreciation for the layers of meaning woven into Theseus' narrative, we embark on a comprehensive exploration of the hero's myth and legacy. Engaging in rigorous analysis and thought-provoking discussion, we shall gain a deeper understanding of Theseus as a multifaceted figure who transcends time and continues to inspire and challenge us as a symbol of human valor, leadership, and enduring cultural significance.

Helen of Troy

Helen of Troy, the enigmatic figure at the heart of one of the most captivating episodes in Greek mythology, has left an indelible mark on the collective consciousness of human history. Renowned for her unparalleled beauty, she became the unwitting catalyst for the legendary Trojan War, a conflict that shaped the course of ancient Greek history. This section will delve into the multifaceted narrative of Helen, exploring her role as the "face that launched a thousand ships," her connection to the epic Trojan War and its far-reaching consequences, her abduction, and her symbolic significance as a representation of beauty and tragic destiny.

The "Face that Launched a Thousand Ships"

Helen's beauty is often epitomized by the famous phrase "the face that launched a thousand ships." This evocative description encapsulates the profound impact of her allure and the extent to which it influenced the course of history. Her marriage to Menelaus, King of Sparta, drew the attention of various suitors, among whom stood the princes and kings of Greece. The eventual elopement of Helen with Paris, the prince of Troy, sparked a chain of events that culminated in the legendary Trojan War. We shall analyze the cultural and psychological significance of beauty as a catalyst for war and explore the complexities of desire and its consequences in the context of ancient Greek society.

The Trojan War and Its Consequences

The Trojan War, an epic conflict between the Greeks and the Trojans, was fought not only for territorial conquest but also to reclaim Helen, whose abduction had ignited the flames of war. This section will explore the various versions of the Trojan War's origins, including the different retellings found in the works of Homer, Euripides, and other ancient writers. We will examine the motives and actions of key figures such as Agamemnon, Menelaus, and Achilles, shedding light on the complexities of human character and the tragic implications of their choices.

Moreover, we shall analyze the far-reaching consequences of the war, which extended beyond the fall of Troy. From exploring the impact of divine intervention to the psychological toll on the heroes and their families, we will uncover the profound implications of the war and its aftermath.

Helen's Abduction and Role in Greek Mythology

The abduction of Helen by Paris is a pivotal event in Greek mythology, igniting a web of intrigue, betrayal, and divine intervention. This section will explore the differing accounts of Helen's abduction, including the contrasting portrayals in various literary sources such as Homer's "Iliad" and Euripides' "Helen." We will analyze the role of the gods in shaping the narrative and the complex interplay between mortal actions and divine will.

Furthermore, we will delve into Helen's characterization, examining her agency, motivations, and the complexities of her identity as both a woman of passion and a pawn in the hands of fate. By exploring the variations in her portrayal, we will gain insight into the evolving perceptions of women in ancient Greek society and the tensions between beauty, desire, and autonomy.

Symbol of Beauty and Tragic Destiny

Helen's story stands as a poignant symbol of beauty and its entangled relationship with destiny. Her allure, while captivating, led to a fate entangled with war, suffering, and loss. This section will critically analyze the notion of beauty as a double-edged sword, exploring its capacity to inspire love, admiration, and conflict simultaneously. We will also contemplate the concept of tragic destiny in the context of Greek mythology, pondering the idea of inexorable fate and the interplay between free will and predestination.

Moreover, we will examine the enduring legacy of Helen in art, literature, and culture, where she remains an emblem of both physical beauty and the complexities of human nature. We will explore how her story continues to resonate with contemporary audiences, inspiring contemplation on themes of desire, morality, and the intertwining of beauty and sorrow.

In conclusion, the tale of Helen of Troy encapsulates a captivating narrative that extends beyond the confines of ancient Greek mythology. Through rigorous analysis and thought-provoking discussion, we shall journey through the labyrinthine depths of her story, engaging in critical examination of her role in shaping Greek culture and exploring the timeless themes she represents. As we embark on this exploration, we invite students to delve into the complexities of human nature and the enduring allure of mythological tales that continue to captivate our imaginations and hearts.

Dionysus

In the captivating pantheon of ancient Greek deities, one figure stands out as a fascinating embodiment of both divine and mortal elements - Dionysus. Revered as the god of wine, revelry, and ecstasy, Dionysus weaves together a tapestry of contradictions and complexities that have captured the imaginations of scholars and storytellers for millennia. From his extraordinary birth to his role in shaping Greek culture and religious practices, Dionysus stands as a vibrant and enigmatic symbol of both pleasure and peril, liberation and restraint.

As we embark on a journey to explore the mythological world of Dionysus, we are drawn into the realms of divine intrigue and mortal tribulations. His parentage, born of both mortal and immortal origins, sets the stage for a character who defies easy categorization. Dionysus emerges as a figure who bridges the gap between the divine and the human, embodying the very essence of the natural world he so fervently represents.

Central to the persona of Dionysus is his divine portfolio as the god of wine and ecstasy. Through the cultivation and consumption of wine, Dionysus holds sway over the revelry and excesses that mark human existence. His influence on the grapevines and the transformative nature of wine serve as metaphors for life's dichotomies - the joys of celebration and the dangers of hedonism.

Yet, Dionysus is more than a mere deity of intoxication. His realm extends to the realm of spiritual transcendence, where the frenzied dances and ecstatic rituals of his worshippers unlock the doors to divine communion. These Dionysian rites grant mortals a glimpse into the mysteries of the cosmos, fostering a deeper connection to the natural world and to each other.

The ambiguous status of Dionysus, straddling the line between demigod and Olympian deity, piques our intellectual curiosity. As we delve into the question of his divine identity, we unravel the intricacies of mythological classification and contemplate the fluidity of roles within the pantheon of gods.

In the course of this exploration, we encounter Dionysus' influence on the religious and cultural life of ancient Greece. His vibrant cult and celebratory festivals brought communities together in communal revelry and emotional expression. Through the lens of Dionysian worship, we gain insights into the psychological and social dimensions of ancient Greek religious practices.

As we embark on this journey to uncover the mysteries of Dionysus, we are guided by the hands of scholars and experts in Greek mythology. Our quest for knowledge takes us beyond the surface of myth and delves into the heart of human nature, revealing the complexities of ancient beliefs and the enduring power of mythological narratives.

With each step, we find ourselves entwined in the intoxicating world of Dionysus, a world of passion, ecstasy, and the eternal dance between the mortal and the divine. Through rigorous exploration and critical thinking, we aim to unveil the profound significance of Dionysus in the ancient Greek psyche and his enduring legacy in the realms of literature, art, and cultural expression. Let us raise our cups to Dionysus, the god who unlocks the gates of perception and invites us to partake in the eternal mysteries of life itself.

Dual Parentage and Immortal Birth

Dionysus, a captivating and enigmatic figure in Greek mythology, occupies a unique position among the Olympian deities due to his dual parentage. Born to the mortal Semele and the divine Zeus, his conception and birth were marked by divine intervention and tragedy. Zeus, smitten with Semele's beauty, revealed his true form as the god of thunder and lightning, an overwhelming sight that resulted in Semele's demise. However, Zeus managed to save the unborn Dionysus by sewing him into his thigh until the god of wine was fully matured. This act of divine birth sets Dionysus apart from his Olympian counterparts, and his unique origin story serves as a compelling introduction to the complexities of his character.

God of Wine and Ecstasy

Dionysus is renowned as the god of wine, revelry, and ecstasy. His influence on the cultivation and consumption of wine is a testament to his role in shaping Greek culture and social practices. As the deity responsible for the growth of grapevines and the production of wine, Dionysus embodies the life-giving and transformative aspects of nature. Wine, with its intoxicating properties, symbolizes both the pleasures and dangers of indulgence, offering a profound metaphor for the balance between moderation and excess in life.

Moreover, Dionysus is associated with ecstatic rituals and wild celebrations, particularly in the form of ecstatic, frenzied dances known as Bacchic or Dionysian rites. These rituals served as a means of transcendence, enabling participants to experience a connection with the divine and the natural world. The Dionysian cult fostered a sense of community and liberation, inviting adherents to shed societal constraints and embrace a more primal and uninhibited state of being.

Demigod or Olympian Deity?

Dionysus' status as both a demigod and an Olympian deity is a subject of scholarly debate. His mortal lineage through his mother, Semele, places him in the category of demigods, those born from the union of a divine parent and a mortal. However, the extraordinary circumstances of his birth and his eventual ascension to Mount Olympus alongside the other major gods have led some to argue for his full status as an Olympian deity.

The ambiguous nature of Dionysus' origins and his ability to bridge the mortal and divine realms invite students to explore the intricate nuances of mythological classification. This discussion can further extend to the broader themes of identity and belonging in the pantheon of gods, prompting critical thinking about the fluidity and complexity of divine roles in ancient Greek religion.

Role in Ancient Greek Religion and Festivals

Dionysus held a prominent role in ancient Greek religious practices and festivals. His cult, known as the Dionysian Mysteries, was one of the most widespread and fervently celebrated in the Hellenistic world. These rites involved elaborate processions, theatrical performances, and ecstatic ceremonies held in honor of the god. The Dionysian festivals, such as the Dionysia and the Lenaia, featured theatrical performances, including tragic and comedic plays, fostering a vibrant cultural and artistic environment.

Additionally, Dionysus played a crucial role in the communal and religious life of the ancient Greeks. As the god of revelry and shared experiences, he brought communities together and allowed them to express their emotions, fears, and hopes collectively. Students can delve into the social and psychological dimensions of

Dionysian worship, examining its significance in fostering a sense of unity and belonging among the ancient Greeks.

In conclusion, Dionysus stands as a multifaceted and dynamic deity in Greek mythology, embodying the themes of dual parentage, wine and ecstasy, ambiguous divine status, and profound religious significance. This section invites students to immerse themselves in the complexities of Dionysus' character and role in ancient Greek culture, encouraging critical analysis and discussion of the diverse facets of this captivating god. Through a rigorous exploration of Dionysus, students will gain a deeper understanding of the intricate tapestry of ancient Greek religion and the lasting impact of mythological narratives on human thought and culture.

Pollux (Polydeuces) and Castor

In the vast tapestry of ancient Greek mythology, few figures hold a more captivating and unique place than the divine twins, Pollux (Polydeuces) and Castor. Born from the extraordinary union of the Spartan queen Leda and the mighty god Zeus, these brothers embody a profound synthesis of mortal and immortal essence. Revered as the Dioscuri, their legendary exploits, divine lineage, and inseparable bond have left an indelible mark on the cultural and religious fabric of ancient Greece.

Blessed with dual parentage, Castor was the mortal son of Leda and King Tyndareus of Sparta, while Pollux derived his immortality from his divine father, Zeus. This dual heritage bestowed upon the twins a distinctiveness that sets them apart from other mythical figures, as they embody the entwined nature of the human and divine realms.

Their preeminent status as horsemen is a testament to their legendary horsemanship, unrivaled in the annals of Greek mythology. The Dioscuri's exceptional equestrian skills have been celebrated in various myths and artistic portrayals, elevating them to the ranks of revered heroes.

The heroic exploits of Pollux and Castor are nothing short of legendary. Their participation in the perilous quest for the Golden Fleece alongside the Argonauts showcased their unmatched courage and resourcefulness. Beyond their valiant feats, the Dioscuri's role as protectors of sailors and travelers garnered them widespread veneration across Greece. Communities sought their divine aid during treacherous journeys, forging an enduring bond between the twins and the people they safeguarded.

In this comprehensive exploration of Pollux and Castor's mythology, we shall delve deep into the rich tapestry of their stories, unearthing the nuances of their divine and mortal natures. We shall traverse their legendary journeys, exploring the impact of their heroism on ancient Greek society and the enduring significance of their worship. Their transformation into the constellation Gemini further immortalized their bond, reminding the world of the enduring allure of mythic narratives.

As we embark on this journey, we shall witness the complexities of their divine lineage, the profound themes of brotherhood and loyalty, and the intertwining of the human and divine within the realm of ancient Greek mythology. The tale of the Dioscuri, Pollux and Castor, serves as an emblematic representation of the intricate relationship between gods and mortals, illustrating the timeless allure and power of myth in shaping the human understanding of the world.

Divine Twins - The Dioscuri

In the annals of Greek mythology, the divine twins, Pollux and Castor, occupy a prominent and revered position as the Dioscuri. Born from the union of the Spartan queen Leda and the god Zeus, the twins' parentage intertwines both mortal and immortal heritage. Castor, the mortal son, is credited to Leda's husband, King Tyndareus of Sparta, while Pollux, the immortal son, stems from Zeus's divine seed.

The unique and harmonious blending of divine and mortal elements grants the Dioscuri a distinctive status among the mythical figures of ancient Greece. As demi-gods, they represent a dynamic duality - one immortal and one mortal - each contributing their unique qualities to the legendary tales that weave their narrative.

Legendary Horsemanship and Heroic Exploits

The Dioscuri, renowned for their equestrian prowess, are hailed as peerless horsemen in Greek mythology. Their unrivaled skill in taming and riding horses has been immortalized in numerous myths and artistic representations. Pollux, as the immortal twin, is often depicted as the more skilled and superior horseman, benefitting from his divine lineage. Castor, the mortal twin, displays remarkable abilities as well, demonstrating the prowess and courage that befits a hero of his stature.

The Dioscuri's heroic exploits span a multitude of legendary adventures, ranging from battles with formidable foes to embarking on epic quests. Among their most celebrated feats is their participation in the Argonauts' quest for the Golden Fleece, where their bravery and resourcefulness solidified their status as revered heroes of ancient Greece.

Protective Role and Worship in Greek Society

Beyond their valiant deeds, the Dioscuri assumed a protective and benevolent role in Greek society. Revered as patrons of sailors and protectors of travelers, they were believed to provide assistance and safety to those undertaking perilous journeys at sea or on land. The divine twins' auspicious presence was invoked during voyages, where their watchful eyes were sought to guide mariners safely to their destinations.

This protective aspect of the Dioscuri found expression in various festivals and religious observances dedicated to their worship. In regions like Sparta, their native city, and throughout Greece, the Dioscuri were venerated through rituals and sacrifices. Their cult gained popularity, especially among seafaring communities and individuals seeking divine aid in times of danger or adversity.

Immortalization in the Stars

The legacy of the Dioscuri extends beyond the realms of myth and worship, as they were ultimately immortalized among the stars. According to ancient Greek belief, the Dioscuri were transformed into the constellation Gemini upon their death. The celestial bond between the twins is eternally preserved in the night sky, a symbol of their inseparable bond and immortal legacy.

Throughout this exploration of the Dioscuri's mythology, we shall unravel the multifaceted nature of their divine personas, the depth of their heroism, and the profound impact they had on the cultural and religious landscape of ancient Greece. We shall engage in critical analysis, delve into the nuances of their legends, and examine their significance within the broader context of Greek mythology and society. The tale of Pollux and Castor, the Dioscuri, shall serve as a compelling testament to the rich tapestry of ancient Greek beliefs, the complexities of human-divine relationships, and the enduring allure of mythic narratives in the human psyche.

Persephone

In the realm of ancient Greek mythology, amidst the grand pantheon of gods and goddesses, one figure stands out as a symbol of both life's vibrancy and the shadowed depths of death. Persephone, the daughter of Zeus and Demeter, reigns as the enigmatic Queen of the Underworld, commanding the transitions of the seasons and the cycles of life and death. Her story, woven with threads of divine intrigue and mortal sorrow, has captivated the hearts and minds of generations, leaving an indelible mark on the tapestry of human culture.

As we embark on this journey into the myth of Persephone, we shall explore the multifaceted layers of her character and the profound significance of her role in ancient Greek religion and society. Born to the mightiest of the gods, Zeus, and the nurturing goddess of agriculture, Demeter, Persephone's lineage casts her as a bridge between the divine and mortal realms. Her divine parentage gifted her with a unique blend of power and vulnerability, making her an essential figure in the ancient pantheon.

At the heart of Persephone's myth lies the fateful moment of her abduction by Hades, the god of the Underworld, and her transformation into the Queen of Shadows. This pivotal event shapes the very fabric of the cosmos, heralding the changing seasons and the cyclical nature of life's ebbs and flows. The story of Persephone's descent into the Underworld mirrors the cycles of death and rebirth found in the natural world, infusing ancient Greek culture with a profound connection to the rhythms of nature and the agricultural cycles that sustained their lives.

Throughout this exploration, we shall venture into the symbolic depths of Persephone's tale, delving into themes of light and darkness, life and death, and the eternal union between the divine and mortal realms. Her story serves as a bridge between the human experience and the realm of the gods, delving into the depths of human emotions, desires, and the mysteries of existence.

Moreover, Persephone's myth is not merely a story of divine beings but also a reflection of the human condition. It explores themes of loss, separation, and transformation, resonating with the complexities of human emotions and experiences. Through her journey, we gain insights into the ancient Greeks' understanding of the complexities of life and the enigmatic nature of the afterlife, providing us with a glimpse into their beliefs and rituals surrounding death and the afterlife.

Join us as we embark on this in-depth exploration of Persephone, the Queen of the Underworld, and uncover the timeless allure and wisdom embedded within her myth. From her dual roles as daughter and wife to her profound impact on Greek religious practices and cultural beliefs, Persephone's story serves as a guiding beacon through the vast expanse of ancient Greek mythology, enriching our understanding of the human experience and the enduring power of myth in shaping our perceptions of the world around us.

The Daughter of Zeus and Demeter

In the intricate tapestry of Greek mythology, Persephone stands as a central and enigmatic figure, her story intertwined with both divine and mortal realms. Born to Zeus, the king of the gods, and Demeter, the goddess of agriculture and fertility, Persephone's lineage positioned her amidst the Olympian pantheon. Her divine parentage granted her remarkable powers and bestowed upon her a unique place in the realm of the immortals.

Her Role as Queen of the Underworld

A pivotal moment in Persephone's tale arises when she is abducted by Hades, the god of the Underworld, and becomes his reluctant bride. This pivotal event transforms her into the Queen of the Underworld, reigning alongside Hades in the realm of shadows. Persephone's descent into the Underworld marks the onset of winter, as her mother, Demeter, mourns her absence, plunging the world into a season of barrenness. Her return to the world of the living in spring heralds the rejuvenation of nature and the rebirth of life, symbolizing the cyclical nature of the seasons.

Connection to the Seasons and Agricultural Cycles

Persephone's myth assumes great significance in the context of agricultural cycles and the seasonal changes that shaped ancient Greek society. The ancient Greeks observed the rhythm of nature and its profound connection to their agricultural practices. The story of Persephone's abduction and subsequent return served as an explanation for the changing seasons. Her time spent in the Underworld mirrored the barrenness of winter, while her return to the surface marked the arrival of spring and the return of fertility to the land.

Symbolism of the Divine and Mortal Union

Persephone's story is rich with symbolism, portraying themes of both life and death, light and darkness, and the eternal union of the divine and mortal realms. Her dual role as both Queen of the Underworld and goddess of fertility embodies the paradoxical nature of existence itself. Persephone's journey into the Underworld represents the cyclical nature of life, death, and rebirth, reflecting the eternal dance between mortality and immortality.

In this comprehensive exploration of Persephone's myth, we shall delve deep into the complexities of her character and the significance of her role as both daughter and wife to prominent deities. We shall analyze the implications of her connection to the changing seasons and agricultural cycles, illuminating the profound influence of her story on ancient Greek religious beliefs and practices.

As we unravel the enigma of Persephone, we will gain insights into the ancient Greeks' understanding of life, death, and the delicate balance between the forces of light and darkness. Through Persephone's tale, we shall explore the intricate web of relationships between gods and mortals, unveiling the timeless allure and relevance of ancient myths in shaping human perspectives on the mysteries of existence.

Minos

In the annals of ancient Greek mythology, few figures hold as complex and enigmatic a place as King Minos of Crete. Son of the mighty god Zeus and mortal princess Europa, Minos ascends the throne of Crete, ruling over a prosperous and powerful kingdom that played a significant role in shaping the narrative of Greek mythology. His myth intertwines with themes of divine lineage, labyrinthine mysteries, and the delicate balance between justice and power. As we venture into the depths of Minos' story, we shall unravel the multifaceted layers of his character, exploring his legendary exploits and the lasting impact of his rule on the mythical landscape.

King of Crete and Son of Zeus

Born from the union of Europa and Zeus, Minos inherits his divine heritage, becoming the rightful heir to the throne of Crete. His lineage connects him to the illustrious pantheon of gods, rendering him not merely a mortal king but also a figure of divine significance. This divine association underscores his authority and sets him apart from other mortal rulers, imbuing his actions and decisions with an aura of both power and responsibility.

The Labyrinth and the Minotaur

Minos' myth is inextricably linked to the legend of the Labyrinth, a mystifying maze constructed by the master craftsman Daedalus to imprison the fearsome Minotaur – a monstrous creature with the body of a man and the head of a bull. The enigmatic Labyrinth, an architectural marvel, serves as a symbol of Minos' power and control over the forces of chaos and terror. It represents the intersection of divine will, human ingenuity, and the intricate web of destiny, encapsulating the themes of confinement and liberation.

Just and Wise Ruler in Greek Mythology

In Greek mythology, Minos is often portrayed as a just and wise ruler, known for his adherence to divine laws and his commitment to the equitable governance of his kingdom. The famous myth of the Minotaur and the Athenian tribute underscores his sense of justice, enforcing a harsh punishment for the sacrilegious murder of his son, Androgeus. This reputation as a just ruler is further emphasized in his encounters with the Athenian hero Theseus, showcasing his adherence to fair judgement and his dedication to upholding the cosmic order.

Influence on Mythological Narrative

Minos' myth plays a significant role in shaping the broader tapestry of Greek mythology. From the labyrinthine symbolism that permeates various narratives to the themes of divine parentage and heroism, Minos' story weaves its threads into the complex narratives of ancient Greece. The myths surrounding Minos, the labyrinth, and the Minotaur continue to inspire art, literature, and philosophical contemplations, serving as a reflection of the human condition and the complexities of power and governance.

In this exploration of King Minos, we shall delve into the interplay of divine heritage and mortal rulership, the intricacies of justice and power, and the enigmatic world of the labyrinth that has captivated the imagination of generations. As we journey through the realms of myth and history, we shall gain a deeper understanding of the intricacies of ancient Greek culture and its lasting influence on the human quest for knowledge, justice, and meaning.

Sarpedon

In the vast tapestry of Greek mythology, Sarpedon emerges as a captivating and complex figure. The son of Zeus, king of the gods, and Laomedon's daughter, Laodamia, Sarpedon inherits both divine lineage and mortal heritage. His journey encompasses heroic feats on the battlefields of the Trojan War, entwined with the inexorable threads of fate that weave a tragic conclusion. As we explore the multifaceted narrative of Sarpedon, we shall uncover the intersections of divine and mortal realms, the pursuit of glory on the battlefield, and the inexorable forces of destiny that ultimately shape his legacy.

Son of Zeus and Laomedon's Son, Laodamia

Born as the son of Zeus, Sarpedon enjoys a divine lineage that connects him to the Olympian pantheon. His mother, Laodamia, is the daughter of King Laomedon of Troy, adding a mortal aspect to his identity. The duality of his parentage signifies the delicate balance between the divine and the mortal, a theme frequently encountered in Greek mythology. As a result of this divine parentage, Sarpedon is bestowed with exceptional abilities and heroic potential that set him apart from ordinary mortals.

The Heroic Role in the Trojan War

Sarpedon's most prominent appearance in Greek mythology is during the Trojan War, where he stands as a formidable warrior and leader of the Lycian forces. Allied with the Trojans, Sarpedon fights valiantly on the battlefield, displaying martial prowess and strategic acumen. His heroic exploits exemplify the qualities valued in ancient Greek culture, including bravery, honor, and loyalty. Throughout the epic conflict, Sarpedon emerges as a symbol of heroic virtue, embodying the essence of the warrior ethos in ancient Greek society.

Fate and Tragic End

Despite his heroic prowess, Sarpedon is not immune to the workings of fate that govern the lives of mortals and immortals alike. In the epic narrative, Sarpedon's fate is inextricably linked to the fulfillment of divine prophecies and the cosmic order. The tragic elements of his story unfold as the implacable wheels of destiny lead him towards an untimely end on the battlefield. This convergence of heroism and tragedy serves as a poignant reminder of the inexorable nature of fate and the vulnerability of even the most illustrious figures in Greek mythology.

The Legacy of Sarpedon in Greek Epics

Sarpedon's legacy extends beyond the boundaries of the Trojan War, leaving an indelible mark on Greek epics and the broader cultural consciousness. His character appears in various works of literature, including Homer's "Iliad" and other epic poems, reinforcing the significance of his role in Greek mythology. The portrayal of Sarpedon's fate and his divine heritage contributes to broader philosophical contemplations about the relationship between gods and mortals, the concept of heroism, and the nuances of life and death.

In delving into the life and fate of Sarpedon, we shall encounter the nuances of divine lineage and mortal struggle, the valor and tragedy of the battlefield, and the profound philosophical questions that underpin the human experience. Through the lens of this enigmatic figure, we gain insights into the complexities of ancient Greek culture, the interplay of fate and free will, and the enduring allure of mythological narratives that continue to captivate and inspire generations of scholars and enthusiasts alike.

Lacedaemon

Amidst the intricate tapestry of Greek mythology, Lacedaemon emerges as a central figure in the founding narrative of one of the most renowned city-states of ancient Greece: Sparta. Born as the son of Zeus and Taygete, Lacedaemon's lineage intertwines with divine heritage, endowing him with unique status and significance. As we embark on an exploration of Lacedaemon's life and legacy, we shall unravel the mythological origins of Sparta, the connections between Lacedaemon and Spartan culture, and the enduring legacy of his heroic ancestry that echoes throughout the annals of Greek history.

Son of Zeus and Taygete

Lacedaemon's parentage is marked by illustrious divinity, for he is the son of Zeus, the supreme deity of Greek mythology, and Taygete, one of the Pleiades, daughters of the Titan Atlas. This divine lineage elevates Lacedaemon's standing, as it establishes a direct link between him and the Olympian pantheon. The association with the Pleiades, a cluster of stars that captivated the imagination of ancient observers, also adds celestial symbolism to his character, further accentuating the divine nature of his birth.

Founder of Sparta and the Spartan Royal Lineage

Lacedaemon's most significant contribution to Greek mythology lies in his role as the founder of Sparta. According to legend, Lacedaemon established the city-state that would become synonymous with martial prowess, discipline, and resilience. His name would become synonymous with the land itself, as the region came to be known as Lacedaemonia or Laconia. Additionally, Lacedaemon's descendants, the Heracleidae, claimed a prominent position in the Spartan royal lineage, tracing their ancestry to the renowned hero Heracles. This connection to Heracles bestowed legitimacy upon the Spartan rulers, enhancing the prestige of the city-state and reinforcing its heroic legacy.

Connections to Spartan Culture and Society

Lacedaemon's influence extended beyond mere legendary origins, permeating the very fabric of Spartan culture and society. Spartan identity was deeply intertwined with mythological narratives, and the city's citizens perceived themselves as descendants of Lacedaemon and the Heracleidae. These mythological associations played a pivotal role in shaping Spartan ideals and values, including martial prowess, discipline, and loyalty to the state. The Spartans sought to emulate their heroic forebear, embodying the virtues that their legendary founder symbolized.

Heroic Legacy and Ancestry

Lacedaemon's heroic legacy extended beyond the realm of Sparta, for his divine ancestry linked him to the broader landscape of Greek mythology. As the son of Zeus, Lacedaemon is emblematic of the interplay between gods and mortals in ancient Greek culture. His mythological lineage reflects the profound fascination with heroism, divine heritage, and the connections between humans and the divine. Lacedaemon's position as a revered figure in Spartan society further highlights the significance of mythological narratives in shaping ancient Greek beliefs, values, and social structures.

In exploring the mythological tale of Lacedaemon, we gain insights into the foundations of Spartan culture, the interplay of divine and mortal realms in Greek mythology, and the enduring power of heroic ancestry in shaping the identities of ancient city-states. Lacedaemon's legacy serves as a testament to the enduring allure and impact of mythological narratives, which continue to captivate the imagination of scholars and enthusiasts alike, while providing a deeper understanding of the complexities of ancient Greek society and its cherished myths.

Arcas

In the rich tapestry of Greek mythology, Arcas emerges as a significant figure closely tied to both divine lineage and regional prominence. As the son of Zeus and Callisto, Arcas' parentage elevates him to a position of esteemed heritage, connecting him to the realm of gods. However, it is his role as the king of Arcadia and the founding figure of the Arcadian dynasty that truly highlights his historical and mythological significance. This section delves into the life of Arcas, exploring his divine lineage, the establishment of the Arcadian dynasty, the myths and legends surrounding his persona, and the integration of Arcas into local cults and worship in ancient Greece.

Son of Zeus and Callisto

Arcas' parentage lies in the divine realm, for he is the son of Zeus, the omnipotent ruler of the Greek pantheon, and Callisto, a nymph and attendant of the goddess Artemis. The story of Zeus' seduction of Callisto and the subsequent birth of Arcas is emblematic of the interplay between gods and mortals, an intricate theme that characterizes numerous tales in Greek mythology. Arcas' divine lineage imbues him with a special status, as he stands at the intersection of the mortal and immortal worlds.

The King of Arcadia and the Arcadian Dynasty

Arcas' ascent to the throne of Arcadia, a region in the Peloponnese known for its rugged terrain and pastoral beauty, marks a critical moment in his life. As the king of Arcadia, Arcas founded the Arcadian dynasty, which would hold sway over the region for generations to come. The establishment of a royal lineage tied to a divine heritage lent legitimacy and authority to Arcas and his descendants, solidifying their position as rulers and guardians of Arcadia's land and people.

Myths and Legends Surrounding Arcas

Arcas' mythological narrative extends beyond his divine parentage and kingly role, encompassing various myths and legends that enrich his character. One such tale revolves around Arcas' involvement in the Calydonian Boar Hunt, an epic hunt that brought together famed heroes from across ancient Greece. Arcas' participation in this perilous endeavor showcased his bravery and heroic nature, further cementing his status as a legendary figure in Greek mythology.

Another prominent myth surrounding Arcas is his involvement in the conflict between his mother Callisto and Hera, the jealous queen of the gods. Hera, angered by Zeus' infidelity with Callisto, transformed her into a bear. Arcas, unaware of his mother's transformation, nearly killed her while hunting. However, Zeus intervened, immortalizing Callisto as the constellation Ursa Major, and Arcas as Ursa Minor, forever linking mother and son in the night sky.

Integration into Local Cults and Worship

As a central figure in Arcadia, Arcas became an essential component of local cults and religious practices. In the region, he was venerated as a divine ancestor, and his heroic exploits were celebrated in various festivals and rituals. Arcas' divine lineage, coupled with his legendary achievements, served as a source of inspiration and guidance for the people of Arcadia, reinforcing their connection to the divine and the heroic.

Conclusion

Arcas' tale embodies the intricate interplay between gods and mortals, showcasing the complex interactions and relationships within Greek mythology. His dual identity as a divine figure and a regional king highlights the nuanced ways in which ancient Greek culture integrated mythological narratives into their societal structures. Arcas' legacy, intertwined with local cults and worship, exemplifies the enduring impact of mythological figures on ancient Greek religious practices and traditions. As we delve into the life of Arcas, we gain deeper insights into the fusion of divine lineage, heroic exploits, and regional identity that characterized the multifaceted nature of ancient Greek mythology.

Conclusion

In this chapter, we embarked on an illuminating journey through the pantheon of Greek mythology, beginning with the primordial Titans, the ancient and formidable deities who predated the Olympian gods. From Oceanus, the personification of the vast and ever-flowing ocean, to Mnemosyne, the symbol of memory and oral tradition, we encountered a diverse array of divine beings, each associated with distinct natural phenomena and cosmic forces.

Transitioning to the Olympian gods, we delved into the captivating realm of Zeus, the king of the gods, and his divine siblings, including Hera, Poseidon, Hades, and Demeter. We explored the complexities of their domains, from the skies and seas to the underworld and the earth, understanding their pivotal roles in the cosmic order and the unfolding of human destinies.

Our exploration culminated with the demigods, the extraordinary offspring of the divine unions between the Olympian gods and mortal women. These demigods, caught between the mortal and divine worlds, demonstrated heroism, courage, and virtue as they embarked on quests and faced formidable challenges, leaving an indelible mark on Greek culture and society.

Throughout this chapter, we have witnessed the enduring significance of Greek mythology in shaping the cultural, religious, and philosophical landscape of ancient Greece. The tales of these deities and demigods have inspired awe, reverence, and contemplation, serving as a foundation for religious practices, artistic expressions, and moral ideals.

As we progress in our exploration of Greek mythology, we will continue to unravel the intricate tapestry of these divine figures, seeking to understand the complexities of human nature and the perennial themes that transcend time. In doing so, we invite you, the reader, to engage critically and thoughtfully with the rich mythological heritage that has profoundly impacted the course of human history and continues to resonate with us in the modern world.

Themes and Patterns in the Stories of Zeus's Demigod Children

The narratives of Zeus's demigod children present a captivating tapestry of themes and patterns that reflect the complexities of ancient Greek society and the human condition. One overarching theme prevalent in these stories is the intricate relationship between gods and mortals. The divine parentage of Zeus's offspring blurs the boundaries between the mortal and immortal worlds, symbolizing the interconnectedness and interdependence of both realms. The demigods' struggles with their mortal and divine identities underscore the existential challenges faced by individuals caught between two vastly different worlds.

Furthermore, the motif of heroism permeates the tales of Zeus's progeny. As heroic figures, these demigods embark on quests and face trials of great magnitude, demonstrating courage, determination, and virtue. Their extraordinary feats, such as Heracles' Twelve Labors and Perseus' slaying of Medusa, serve as models of heroism and inspire admiration and emulation among ancient Greeks. The demigods' heroism reflects the idealized qualities valued in ancient Greek society, emphasizing the importance of bravery and nobility in the face of adversity.

Impact and Influence of Demigods on Ancient Greek Society

The influence of Zeus's demigod children on ancient Greek society transcends the realm of mythology and seeps into various aspects of cultural, religious, and social life. Their stories, perpetuated through oral tradition and later recorded in literature, became an integral part of the Greek collective memory. The tales of demigods played a significant role in shaping Greek cultural identity, instilling shared values, and fostering a sense of community and belonging.

Religiously, the demigods bridged the gap between the divine and the human, serving as intermediaries and guardians. Local cults and festivals dedicated to demigods provided opportunities for communities to seek protection, guidance, and divine favor. Moreover, their cults often integrated with preexisting religious practices, enriching the religious landscape of ancient Greece.

The societal impact of demigods also extended to the realm of politics and power dynamics. The lineage of divine parentage granted legitimacy and authority to certain rulers and dynasties, as seen with the establishment of royal lineages descending from Zeus's demigod children. Additionally, the tales of heroic exploits served as cautionary tales and moral lessons for rulers and citizens alike, underscoring the importance of just and noble leadership.

The Enduring Legacy of Zeus's Progeny in Mythology and Modern Culture

The legacy of Zeus's demigod children endures through the ages, as their stories continue to captivate audiences and influence modern culture. Greek mythology, with its rich tapestry of gods and heroes, remains a wellspring of inspiration for literature, art, theater, and popular culture. The archetypal figures of demigods embody timeless themes of heroism, identity, and the struggle between mortality and immortality, resonating with contemporary audiences.

In literature and cinema, the tales of Zeus's demigod children have been reimagined and adapted into countless retellings, exploring new dimensions of these ancient characters. The enduring appeal of figures like Heracles and Perseus demonstrates their relevance in exploring human nature and the complexities of the human experience.

Beyond entertainment, the influence of Zeus's progeny extends into the realm of psychology and self-discovery. Jungian psychologists and modern mythologists draw upon the archetypes present in Greek mythology, including the demigod hero, to explore the depths of the human psyche and the collective unconscious.

In conclusion, the stories of Zeus's demigod children reveal not only the multifaceted nature of Greek mythology but also the profound impact of these figures on ancient Greek society and their enduring legacy in contemporary culture. As we delve into the complex tales of these divine and mortal beings, we gain insight into the human condition and the timeless themes that continue to resonate with humanity. The demigods' journeys of heroism, identity, and the quest for meaning transcend time and space, inspiring critical thinking and exploration of the human experience in both ancient and modern contexts.

The divine hierarchy and the role of gods in human affairs

In the intricate tapestry of ancient Greek mythology, the divine hierarchy played a pivotal role in shaping the cosmos and influencing the course of human affairs. The pantheon of Greek gods and goddesses constituted a complex web of relationships, powers, and responsibilities, with each deity holding domain over distinct aspects of the natural and supernatural realms. This section delves into the fundamental principles that governed the divine hierarchy and explores the multifaceted role of gods in the lives of mortals.

The Olympian Pantheon: A Structured Order of Deities

At the pinnacle of the divine hierarchy stood the Olympian gods, a prominent group of twelve deities who resided on Mount Olympus. Led by Zeus, the king of gods and lord of the heavens, this assembly comprised Hera, Poseidon, Demeter, Athena, Apollo, Artemis, Ares, Aphrodite, Hephaestus, Hermes, and Dionysus. Each Olympian deity presided over specific domains and embodied particular attributes, ranging from wisdom and war to fertility and craftsmanship. This organized structure underscored the significance of divine order and the harmony that governed the cosmos.

The Role of Gods in Human Affairs: Agents of Fate and Free Will

The gods' involvement in human affairs was multifaceted, reflecting the complex interplay between fate and free will in Greek mythology. As celestial beings, the gods possessed vast knowledge and foresight, which often translated into shaping the destinies of mortals. Their influence could be both benevolent and malevolent, as gods sometimes bestowed blessings or inflicted punishments based on human actions and devotion. The concept of moira, or fate, underscored the notion that certain events were predetermined and beyond mortal control, while at the same time, individuals were responsible for their choices and actions, signifying free will.

Divine Intervention and Favor: Rituals and Sacrifices

To appease the gods and seek their favor, ancient Greeks performed elaborate rituals and made sacrificial offerings. Temples and sacred sites were dedicated to specific deities, serving as focal points for worship and religious gatherings. Priests and priestesses acted as intermediaries between mortals and gods, performing sacred rites and interpreting divine will. Such practices aimed to invoke divine benevolence, ensure bountiful harvests, protect against calamities, and gain victory in battles. These rituals also facilitated communal cohesion and contributed to the reinforcement of social norms and values.

The Moral and Ethical Dimension: Gods as Moral Exemplars

Beyond their roles as cosmic entities, the gods served as moral exemplars, showcasing virtues and vices that mirrored human conduct. While some myths illustrated divine qualities to emulate, others depicted gods behaving in capricious or morally ambiguous ways. Such narratives posed thought-provoking questions about the nature of divinity and the relationship between gods and mortals. Greek tragedies and epics often explored ethical dilemmas arising from interactions with the divine, further enriching the moral discourse within Greek society.

Theological Interpretations and Philosophical Inquiries

The divine hierarchy in Greek mythology prompted philosophical inquiries concerning the nature of divinity, cosmology, and metaphysics. Philosophers like Plato and Aristotle explored the ontological status of gods, considering whether they were archetypes or existent entities. Their works, along with the writings of other ancient thinkers, laid the groundwork for theological discussions that continue to inspire philosophical discourse to this day.

Conclusion:

The divine hierarchy and the role of gods in human affairs in ancient Greek mythology were foundational elements of the culture's religious and philosophical landscape. The Olympian pantheon's structured order, the gods' interactions with mortals, and the moral dimensions conveyed through myths provided the ancient Greeks with a profound understanding of the cosmic and ethical dimensions of existence. As students of Greek mythology, we are invited to critically engage with the complexities of the divine hierarchy and explore the enduring questions raised by the interplay of gods and humans in the myths of ancient Greece.

Mythology as a Window to Belief

In the vast tapestry of human history, mythology has emerged as a fascinating and multifaceted subject of study, offering a unique window into the belief systems, values, and worldview of ancient cultures. Mythological narratives, crafted by diverse civilizations across time, serve as a repository of human imagination, wisdom, and spiritual exploration. This section delves into the profound significance of mythology as a lens through which we can explore the religious, philosophical, and social dimensions of ancient societies.

The Nature of Mythology: Myths as Cultural Mirrors

Myths are symbolic narratives that convey the cosmological, moral, and social beliefs of a particular culture or civilization. They often feature gods, heroes, and supernatural beings and provide explanations for the origins of the world, the nature of humanity, and the interactions between mortals and immortals. These stories reflect the cultural values, fears, aspirations, and experiences of the societies from which they arise. As we examine myths, we encounter the rich tapestry of human thought and emotions woven into the fabric of ancient civilizations.

Mythology and Religion: Interplay of the Sacred and Profane

Mythology and religion share a complex relationship, with myths often serving as the foundation of religious beliefs and rituals. The deities and heroic figures depicted in myths are not merely characters in a story but embody the sacred and the divine. Rituals and practices associated with mythological narratives create a sense of continuity and reinforce communal identity. The study of mythology offers insights into the religious practices, cults, and sacred sites that shaped the spiritual landscapes of ancient societies.

Interpretations and Reinterpretations: The Evolving Nature of Myths

As myths are transmitted through generations, they undergo reinterpretations and adaptations to suit the changing needs and contexts of different epochs. These transformations may arise due to shifts in cultural norms, political ideologies, or philosophical inquiries. Scholars, poets, and artists have engaged in the reimagining of myths, adding layers of complexity and nuance to the original narratives. The study of these reinterpretations sheds light on the dynamic nature of mythology and its enduring relevance.

Mythology and Modernity: Insights into Contemporary Culture

Despite the temporal and cultural distance that separates us from ancient societies, mythology continues to resonate in modern times. Myths find echoes in literature, art, music, and popular culture, reflecting the enduring appeal of these timeless stories. The archetypal characters and themes present in myths provide a lens through which we can explore contemporary issues and psychological experiences. Moreover, the study of mythology prompts us to engage critically with our own beliefs, values, and cultural heritage.

Approaching Mythology with Critical Inquiry

As students of mythology, we embark on a journey of critical inquiry, exploring the nuances, complexities, and contradictions within these ancient narratives. We analyze the historical contexts in which myths emerged, the socio-political implications of their transmission, and the ways in which they shaped the collective psyche of their respective civilizations. Through rigorous examination and thoughtful reflection, we uncover the layers of symbolism, ideology, and universal themes embedded in these captivating tales.

Conclusion:

The study of mythology offers us a profound opportunity to understand the beliefs, worldviews, and spiritual aspirations of ancient cultures. As we explore the diverse pantheon of gods, the heroic feats of demigods, and the intricate tapestry of mythical narratives, we gain insights into the human experience across time and space. Through this exploration, we foster critical thinking and engage in meaningful discussions, recognizing the enduring significance of mythology as a window to belief, both in the past and in our contemporary world.

The relationship between myths and religious beliefs in ancient Greek culture

Ancient Greek mythology and religious beliefs were profoundly interconnected, with myths serving as a fundamental expression of the Greeks' religious worldview. This section delves into the intricate relationship between myths and religious beliefs in Greek culture, examining how myths functioned as a medium for communicating divine narratives, elucidating sacred truths, and shaping the spiritual experiences of the ancient Greeks.

Myths as Sacred Narratives

In ancient Greek society, myths were regarded as sacred narratives, conveying stories of gods, goddesses, heroes, and supernatural beings. These myths were not seen as mere works of fiction or entertainment; rather, they were considered to be timeless and profound accounts of the divine. Through myths, the Greeks sought to comprehend the origins of the universe, the creation of the world, the nature of the gods, and the moral guidelines governing human behavior. As such, myths played an integral role in establishing the cosmogonical and theogonical frameworks that underpinned Greek religious beliefs.

Rituals and Festivals Inspired by Myths

Myths were intimately intertwined with religious rituals and festivals in ancient Greece. Many religious ceremonies were directly inspired by the events and characters depicted in mythical narratives. For instance, the myth of Demeter and Persephone formed the basis for the Eleusinian Mysteries, a significant religious festival celebrated in honor of these goddesses. Similarly, the myth of Dionysus, the god of wine and ecstasy, inspired the Dionysian festivals, characterized by revelry and ecstatic worship. These rituals were believed to ensure the favor of the gods, promote fertility, and strengthen the bonds of the community.

Divine Genealogies and Ancestry

Greek mythology abounded with genealogies tracing the lineage of gods and goddesses. These genealogies served to establish the hierarchical order of the divine realm and the interconnectedness of deities within the pantheon. The stories of gods' lineage and ancestry highlighted their divine attributes, immortal nature, and divine authority over various aspects of the cosmos. Moreover, divine genealogies also linked certain city-states or local cults to prestigious deities, fostering a sense of sacred identity and communal pride.

Moral and Ethical Lessons in Myths

Beyond recounting the exploits of deities and heroes, myths often conveyed moral and ethical lessons to guide human behavior. The actions and consequences depicted in these narratives provided the ancient Greeks with a moral framework, reinforcing notions of justice, piety, and hubris. For instance, the myth of Prometheus and the theft of fire conveyed the dangers of challenging divine authority, while the story of Pandora warned against the consequences of human curiosity. Myths served as cautionary tales, prompting individuals to contemplate their actions and strive for moral rectitude.

Challenges and Interpretations

Despite the deeply ingrained connection between myths and religious beliefs, there were instances of variations and reinterpretations of myths across different regions and time periods. Local cults and traditions often modified myths to suit their specific needs and cultural contexts. As a result, myths sometimes presented seemingly contradictory narratives, leading to debates and discussions among ancient Greeks regarding the authenticity and significance of certain myths. The fluidity of mythic narratives added richness and complexity to Greek religious beliefs, fostering an ongoing discourse within the society.

Conclusion:

In ancient Greek culture, myths and religious beliefs were inextricably linked, forming an intricate tapestry that shaped the spiritual and social fabric of the society. Myths served as sacred narratives, conveying divine truths, guiding moral behavior, and inspiring religious rituals and festivals. The stories of gods' genealogies and the exploits of heroes established a hierarchical divine order and forged a sense of communal identity. The enduring relationship between myths and religious beliefs reflects the profound significance of mythology as a conduit for understanding the complexities of ancient Greek spirituality and culture.

Analyzing the function of myths as narratives of cultural values and identity

Myths in ancient Greek culture served as potent vehicles for expressing and preserving cultural values, norms, and identity. This section delves into the multifaceted role of myths as narratives that encapsulate the core beliefs, social ideals, and collective identity of the ancient Greeks. Through a comprehensive analysis of key mythological narratives, we explore how myths functioned as mirrors reflecting the cultural consciousness and shaping the worldview of the society.

Reflection of Cultural Values

Myths were intricately intertwined with the values and ethics of ancient Greek society. Through the portrayal of gods, goddesses, and heroes, myths conveyed a set of moral standards that were upheld by the community. For instance, the myth of Prometheus stealing fire from the gods and gifting it to humanity exemplified the Greeks' reverence for resourcefulness, intelligence, and defiance against divine authority. Similarly, the legend of Hercules and his Twelve Labors exemplified the virtues of bravery, determination, and resilience in the face of adversity. By embodying these virtues in mythic figures, the ancient Greeks not only celebrated individual heroism but also instilled a sense of moral obligation and collective responsibility.

Reinforcement of Social Norms

Myths played a crucial role in reinforcing social norms and hierarchical structures in ancient Greek society. The divine genealogies, in particular, demonstrated the esteemed lineage of certain ruling families, solidifying their authority and legitimacy. Moreover, myths often depicted the consequences of violating societal norms, serving as cautionary tales to deter individuals from deviating from established customs. The myth of Arachne, for instance, warned against the dangers of arrogance and hubris in the face of divine authority. These narratives contributed to the maintenance of order, stability, and social cohesion within the community.

Formation of Collective Identity

Myths were instrumental in forging a sense of collective identity among the ancient Greeks. Shared myths, rituals, and festivals brought communities together, fostering a shared sense of heritage and belonging. The myth of the founding of Athens by Cecrops, for example, solidified the city's identity and origin story, instilling a sense of civic pride and unity among its inhabitants. Similarly, the myths surrounding the Trojan War and the adventures of Odysseus bound the diverse Greek city-states together, creating a pan-Hellenic identity that transcended regional differences. Myths were not only stories of the distant past but living narratives that connected the people to their ancestral roots and cultural heritage.

Cultural Adaptation and Transformation

While myths were deeply rooted in tradition, they also exhibited adaptability and transformation over time. As the Greeks encountered new cultures and absorbed foreign influences, they integrated these elements into their mythic narratives. For instance, the myth of Aphrodite, the goddess of love and beauty, was believed to have been influenced by Near Eastern goddesses like Ishtar and Astarte. Similarly, the cult of Demeter and Persephone, centered on the cycle of vegetation, bore similarities to ancient Near Eastern fertility cults. These adaptations allowed myths to remain relevant and meaningful to changing societal contexts while preserving their core cultural values.

The Polyvalent Nature of Myths

Myths were often polyvalent, capable of carrying multiple meanings and interpretations. Different communities and individuals might understand the same myth in diverse ways, leading to a rich tapestry of meanings. This polyvalence allowed myths to accommodate varying beliefs, viewpoints, and local traditions, ensuring their enduring relevance in a dynamic and diverse society.

Conclusion:

In ancient Greek culture, myths served as powerful narratives that encompassed cultural values, societal norms, and collective identity. They reflected the moral principles, social hierarchies, and cherished virtues of the society while promoting a shared sense of heritage and belonging. Myths were not stagnant relics of the past; rather, they adapted and transformed over time, remaining vital components of Greek culture. Through their polyvalent nature, myths accommodated diverse interpretations, engaging individuals and communities in critical thinking and discussion. As windows to the beliefs and identity of ancient Greece, myths continue to captivate and inspire modern audiences, revealing the timeless complexities of human nature and the enduring power of storytelling.

Ancient Greek Religious Practices

Ancient Greek religious practices form a rich tapestry of beliefs, rituals, and customs that played a central role in the lives of the Greeks. Rooted in the polytheistic worldview, the religious landscape of ancient Greece was populated by a diverse pantheon of gods and goddesses, each presiding over various aspects of human existence and the natural world. This section serves as a gateway to exploring the intricacies of this religious tapestry, delving into the multifaceted dimensions of Greek religiosity and its enduring significance.

Polytheism and Anthropomorphism: The Greek Pantheon

At the heart of ancient Greek religious practices was the worship of an extensive pantheon of gods and goddesses. These divine beings, though immortal and powerful, were often depicted with human attributes and emotions, a concept known as anthropomorphism. Through anthropomorphism, the ancient Greeks bridged the gap between the human and divine realms, making the gods relatable to mortal concerns and aspirations. The pantheon encompassed deities with dominion over various domains, such as Zeus, the king of the gods and god of thunder; Athena, the goddess of wisdom and warfare; Aphrodite, the goddess of love and beauty; and many others. Understanding the diverse roles and attributes of these gods provides invaluable insights into the complexities of Greek religious practices.

Rituals and Offerings: Communing with the Divine

Ancient Greek religious practices were deeply entwined with rituals and ceremonies designed to connect with the gods and seek their favor. These rituals ranged from grand festivals, such as the Olympics in honor of Zeus, to private household ceremonies, like libations and sacrifices, performed to honor the household gods and ancestors. Temples and sacred sites dedicated to specific deities served as focal points for religious activities, drawing pilgrims and devotees from across the Greek world. Understanding the significance of these rituals sheds light on the spiritual and social dimensions of Greek religious life.

Oracle and Divination: Seeking Guidance from the Divine

The Greeks sought divine guidance and insight through various forms of divination and oracular practices. One of the most famous oracles was the Oracle of

Delphi, where the priestess, known as the Pythia, delivered cryptic prophecies inspired by Apollo. These prophetic utterances held great influence, guiding political decisions, military campaigns, and personal matters. The art of divination, including the interpretation of dreams and the examination of animal entrails, provided avenues for individuals to seek divine counsel and navigate the uncertainties of life.

Integration of Religion in Daily Life: Religion as a Cultural Fabric

Ancient Greek religious practices were not confined to temples and rituals; they permeated every aspect of daily life and communal activities. From birth to death, religion was an integral part of Greek culture, shaping traditions, laws, and customs. Religious festivals and processions, such as the Eleusinian Mysteries and the Dionysian celebrations, brought communities together in celebration and spiritual connection. The concept of "eusebeia," or piety, was highly valued, emphasizing reverence and duty towards the gods, family, and the state. Understanding the integration of religion in daily life provides a holistic perspective on the cultural, social, and psychological impact of religious beliefs and practices.

Evolution and Interaction: The Interplay of Local and Pan-Hellenic Traditions

Greek religious practices were not homogenous but evolved over time, influenced by local traditions, interactions with other cultures, and historical events. Different regions and city-states had their unique religious practices and cults, reflecting the diverse landscape of Greek culture. Yet, there were also pan-Hellenic religious festivals and cults that united the Greek world, fostering a sense of common identity and shared heritage. The study of these interactions and variations offers a nuanced understanding of the dynamic nature of Greek religiosity.

Conclusion:

The introduction to ancient Greek religious practices provides a foundation for exploring the multifaceted world of Greek religiosity. From the anthropomorphic pantheon to intricate rituals, from oracular practices to the integration of religion in daily life, the rich tapestry of Greek religious practices shaped the worldview, values, and identity of the ancient Greeks. Understanding these practices allows us to delve into the heart of Greek culture and spirituality, revealing a society deeply connected with the divine and seeking to comprehend the mysteries of existence through their religious beliefs and rituals.

Rituals, sacrifices, and ceremonies: Understanding the role of religious practices in the lives of ancient Greeks

The religious practices of ancient Greeks were integral to their cultural and spiritual identity. These practices encompassed a diverse array of rituals, sacrifices, and ceremonies that played a crucial role in their daily lives and communal activities. The ancient Greeks believed that by performing these religious acts, they could communicate with the gods, seek their favor, and maintain cosmic order and harmony. This section explores the multifaceted dimensions of Greek religious practices and delves into their significance in shaping individual beliefs and societal values.

Rituals and Their Functions

Rituals in ancient Greek religion were carefully prescribed sequences of actions performed in a set order. These rituals were often accompanied by prayers, hymns, and symbolic gestures. Their meticulous observance was believed to maintain the relationship between mortals and deities and uphold the cosmic order. Rituals were conducted in various settings, such as temples, homes, and sacred sites, each serving a specific purpose. Some rituals marked the passage of time, like the annual festivals dedicated to specific gods, while others were performed to mark important life events such as births, marriages, and funerals. Understanding the functions of these rituals provides insight into how the Greeks sought to navigate the complexities of their existence and foster a sense of community and shared purpose.

The Role of Sacrifices

Sacrifices held a central position in Greek religious practices. The act of offering animals, crops, or other valuables to the gods was seen as a form of reciprocity, expressing gratitude and seeking divine favor. Sacrifices were performed for various reasons, including seeking protection, celebrating victories, and appeasing wrathful deities. The choice of offerings varied based on the recipient god and the nature of the request. While sacrifices were seen as a means to establish communion with the gods, they also served to strengthen social bonds, as communal feasting often followed these religious acts. Analyzing the role of sacrifices allows us to understand the intricate connection between religion and social cohesion in ancient Greek society.

Ceremonies and Festivals

Ceremonies and festivals held a prominent place in Greek religious life. Festivals, often held in honor of specific deities, were celebrated with grand processions, athletic competitions, theatrical performances, and elaborate rituals. These festivals not only demonstrated reverence to the gods but also acted as occasions for communal bonding and cultural expression. For example, the Panathenaic Games held in Athens in honor of Athena brought people from all over Greece together to celebrate their shared heritage. Ceremonies, on the other hand, were events that marked significant life moments, such as coming of age or citizenship initiation. Through ceremonies and festivals, the Greeks reinforced their religious beliefs and cultural traditions.

Mysteries and Secret Cults

Apart from the public rituals and festivals, ancient Greece also had secretive religious practices known as mysteries or mystery cults. These cults involved initiation rites and sacred knowledge accessible only to initiates. One of the most famous mystery cults was the Eleusinian Mysteries, dedicated to Demeter and Persephone. The precise details of these rites were closely guarded, and initiates believed that participating in the mysteries offered the promise of a better afterlife and spiritual enlightenment. The existence of mystery cults highlights the diverse range of religious experiences available to the ancient Greeks and their pursuit of deeper spiritual understanding.

Rituals and Personal Piety

Religious practices were not solely confined to state-sanctioned rituals and festivals. Individual piety played a crucial role in Greek religious life. Private households had household shrines, where families would perform daily rituals and offerings to their household gods and ancestors. Additionally, individuals sought personal communication with the gods through prayer, divination, and dream interpretation. Personal piety allowed for a more intimate and personal relationship with the divine, reinforcing the idea that religious beliefs were not only collective but also deeply personal.

Conclusion: The Multifaceted Nature of Greek Religious Practices

The intricate web of rituals, sacrifices, and ceremonies in ancient Greek religion reveals the multifaceted nature of their religious beliefs. These practices were not isolated from everyday life but permeated every aspect of ancient Greek society. They served as a means of communication with the gods, a way to express gratitude, seek protection, and make sense of the complexities of life and death. Through the study of these religious practices, we gain invaluable insights into the spiritual, cultural, and social fabric of ancient Greek civilization. Understanding the significance of rituals, sacrifices, and ceremonies allows us to appreciate the enduring impact of ancient Greek religious beliefs on the development of human thought and cultural practices.

Temples, sanctuaries, and sacred spaces: Examining the physical manifestations of Greek religious devotion

In ancient Greece, religious practices were not confined to abstract beliefs and rituals; they found tangible expressions in the form of temples, sanctuaries, and other sacred spaces. These physical manifestations of religious devotion were central to the religious experience of the ancient Greeks and played a vital role in shaping their spiritual and cultural identity. This section explores the significance of temples, the layout of sanctuaries, and the purpose of sacred spaces in Greek religious life, shedding light on how the physical and spiritual realms intersected in their worship.

Temples: Architectural Marvels and Divine Abodes

Greek temples were architectural masterpieces dedicated to the worship of specific gods and goddesses. These structures served as divine abodes, places where the gods were believed to reside and interact with mortals. Built with meticulous precision and adorned with intricate sculptures and artwork, temples exemplified the artistic and engineering prowess of ancient Greece. Each temple was designed following a specific architectural order, such as Doric, Ionic, or Corinthian, adding a sense of visual harmony to the sacred landscape. Examples of renowned temples include the Parthenon in Athens, dedicated to the goddess Athena, and the Temple of Apollo at Delphi, a sanctuary visited by pilgrims seeking oracles and divine guidance.

Sanctuaries: Centers of Worship and Communal Gatherings

Sanctuaries were enclosed sacred spaces dedicated to the worship of deities and the performance of religious rites. They were often located in natural settings, such as mountains, groves, or coastal areas, believed to be especially favored by the gods. Sanctuaries served as centers of religious activities and were equipped with altars for offerings, statues of the gods, and other religious paraphernalia. Major sanctuaries, such as the Sanctuary of Olympia, the site of the ancient Olympic Games, attracted visitors from all over Greece to partake in festivals, athletic competitions, and religious ceremonies. These communal gatherings fostered a sense of unity and shared spiritual identity among the ancient Greeks.

Oracles and Sacred Sites: Channels to the Divine

Certain locations in ancient Greece were renowned for being oracular centers, where priestesses, known as oracles, delivered divine messages and prophecies. The Oracle of Delphi, dedicated to the god Apollo, was one of the most famous oracular sites. Pilgrims from far and wide sought the counsel of the Oracle of Delphi before making significant decisions, such as going to war or founding colonies. The prophetic utterances of the oracles were highly esteemed and held immense influence over the political and military affairs of the time. These sacred sites acted as channels through which the divine communicated with mortals, shaping their beliefs and actions.

Outdoor Ritual Spaces: Celebrating Nature and Deities

In addition to temples and sanctuaries, the ancient Greeks also conducted religious rituals in outdoor spaces that were considered sacred. These open-air areas, often situated amidst natural surroundings, provided a direct connection to the gods and the divine forces of nature. Examples include the sacred groves dedicated to particular deities, where rituals involving music, dance, and offerings took place. The Greeks believed that these natural spaces allowed for a closer communion with the gods, celebrating the beauty and bounty of the natural world while expressing gratitude to the divine.

Religious Pilgrimages: Journeys of Faith

Religious pilgrimages were a significant aspect of Greek religious practices. Devotees embarked on journeys to visit distant sanctuaries or oracular sites, seeking spiritual enlightenment, healing, or divine guidance. These pilgrimages were not only acts of religious devotion but also opportunities for personal introspection and renewal. Pilgrims often engaged in rituals of purification and introspection before reaching their sacred destination, emphasizing the transformative and introspective nature of these journeys.

Conclusion: The Physical and Spiritual Convergence

The temples, sanctuaries, and sacred spaces of ancient Greece were more than just physical structures; they were tangible expressions of the Greeks' religious fervor and their quest for spiritual connection. These physical manifestations of religious devotion provided a sense of continuity and coherence in the diverse tapestry of Greek religious beliefs and practices. From awe-inspiring temples to mystical oracular sites, each aspect of Greek sacred spaces reflected the enduring bond between mortals and the divine, shaping their worldview and influencing their cultural and social norms. Analyzing the physical manifestations of Greek religious devotion allows us to glimpse into the rich tapestry of ancient Greek spirituality and the profound impact of religious practices on their lives and society as a whole.

Chapter 3: Scope and Goals of the Course

The study of ancient Greek religion is an enriching and multidisciplinary field that delves into the complex tapestry of beliefs, rituals, and practices that defined the spiritual landscape of ancient Greece. In this chapter, we embark on an exploration of the scope and goals of our course, aiming to provide students with a comprehensive understanding of the multifaceted aspects of Greek religious traditions. We will delve into the diverse pantheon of gods and goddesses, the significance of myths and religious narratives, the role of religious practices in ancient Greek society, and the enduring legacy of these ancient beliefs in modern times.

Understanding the Pantheon: Gods and Goddesses of Ancient Greece

The ancient Greek pantheon comprised a plethora of gods and goddesses, each with distinct roles, attributes, and realms of influence. Throughout this course, we will examine the major deities, including Zeus, Hera, Poseidon, Athena, Apollo, Artemis, Aphrodite, and many others. Our exploration will shed light on the divine family tree and the intricate relationships between these gods, as well as the myths and narratives that shaped their identities. By understanding the divine personalities and attributes, we aim to grasp the complexities of Greek religious beliefs and the influence of divine powers on various aspects of human life.

The Power of Myth: Analyzing Religious Narratives

Myths served as the foundation of ancient Greek religion, providing a lens through which the Greeks understood the world, their origins, and their place in the cosmic order. Throughout this chapter, we will closely analyze the rich tapestry of Greek myths, exploring the adventures of gods, heroes, and mythical creatures. By examining these narratives, we aim to discern the underlying cultural values, ethical principles, and philosophical ideas embedded within them. We will also delve into the diverse interpretations of myths across different periods and regions, showcasing how myths were not static but evolved over time, reflecting the changing beliefs and values of Greek society.

Religious Practices: Rituals, Sacrifices, and Ceremonies

In ancient Greece, religious practices were not mere formalities; they formed an integral part of daily life and community cohesion. This section will delve into the diverse religious rituals, sacrifices, and ceremonies conducted by the ancient Greeks. From the elaborate temple rituals to the outdoor festivals and processions, we will examine the symbolic significance and functions of these practices in shaping individual and communal identities. We will also discuss the role of priests, priestesses, and religious specialists in mediating between the mortal and divine realms, fostering a deeper understanding of the complex dynamics of Greek religious life.

The Interaction of Religion and Society

Ancient Greek religion was intricately intertwined with various aspects of society, politics, and culture. In this section, we will explore the impact of religious beliefs on social norms, ethics, and governance. We will discuss how religious festivals and games brought communities together, fostering a sense of unity and shared cultural identity. Moreover, we will examine how religious oracles and sanctuaries influenced important decisions, such as going to war or establishing colonies. By analyzing the interaction of religion and society, we aim to appreciate the profound influence of religious beliefs on shaping the fabric of ancient Greek civilization.

Legacy and Relevance: Ancient Greek Religion in Modern Times

Finally, this chapter will contemplate the enduring legacy of ancient Greek religion in the modern world. We will explore how elements of Greek mythology, religious symbolism, and ethical principles have transcended time and continue to resonate in various fields, such as literature, art, philosophy, and popular culture. Furthermore, we will discuss the influence of ancient Greek religion on the development of Western religious and philosophical traditions, showcasing its enduring relevance and impact on the course of human thought.

Conclusion

In the following chapters, we will delve into each of these topics with a critical and open-minded approach, engaging with different perspectives and interpretations. Through a combination of historical analysis, literary examination, and anthropological insights, we aim to present a comprehensive and thought-provoking exploration of ancient Greek religious practices and beliefs. By the end of this course, students will have gained a deep appreciation for the richness and complexity of ancient Greek religion and its enduring significance in shaping human culture and thought.

Historical Context of Ancient Greece

The study of ancient Greece provides a captivating journey through time, encompassing a vast expanse of history that spans over millennia. In this section, we shall embark on an immersive exploration of the historical context that shaped the vibrant civilization of ancient Greece. To comprehend the religious, social, and cultural facets of this ancient world, it is imperative to first establish a solid foundation by delving into the historical events and developments that defined its trajectory.

The Bronze Age: Minoans and Mycenaeans

The Minoan Civilization: The Precursors of Greek Culture
In the midst of the Bronze Age, the island of Crete emerged as a cradle of an advanced civilization known as the Minoans, who thrived from approximately 2700 to 1450 BCE. The Minoans were a seafaring people, and their civilization was characterized by complex social structures, innovative architecture, and vibrant art, which are manifest in the splendid palace complexes such as the one at Knossos.

The Minoan religious practices, as discerned from archeological findings, indicate a prominent role of nature, fertility, and female deities. The iconic figurines of 'snake goddesses' and symbols associated with fertility are testament to this trend. It is plausible that these Minoan beliefs and practices had a significant influence on the later religious systems of ancient Greece.

Moreover, the Minoan civilization's extensive maritime trade networks underscore its advanced economic organization and technological capabilities. Evidence of Minoan pottery and artifacts across the Mediterranean region attests to these extensive trade connections.

✧ The Mycenaean Civilization: The Dawn of the Hellenic Age

Around 2000 BCE, another civilization began to develop on the mainland of Greece. Known as the Mycenaeans, they reached their zenith between 1400 and 1200 BCE. The Mycenaeans borrowed and adapted many aspects of Minoan culture, including its writing system (Linear A), which they developed into their own script known as Linear B.

The Mycenaean civilization was marked by strong militaristic characteristics, evidenced by the fortifications of their palatial centers and the frequent depiction of warfare in their art. Mycenaean religion, discernible from Linear B tablets, mentions deities that later became part of the Greek pantheon, albeit their characteristics and roles might have been different in this early period.

In essence, the interplay between the Minoan and Mycenaean civilizations contributed to the development of what would later become the distinctive Hellenic culture, influencing various aspects, including religion, art, architecture, and economic organization.

Dark Ages and the Emergence of the Polis

The Greek Dark Ages: Disruption and Transformation
With the sudden collapse of the Mycenaean civilization around 1100 BCE, the progress of the previous eras seemingly reversed. This period, known as the Dark Ages, was characterized by depopulation, deurbanization, and a decline in literacy. The complex political and economic systems of the Mycenaean era gave way to smaller, agrarian communities. Despite this regression, the Dark Ages were not entirely an era of decline. Instead, it was a period of transformation and adaptation to new circumstances.

✧   The Rise of the Polis: A New Dawn

Around the 9th century BCE, as the Dark Ages began to recede, the polis or city-state started to emerge as the principal form of political organization. Each polis was an independent entity, with its unique set of laws, political structure, and patron deities. Two of the most famous city-states were Athens, known for its democratic governance, and Sparta, famous for its military-oriented society.

The rise of the polis marked a critical stage in the evolution of Greek culture. It served as a framework that facilitated the development of a shared cultural identity while maintaining regional variations. This period saw significant advancements in various fields, including politics, philosophy, literature, and the arts, which laid the foundation for the Classical period of Greece.

By exploring these transformative epochs in Greek history, students will gain a deeper understanding of the complex and dynamic nature of societal evolution, offering valuable insights into how civilizations adapt and evolve in response to both internal changes and external pressures.

The Archaic Period: Encounter with the Near East and Colonization

✦ Cultural Interaction and Syncretism

The Archaic period, spanning from the 8th to the 6th century BCE, was a transformative era in Greek history. During this period, the Greeks reestablished contact with the civilizations of the Near East, such as the Persians, Phoenicians, and Egyptians. The commercial and diplomatic interactions facilitated by maritime trade led to a reciprocal exchange of ideas, techniques, and artistic styles.

Evidence of this cross-cultural interaction is visible in the Orientalizing period of Greek art (700-600 BCE), where the adoption of Near Eastern motifs and techniques became increasingly evident. This period also saw the creation of monumental stone sculptures, a concept likely influenced by the monumental art of Egypt and Mesopotamia.

Moreover, the Greeks' exposure to foreign deities and religious practices often led to a form of syncretism, where foreign gods were identified with Greek gods with similar attributes. For instance, the Egyptian god Amun was often equated with Zeus, reinforcing the existing religious structures with new layers of meaning and context.

✦ Expansion and Colonization

Simultaneously, this period was marked by an outward expansion of the Greeks, prompted by the overpopulation of the city-states and the desire for new trade routes and resources. This led to the establishment of colonies across the Mediterranean and the Black Sea. These colonies, such as Syracuse in Sicily or Massalia in modern-day France, not only extended the sphere of Greek influence but also introduced Hellenic culture, language, and religious practices into new regions. It is worth noting that while these colonies maintained connections with their mother city, they operated as independent city-states, each with its own political structure and societal norms.

The Golden Age: Athens and the Birth of Democracy

✦ The Rise of Democracy

The 5th century BCE marks the zenith of Athenian power and culture, a period often referred to as the Golden Age of Athens. Athens emerged as a beacon of democracy under the leadership of Pericles, who instituted reforms that allowed for greater political participation from the citizenry. The introduction of pay for public service enabled even the poorer citizens to participate in the city's governance, thereby consolidating the democratic structure of the polis.

✧ Cultural and Intellectual Blossoming

During the Athenian Golden Age, cultural and intellectual life flourished. The period was marked by advancements in philosophy, drama, history, architecture, and sculpture. The works of playwrights such as Aeschylus, Sophocles, and Euripides; the philosophical insights of Socrates, Plato, and Aristotle; the historical accounts of Herodotus and Thucydides, all belong to this remarkable period of intellectual exploration and refinement.

Moreover, religion played a pivotal role in the life of the polis, with religious festivals such as the Panathenaia and Dionysia serving not only as acts of collective worship but also as important civic events. The period also saw the construction of iconic temples such as the Parthenon, a monument dedicated to Athena, the patron goddess of Athens.

In sum, the Archaic period and the Golden Age of Athens illustrate the dynamic interaction between economic interests, cultural exchange, political reforms, and religious practices, contributing significantly to the shaping of the ancient Greek world. It is this intricate web of influences and exchanges that underscores the richness and complexity of ancient Greek history, offering invaluable insights for the contemporary study of historical processes and societal transformation.

The Peloponnesian War and Its Aftermath

The rivalry between Athens and Sparta culminated in the devastating Peloponnesian War, which reshaped the course of Greek history. The war's aftermath witnessed the decline of Athens as a dominant power and the rise of other city-states vying for supremacy. These turbulent times saw the emergence of powerful military leaders, philosophers, and thinkers who explored profound questions about human existence, ethics, and the divine. It was during this era that Plato, Aristotle, and other philosophers laid the foundations of Western philosophy, encompassing discussions about the nature of gods and the cosmos.

The Hellenistic Era: The Age of Alexander the Great

The death of Alexander the Great marked the beginning of the Hellenistic period, during which Greek culture spread across vast territories, creating a new cosmopolitan world. The intermingling of Greek, Egyptian, and Persian traditions fostered a rich syncretism in religious practices, leading to the formation of new cults and belief systems. The diverse pantheon of gods grew to encompass deities from various cultures, reflecting the interconnectedness of the Hellenistic world.

Conclusion: The Tapestry of Ancient Greek History

As we immerse ourselves in the historical context of ancient Greece, we gain a profound appreciation for the dynamic and transformative nature of this civilization. The interplay between cultures, the rise and fall of city-states, and the enduring impact of religious beliefs and practices all contribute to the intricate tapestry that is ancient Greek history. As we proceed with our study, let us endeavor to understand the interconnections between historical events, religious practices, and cultural developments, fostering a holistic comprehension of the rich and diverse heritage of ancient Greece.

A chronological overview of significant historical periods relevant to the study of Greek religion

To comprehend the rich tapestry of Greek religion, it is essential to embark on a chronological journey through the significant historical periods that shaped and influenced the beliefs, practices, and cultural expressions of the ancient Greeks. From the Bronze Age civilizations to the Hellenistic era, each epoch left an indelible mark on the religious landscape of ancient Greece. In this section, we shall navigate through these pivotal periods, illuminating their impact on the religious worldview, rituals, and the divine pantheon of the ancient Greeks.

The Bronze Age: Minoans and Mycenaeans (c. 3000 BCE - c. 1100 BCE)

The Bronze Age witnessed the emergence of two major civilizations in the Aegean region: the Minoans on the island of Crete and the Mycenaeans on the Greek mainland. The Minoans, known for their advanced maritime trade and vibrant artistic expressions, offered insights into the early religious practices of the region. Intriguing artifacts, such as the Snake Goddess figurines and the mysterious Linear A script, hint at their devotion to a pantheon of nature deities and goddesses.

The Mycenaeans, with their fortified citadels and warrior culture, inherited and adapted aspects of Minoan religion while infusing it with their martial focus. The surviving Linear B tablets reveal the worship of powerful deities such as Zeus, Poseidon, and Hera, reflecting the gradual establishment of a more cohesive pantheon.

The Dark Ages and the Rise of the Polis (c. 1100 BCE - c. 800 BCE)

Following the collapse of the Mycenaean civilization, Greece entered a period known as the Dark Ages, characterized by a decline in urbanization, trade, and literacy. With the fragmentation of the centralized Mycenaean power, communities sought new ways of organizing themselves. The rise of the polis, or city-state, heralded a profound shift in Greek society, politics, and religious practices. Each polis developed its unique cults and rituals, honoring local deities and heroes that represented the city's identity.

The Archaic Period: Encounter with the Near East and Colonization (c. 800 BCE - c. 480 BCE)

The Archaic period marked a phase of increased contact and cultural exchange between the Greeks and the Near East. As Greek merchants ventured to distant lands, they encountered foreign religious practices and divinities, influencing their own belief systems. New cults emerged, and gods from different regions were assimilated into the Greek pantheon.

This period also witnessed significant colonization, as Greek city-states founded colonies in the Mediterranean and beyond. The establishment of these colonies brought about an amalgamation of indigenous beliefs with Greek religious practices, resulting in the syncretism of diverse cults.

The Golden Age: Athens and the Birth of Democracy (c. 480 BCE - c. 323 BCE)

The 5th century BCE, often referred to as the Golden Age of Greece, was marked by the rise of Athens as a dominant cultural and political power. The flourishing of arts, philosophy, and democratic governance had a profound impact on religious expression. Athenian religious festivals, such as the Panathenaia, celebrated the city's patron goddess, Athena, and fostered a sense of civic identity.

The Peloponnesian War and Its Aftermath (431 BCE - 404 BCE)

The Peloponnesian War, a protracted conflict between Athens and Sparta, brought about significant political and social upheaval in Greece. The war's aftermath witnessed the weakening of Athenian power and the rise of other city-states. This period of political instability saw the emergence of philosophers like Socrates, Plato, and Aristotle, whose philosophical inquiries delved into the nature of gods and their relationship with human affairs.

The Hellenistic Era: The Age of Alexander the Great (c. 323 BCE - c. 31 BCE)

With the conquests of Alexander the Great, the Hellenistic era began, ushering in an era of unprecedented cultural exchange across vast territories. Greek culture, including religious beliefs and practices, spread far and wide, resulting in a diverse religious landscape. Cults of individual gods and mystery religions gained popularity, offering devotees personal salvation and mystical experiences.

Conclusion: Unraveling the Historical Threads of Greek Religion

The chronological overview of these significant historical periods demonstrates the dynamic and evolving nature of Greek religion. From the ancient Minoans and Mycenaeans to the cosmopolitan Hellenistic era, the religious beliefs and practices of the ancient Greeks underwent continuous transformation, reflecting their encounters with foreign cultures and their quest for understanding the divine. As we delve deeper into the subsequent chapters, we shall examine how these historical epochs influenced the pantheon of gods, the conduct of rituals, and the interconnectedness of Greek religion with various aspects of ancient life. Through rigorous analysis and critical thinking, students will gain a holistic understanding of the interplay between history, religious beliefs, and cultural expressions in the fascinating world of ancient Greek religion.

The influence of social, political, and cultural factors on religious development

The religious landscape of ancient Greece was not isolated from the broader social, political, and cultural context in which it flourished. Rather, it was intricately intertwined with various facets of Greek society, evolving in response to historical events, political shifts, and cultural exchanges. In this section, we shall embark on a comprehensive exploration of how social, political, and cultural factors influenced the development of Greek religion. By analyzing the interplay between religious beliefs and the broader societal context, we aim to elucidate the complex relationship between religion and various aspects of ancient Greek life.

Social Factors: Rituals, Practices, and Community Identity

Social factors played a crucial role in shaping the religious practices and rituals of ancient Greeks. Religion was a communal affair, and the performance of rituals brought individuals together, reinforcing a sense of shared identity within the polis. Festivals like the Eleusinian Mysteries, dedicated to Demeter and Persephone, provided an opportunity for the entire community to participate in sacred rites, fostering a sense of cohesion and belonging.

Additionally, the role of social institutions, such as the family and gender dynamics, significantly impacted religious practices. Household rituals, devoted to gods like Hestia and Zeus, reinforced familial bonds and responsibilities. Moreover, gender roles within religious activities, such as the exclusion of women from certain cults like the Dionysian mysteries, were reflective of wider societal norms and hierarchies.

Political Factors: The Divine and Mortal Rulers

The relationship between gods and mortals was closely intertwined with the political structure of ancient Greek society. The divine and mortal realms were believed to be interconnected, and divine favor or wrath often influenced political decision-making. Leaders sought the favor of gods through religious ceremonies and dedications, with certain cults enjoying state patronage.

Additionally, the ruler cult, prevalent in various city-states, exemplified the close association between politics and religion. Divine honors were accorded to leaders like Alexander the Great, who claimed divine lineage, blurring the boundaries between the divine and the mortal. Such practices served to legitimize and consolidate political power, fostering loyalty and devotion among the populace.

Cultural Factors: Syncretism and Panhellenism

Greek religion was remarkably adaptable, assimilating elements from various cultures through cultural exchanges. Syncretism, the merging of different religious beliefs and practices, was particularly evident during the Hellenistic period, as Greek culture spread across different regions. For example, the cult of Serapis, a deity combining Egyptian and Greek elements, gained popularity in Egypt and beyond.

Furthermore, the concept of Panhellenism, the idea of shared Greek identity and culture, transcended political boundaries and influenced religious practices. Panhellenic festivals, such as the Olympic Games and the Pythian Games, not only celebrated athletic prowess but also served as opportunities for Greeks to unite in religious devotion and cultural exchange.

Conclusion: Unraveling the Complex Tapestry of Religious Development

The influence of social, political, and cultural factors on religious development in ancient Greece is multifaceted and nuanced. By examining the intricate interplay between religious beliefs and the broader societal context, students can gain a deeper understanding of the complexities that shaped Greek religion. As we delve into the subsequent chapters, we shall further investigate specific examples and case studies to illuminate how these factors influenced the pantheon of gods, the conduct of rituals, and the sacred spaces that defined ancient Greek religious life. Through critical analysis and thoughtful exploration, students will come to appreciate the intricate relationship between religion and the multifaceted tapestry of ancient Greek civilization.

Cultural and Philosophical Background

To comprehend the religious landscape of ancient Greece fully, it is essential to explore the cultural and philosophical milieu in which Greek religion thrived. The rich and diverse cultural heritage of the Greeks, coupled with their philosophical inquiry, contributed significantly to the development and interpretation of religious beliefs and practices. In this section, we embark on an in-depth examination of the cultural and philosophical background that influenced Greek religion. By delving into the intricacies of Greek thought, art, literature, and philosophical musings, we aim to shed light on the complex interplay between culture, philosophy, and religious expression in ancient Greece.

The Influence of Myth and Epic Poetry

Greek mythology and epic poetry were foundational to the cultural identity of the ancient Greeks. Myths, narratives of divine and heroic beings, permeated all aspects of Greek life, providing explanations for natural phenomena, the origins of gods and mortals, and the moral principles that governed human conduct. Iconic works like Homer's Iliad and Odyssey shaped not only literary traditions but also the conceptualization of divinity, heroism, and the human condition.

Mythical figures, such as Zeus, Hera, and Athena, were not only deities but also archetypes of human attributes, desires, and flaws. The portrayal of gods with human emotions and frailties challenged the perception of divine perfection, prompting philosophical inquiries into the nature of divinity and the relationship between gods and mortals.

Philosophical Underpinnings: The Quest for Knowledge and Wisdom

Philosophy, a defining hallmark of Greek intellectual achievement, fostered a rational and inquisitive approach to understanding the cosmos and the divine. Philosophers like Pythagoras, Plato, and Aristotle sought to explain the nature of reality, the origins of the universe, and the place of humanity within it. Their speculations on metaphysics, ethics, and epistemology inevitably intersected with religious notions, raising questions about the existence of gods, the concept of the divine, and the moral foundations of religious beliefs.

For instance, Plato's "Theory of Forms" postulated the existence of abstract, perfect forms of objects and concepts, including divine beings. This philosophical exploration challenged traditional religious representations of gods and propelled debates on the essence of divine entities.

Art, Rituals, and Sacred Spaces

Greek art, whether in the form of sculpture, pottery, or architecture, was infused with religious symbolism and spiritual significance. Temples, the most prominent architectural representation of religious devotion, stood as physical manifestations of the divine presence and focal points for rituals and ceremonies. Elaborate sculptures and frescoes adorned these sacred spaces, depicting gods, heroes, and mythical scenes, thereby reinforcing religious beliefs and narratives.

Moreover, rituals and festivals were central to Greek religious life, and their performance provided an avenue for artistic expression and cultural celebration. Dionysian festivals, for instance, featured dramatic performances like tragedies and comedies, exploring profound philosophical themes and moral dilemmas.

Conclusion: Understanding the Intersection of Culture and Religion

The cultural and philosophical background of ancient Greece significantly shaped the religious beliefs, practices, and expressions of the ancient Greeks. The interplay between myth, philosophy, art, and religious rituals facilitated a dynamic and evolving religious landscape that was deeply ingrained in the fabric of Greek society. As students delve further into the subsequent chapters, they will continue to unearth the profound impact of culture and philosophy on Greek religion. By engaging in critical analysis and discussion, students can gain a comprehensive understanding of the multifaceted relationship between the intellectual and artistic achievements of the Greeks and the religious tapestry that enriched their lives.

Philosophical influences on religious thought in ancient Greece (e.g., Plato, Aristotle)

The intellectual milieu of ancient Greece was shaped by the profound contributions of philosophical thinkers like Plato and Aristotle. These philosophical luminaries sought to explore the fundamental questions of existence, knowledge, and morality, which inevitably intersected with religious beliefs and practices. In this section, we embark on an in-depth analysis of the philosophical influences on religious thought in ancient Greece. By delving into the ideas and theories put forth by Plato, Aristotle, and other philosophers, we aim to shed light on the intricate interplay between philosophy and religion, and how these influential thinkers shaped the understanding of the divine and the human experience.

A. Plato: The World of Forms and the Nature of Divinity

Plato's philosophical exploration centered on the concept of Forms or Ideas, which he believed were eternal and perfect representations of objects and abstract concepts. In "The Republic," Plato expounded on the "Allegory of the Cave," where he postulated a world of transcendent Forms that represented the true essence of reality. This metaphysical view of the world had profound implications for religious thought.

Within this philosophical framework, Plato also contemplated the nature of divinity. He perceived the gods as manifestations of the highest Forms, representing the ideal attributes of goodness, justice, and wisdom. However, Plato's view of the gods transcended traditional anthropomorphic representations, as he emphasized their incorporeal and immutable nature. This departure from conventional religious imagery challenged prevailing beliefs about the gods' physical forms and prompted a philosophical inquiry into the essence of divinity.

Aristotle: The Prime Mover and the Unity of God

Aristotle, a pupil of Plato, further contributed to the philosophical landscape of ancient Greece. In his "Metaphysics," Aristotle introduced the concept of the Prime Mover, an unmoved and eternal entity that set the cosmos in motion. While Aristotle did not explicitly attribute this Prime Mover to any specific deity, the concept had implications for religious thought.

Aristotle's philosophical discussions also centered on the notion of a single, supreme deity that governed the unity of the cosmos. His concept of the "Unmoved Mover" resonated with the idea of a divine force that provided order and purpose to the universe. This philosophical view of a singular divine principle contributed to the development of monotheistic perspectives and influenced subsequent religious philosophies.

Influence on Religious Practitioners and Thought

The philosophical ideas of Plato and Aristotle had a profound impact on religious practitioners and intellectuals in ancient Greece. As intellectuals engaged in dialogue and debates, their philosophical inquiries influenced religious practices and interpretations. The concept of transcendent Forms and the Prime Mover encouraged contemplation on the nature of the divine, the immortality of the soul, and the concept of a higher purpose in human existence.

Religious scholars and practitioners sought to reconcile these philosophical ideas with traditional religious beliefs, leading to syncretism and the evolution of religious thought. Moreover, philosophical schools like the Academy and the Lyceum fostered an intellectual environment where religious and philosophical discourses coexisted and intersected, shaping the religious landscape of ancient Greece.

Conclusion: The Complex Relationship between Philosophy and Religion

The philosophical influences on religious thought in ancient Greece showcased a dynamic interplay between intellectual inquiry and religious beliefs. Plato and Aristotle, among others, contributed significant insights into the nature of divinity, the cosmos, and the human condition, which influenced religious practices and interpretations. As students continue their exploration of Greek religious thought, they will gain a deeper appreciation for how philosophy enriched religious perspectives and fostered critical engagement with questions of the divine. By engaging in discussions and exercises that explore the interface between philosophy and religion, students can grasp the intricacies of this dynamic relationship and its lasting impact on ancient Greek culture.

The concept of the soul and its connection to religious beliefs

The concept of the soul is central to ancient Greek religious beliefs and has been a subject of profound philosophical and theological contemplation. In this section, we embark on an in-depth analysis of the soul's significance in Greek religious thought, exploring its various dimensions, roles, and connections to religious practices. Through an interdisciplinary approach that draws from philosophy, mythology, and religious practices, we aim to provide students with a comprehensive understanding of how the ancient Greeks conceptualized the soul and its impact on their religious beliefs.

Defining the Soul: A Multifaceted Entity

The Greek concept of the soul, known as "psūkhē," is a complex and multifaceted entity that extends beyond physical existence. Unlike the modern notion of the soul as a singular and indivisible essence, the ancient Greeks held diverse perspectives on the nature of the soul. Philosophers, such as Plato and Aristotle, proposed various theories about the soul's immortality, its relationship with the body, and its connection to the divine.

Immortality and the Afterlife

In ancient Greek religious beliefs, the soul was often perceived as immortal and everlasting. According to some interpretations, the soul was thought to endure after death, transitioning to the realm of the afterlife. This notion influenced religious practices, such as burial rites and funerary customs, as the ancient Greeks sought to ensure a proper passage for the soul to the realm of the deceased ancestors or the domain of the gods.

The Role of the Soul in Human Experience

The concept of the soul played a pivotal role in shaping Greek perspectives on human experience. It was believed that the soul encompassed the essence of an individual's character, emotions, and intellect. This understanding influenced moral and ethical frameworks, as individuals were encouraged to cultivate virtues and wisdom to nourish the soul's growth and evolution.

Connection to Religious Practices

Religious practices in ancient Greece were deeply intertwined with the concept of the soul. Rituals, sacrifices, and ceremonies were conducted to honor the gods and ensure their favor. The soul's role in these practices lay in its intermediary function, connecting humans to the divine realm. Offerings and supplications were made to secure divine blessings and protection for the soul's well-being, both in life and the afterlife.

Philosophical Perspectives on the Soul

Philosophers like Plato and Aristotle offered contrasting views on the soul's nature and purpose. Plato, in his dialogues, explored the soul's immortality and its journey through different reincarnations, seeking a return to the world of the Forms. On the other hand, Aristotle emphasized the soul as the vital principle that bestowed life upon living beings and classified souls based on their faculties and functions.

Diversity of Interpretations

While the concept of the soul was central to Greek religious beliefs, its interpretation varied across regions and cultural practices. Mystery cults, such as the Orphic Mysteries, offered esoteric views on the soul's divine origins and its journey of purification. Similarly, philosophical schools, such as the Stoics and the Epicureans, presented distinct perspectives on the soul's relationship to virtue and happiness.

Conclusion: A Profound Intersection of Philosophy and Religion

The concept of the soul served as a crucial link between philosophical inquiry and religious beliefs in ancient Greece. It influenced religious practices, ethical frameworks, and notions of the afterlife. Philosophers and religious practitioners alike engaged in discussions and rituals that revolved around the soul's nature and its connection to the divine. By exploring the diverse interpretations of the soul and its significance in religious thought, students can gain a profound appreciation for the rich tapestry of ancient Greek beliefs and the complexities of the human spirit. This comprehensive understanding encourages critical thinking and discussions on the soul's enduring legacy in both ancient and modern perspectives on religion and spirituality.

Religious Syncretism and Interaction

Religious syncretism and interaction in the context of ancient Greek civilization represent a fascinating aspect of the Hellenic religious landscape. This section delves into the intricate interplay of diverse religious beliefs and practices, exploring how various cultures, traditions, and deities interacted and influenced one another. By critically examining the processes of religious syncretism and the dynamics of religious interactions, students can gain a deeper understanding of the complex and evolving nature of ancient Greek spirituality.

The Essence of Religious Syncretism

Religious syncretism, at its core, entails the blending and merging of different religious beliefs, deities, and rituals. Throughout ancient Greek history, this phenomenon was shaped by an array of factors, including cultural exchanges, trade networks, and conquests. As different cultures and city-states encountered one another, they shared and integrated religious practices, leading to the coexistence and amalgamation of diverse spiritual traditions.

The Rise of Mystery Cults

Among the various religious developments in ancient Greece, mystery cults played a significant role in promoting religious syncretism. Mystery cults were characterized by their secret rituals, initiation ceremonies, and promises of spiritual salvation. These cults often attracted members from different social strata and city-states, fostering a sense of shared spiritual experience and transcending regional boundaries.

The Pantheon and Divine Assimilation

The Greek pantheon, consisting of numerous gods and goddesses, was not fixed but rather adaptable and open to assimilation. As a result, various deities from local cults and foreign regions were incorporated into the broader pantheon through religious syncretism. For example, the Anatolian goddess Cybele found her place in the Greek pantheon as a deity known as Magna Mater, representing the merging of religious traditions.

Cultural Exchanges and Conquests

The expansion of the Greek world through colonization and conquest facilitated extensive cultural exchanges and interactions. Greek colonies established in foreign lands encountered diverse belief systems, leading to the blending of local and Greek religious elements. These interactions resulted in the development of unique syncretic deities and practices that reflected the shared beliefs and experiences of these regions.

The Challenge of Preserving Tradition

While religious syncretism fostered cultural exchange and inclusivity, it also faced resistance from traditionalists who sought to preserve the purity of their native beliefs. This tension between syncretism and tradition created a dynamic religious landscape where different ideologies coexisted and vied for prominence.

Case Study: Serapis and Isis

One prominent example of religious syncretism in ancient Greece is the cult of Serapis and Isis. Serapis, a syncretic deity combining elements of Greek and Egyptian religious traditions, exemplified the blending of foreign and local beliefs. The cult of Isis, originating in Egypt, also gained popularity throughout the Greek world, showcasing the adaptability of religious practices to different cultural contexts.

Religious Syncretism in the Roman Empire

The concept of religious syncretism extended beyond the borders of ancient Greece and influenced the religious landscape of the Roman Empire. As the Roman Empire expanded its territories, it encountered diverse cultures and belief systems, resulting in the assimilation and integration of foreign deities into the Roman pantheon.

Conclusion: A Diverse and Dynamic Spiritual Landscape

Religious syncretism and interaction in ancient Greece exemplify the adaptability and interconnectedness of human religious experiences. The blending of diverse beliefs and practices enriched the spiritual lives of ancient Greeks, fostering a sense of interconnectedness and cultural exchange. The study of religious syncretism encourages students to engage critically with the dynamic nature of ancient Greek spirituality and its impact on subsequent religious traditions. By exploring the complexities of religious interactions, students can gain a deeper appreciation for the enduring legacy of syncretic religious practices in shaping ancient Greek society and the broader Mediterranean world.

Examining the assimilation of foreign religious elements and the blending of diverse traditions

In the rich tapestry of ancient Greek religious practices, the assimilation of foreign religious elements and the blending of diverse traditions played a pivotal role in shaping the spiritual landscape. This section delves into the complexities of how foreign deities, cults, and rituals were incorporated into the Greek religious framework, fostering religious syncretism and cultural exchange. Through the exploration of case studies and historical examples, students can gain a comprehensive understanding of the dynamic nature of ancient Greek spirituality and its interactions with other cultures.

Cultural Encounter and Adaptation

The ancient Greeks' extensive cultural encounters, facilitated by trade, colonization, and conquest, provided fertile ground for the assimilation of foreign religious elements. As Greek city-states established connections with distant regions, they encountered a wide array of deities and religious practices. The adaptability of Greek religion allowed for the incorporation of foreign elements into existing belief systems, leading to the emergence of syncretic deities and new religious practices.

Case Study: The Cult of Dionysus

The cult of Dionysus serves as a compelling example of the assimilation of foreign religious elements into the Greek religious sphere. Originating in the Near East and Egypt, the worship of Dionysus, the god of wine and ecstasy, found its way into Greece. As the cult spread, it absorbed aspects of various local beliefs, leading to a diverse range of Dionysian rituals, including ecstatic dances and Bacchanalian festivities.

The Mystery Cults and Spiritual Initiations

Mystery cults, characterized by their secret rites and initiation ceremonies, exemplify how foreign religious elements were embraced and integrated into Greek spirituality. Initiates underwent transformative experiences that transcended their cultural and social backgrounds, promoting a sense of spiritual unity beyond regional boundaries. The Eleusinian Mysteries, dedicated to Demeter and Persephone, and the cult of Isis, originating in Egypt, were notable examples of mystery cults that attracted adherents from diverse backgrounds.

The Syncretic Deities: Serapis and Cybele

Serapis and Cybele represent prominent instances of syncretic deities resulting from the blending of foreign religious elements with Greek tradition. Serapis, a combination of Egyptian and Greek elements, was worshiped as a universal god embracing attributes of fertility, death, and the afterlife. Similarly, Cybele, a goddess of Anatolian origin, became integrated into the Greek pantheon as Magna Mater, representing both earth and cosmic divinity.

The Role of Philosophy and Interpretation

Philosophical schools, such as Neoplatonism, contributed to the assimilation of foreign religious elements by interpreting myths and deities allegorically. Philosophers sought to reconcile diverse religious traditions through rational discourse, emphasizing the underlying spiritual truths rather than literal interpretations. This intellectual approach fostered a greater understanding and appreciation for the interconnectedness of different belief systems.

Challenges and Resistance

While assimilation and blending were prevalent, challenges and resistance to the incorporation of foreign religious elements also emerged. Traditionalists and religious purists sought to preserve the purity of native beliefs, and conflicts between different religious ideologies occasionally arose.

Conclusion: A Fluid and Evolving Spiritual Landscape

The assimilation of foreign religious elements and the blending of diverse traditions in ancient Greece exemplify the fluid and evolving nature of human spirituality. The Greek religious landscape was enriched by the integration of foreign deities and rituals, demonstrating the ancient Greeks' willingness to engage with diverse belief systems. The study of religious assimilation encourages critical thinking about cultural encounters and the complexities of religious interactions. By examining the assimilation process, students can gain insights into the adaptability and inclusivity of ancient Greek religion, as well as its lasting impact on subsequent religious and philosophical traditions.

The impact of contact with other Mediterranean cultures on Greek religious practices

Ancient Greece was a vibrant crossroads of cultures, and its religious practices were deeply influenced by contact with other Mediterranean civilizations. This section explores how interactions with neighboring societies, including the Egyptians, Phoenicians, and Persians, contributed to the evolution and diversification of Greek religious beliefs and rituals. By examining the exchange of ideas, cults, and religious symbols, students can gain valuable insights into the complex interplay of religious practices and the cultural milieu of ancient Greece.

Cultural and Religious Exchange in the Mediterranean

The Mediterranean Sea served as a conduit for cultural exchange, fostering connections between diverse societies. As Greek traders, explorers, and colonists ventured into new territories, they encountered foreign religious traditions and integrated aspects of these beliefs into their own practices. This cultural and religious cross-pollination enriched Greek spirituality and contributed to the development of syncretic deities and rituals.

Case Study: The Cult of Aphrodite

The cult of Aphrodite, the goddess of love and beauty, offers a compelling example of how contact with other Mediterranean cultures influenced Greek religious practices. Aphrodite's origins can be traced to the ancient Near East, where she was worshipped as Ishtar and Astarte. Through contact with Phoenician and Cypriot civilizations, the Greek perception of Aphrodite underwent transformation, assimilating various aspects of these foreign goddesses.

The Influence of Egyptian Religion

Egypt, with its rich religious tradition, had a profound impact on Greek religious practices. Egyptian deities such as Isis and Serapis were assimilated into the Greek pantheon, resulting in new religious syncretisms. Temples dedicated to Egyptian gods were established in Greek cities, and mystery cults, like that of Isis, attracted a devoted following. Egyptian religious symbols and practices also found their way into Greek magic and divination.

The Persian Connection

The Achaemenid Persian Empire exerted cultural and religious influence on the Greeks during the Persian Wars and subsequent periods of contact. The cult of Mithras, originating in Persia, gained popularity among soldiers and the upper echelons of society in the Roman Empire, including Greece. The worship of Mithras spread throughout the Mediterranean and persisted as a significant religious phenomenon.

Religious Syncretism and Cultural Adaptation

The process of religious syncretism and cultural adaptation was not one-sided; the Greeks also influenced the religious practices of their neighbors. In regions with significant Greek settlements, such as Magna Graecia (southern Italy), the local religious landscape absorbed Greek elements, leading to a dynamic fusion of traditions.

Challenges and Conflicts

Despite the many instances of religious syncretism and cultural exchange, interactions with other Mediterranean cultures also gave rise to challenges and conflicts. In some cases, the assimilation of foreign deities faced resistance from traditionalists who sought to preserve native beliefs.

Conclusion: A Diverse and Interconnected Spiritual Milieu

The impact of contact with other Mediterranean cultures on Greek religious practices reflects a diverse and interconnected spiritual milieu. Through encounters with foreign deities, rituals, and beliefs, the ancient Greeks demonstrated their adaptability and receptiveness to different religious traditions. The blending of diverse elements enriched Greek religious practices and fostered a sense of interconnectedness between the ancient Mediterranean civilizations. The study of these interactions encourages students to engage critically with the complexities of cultural encounters and to appreciate the dynamic nature of religious practices in ancient Greece.

Chapter 4: Importance of Studying Ancient Greek Religion

Chapter 4 delves into the profound importance of studying ancient Greek religion, exploring its impact on various aspects of society, culture, and human psychology. By investigating the multifaceted roles of religion in the lives of ancient Greeks, students can gain a comprehensive understanding of the interconnectedness between religious beliefs and the broader fabric of ancient Greek civilization.

Shaping Worldviews and Identity

Ancient Greek religion was not merely a collection of myths and rituals; it formed the foundation of the Greek worldview and played a pivotal role in shaping individual and communal identities. The beliefs in powerful deities, the afterlife, and divine intervention in human affairs influenced how the ancient Greeks perceived the world, their place within it, and their purpose in life.

Religious Practices and Cultural Norms

The study of ancient Greek religion offers valuable insights into the interplay between religious practices and cultural norms. Rituals and festivals honoring deities were intricately woven into the fabric of daily life, permeating various aspects of ancient Greek society, from politics and governance to art, literature, and architecture.

Moral and Ethical Frameworks

Religious narratives and moral teachings provided the ancient Greeks with ethical frameworks and guidelines for righteous conduct. The stories of virtuous heroes and divine retribution underscored the significance of leading a life in accordance with the gods' will and moral principles.

Political and Civic Life

Religion and politics were inextricably linked in ancient Greece. The role of priests, priestesses, and religious institutions in civic affairs, the establishment of sanctuaries, and the practice of divination to guide political decisions demonstrate the centrality of religion in governance and statecraft.

Psychological Aspects of Worship

The psychological dimensions of ancient Greek religion are equally crucial to understanding human nature and behavior. The rituals of catharsis, the veneration of healing deities like Asclepius, and the use of divination for guidance reflect how religion provided solace and a sense of purpose in the face of adversity and uncertainty.

Influence on Art, Literature, and Philosophy

The study of ancient Greek religion also illuminates its profound influence on artistic expression, literary works, and philosophical thought. From the portrayal of mythological themes in sculpture and pottery to the exploration of divine concepts in the works of philosophers like Plato and Aristotle, religious motifs permeated various cultural forms.

Connection to Modern Religious Practices

Understanding ancient Greek religion fosters an appreciation for its enduring legacy in modern religious practices. The continuity of certain beliefs and rituals, as well as the adoption of ancient Greek deities and symbols in neo-paganism and other contemporary spiritual movements, exemplify the enduring influence of ancient Greek religion on modern spiritual landscapes.
religion and its far-reaching implications for the ancient world and beyond.

Contributions to Western Civilization

Chapter 4 explores the profound contributions of ancient Greek religion to Western civilization. Ancient Greece, often regarded as the cradle of Western culture, bestowed upon the world a rich legacy of religious beliefs, practices, and ideas that continue to influence modern societies in myriad ways. From philosophy and art to governance and ethics, the impact of ancient Greek religion on Western civilization is both far-reaching and enduring.

✧ Philosophy and the Quest for Knowledge

The quest for knowledge and the pursuit of wisdom have been fundamental aspects of human inquiry since time immemorial. In ancient Greece, this search for understanding found expression not only in religious thought but also in the burgeoning field of philosophy. The interplay between religious beliefs and philosophical inquiry laid the foundation for Western philosophical thought, with early philosophers grappling with questions that were deeply intertwined with religious concepts. This section explores the profound influence of religious thought on the early philosophers of ancient Greece and how their inquiries into the nature of the universe and existence were shaped by their contemplation of the divine.

✧ Ancient Greek Religion and the Birth of Philosophy

The Presocratics and the Nature of the Cosmos

The Presocratic philosophers, including Thales, Anaximander, and Pythagoras, sought to understand the underlying principles governing the natural world. Their inquiries were deeply rooted in religious questions about the origins of life and the nature of the universe. Thales' exploration of the fundamental principle or "arche" was akin to seeking the ultimate source or divine origin of all existence. Anaximander's cosmological theories, proposing a boundless, indeterminate substance as the origin of all things, reflected an attempt to comprehend the divine order in the cosmos. Pythagoras' fascination with numerical relationships and the harmony of the celestial spheres was intertwined with his belief in a divine mathematical order governing the universe.

The Divine and Metaphysical Aspects in Plato's Philosophy

Plato, one of the most influential philosophers in history, delved into the metaphysical realm and explored the relationship between the physical world and higher realities. Central to his philosophy were the "Forms" or "Ideas," which he posited as perfect, eternal, and abstract entities representing the true essence of everything in the material world. Plato's concept of the Forms had a profound religious undertone, reminiscent of the transcendent nature of gods in ancient Greek religion. His allegory of the cave further underscored the notion of seeking a higher truth beyond the physical realm, akin to the quest for divine knowledge.

✧ Aristotle's Integration of Religion and Philosophy

The Prime Mover and Unmoved Mover

Aristotle, a student of Plato, approached philosophical inquiry from a different perspective but remained deeply connected to religious themes. In his philosophy, the concept of the Prime Mover or Unmoved Mover played a crucial role. Aristotle proposed the existence of a divine and eternal being that initiated the movement and changes in the world, yet itself remained unchanging and immaterial. This notion reflected Aristotle's contemplation of the ultimate cause of all things, which he saw as inherently connected to the divine.

Teleology and the Natural World

Aristotle's concept of teleology, the idea that everything in nature has a purpose or final cause, also showcased the influence of religious thought on his philosophical framework. The idea of purpose and design in the natural world mirrored the ancient Greek belief in divine agency shaping the course of events. Aristotle's understanding of nature as imbued with inherent purposes aligned with the idea of gods overseeing and guiding the cosmos.

Conclusion

The early philosophers of ancient Greece were deeply influenced by the religious beliefs and inquiries prevalent in their society. Their quest for knowledge and understanding of the natural world was intricately interwoven with religious questions about the divine, the universe's origin, and the nature of existence. Thales, Anaximander, Pythagoras, Plato, and Aristotle all sought to unravel the mysteries of existence by contemplating the divine order in the cosmos. By recognizing the profound influence of religious thought on the birth of Western philosophy, students gain a deeper appreciation for the interconnectedness of these ancient disciplines and the enduring impact of their inquiries on the evolution of human knowledge and wisdom.

+

Art, Literature, and Drama

The art of ancient Greece was imbued with representations of mythology, reflecting the rich tapestry of religious beliefs and narratives that shaped the culture. From sculpture to pottery and literature to drama, mythological themes permeated various forms of artistic expression, serving as a means to celebrate the divine, portray heroic exploits, and convey moral lessons. This section delves into the representation of mythology in ancient Greek art and its significance in preserving religious narratives while imparting cultural ideals and moral values.

✧   Sculpture, Pottery, and Painting: Depictions of Divine and Heroic Stories

Divine Pantheon in Sculpture

Greek sculpture beautifully captured the various gods and goddesses of the pantheon, immortalizing their divine attributes and roles. For example, Zeus, the king of the gods, was often portrayed with regal authority and power, wielding a thunderbolt as a symbol of his dominion over the cosmos. Similarly, the graceful forms of Aphrodite celebrated the goddess of love and beauty, emphasizing the allure and charm she bestowed upon mortals.

Pottery and Mythological Narratives

Greek pottery served as a canvas for mythological storytelling, with intricate depictions of heroic exploits and divine episodes. Scenes from the Trojan War, the labors of Heracles, and the adventures of the Argonauts adorned amphorae, kraters, and other vessels. These depictions not only entertained but also educated viewers about cultural heroes and the values they embodied.

Mythological Themes in Painting

Though much of ancient Greek painting is lost, literary references and surviving examples indicate that mythology was a significant theme. Wall paintings and frescoes adorned temples and public buildings, featuring scenes from mythological narratives. These paintings contributed to the aesthetic and spiritual atmosphere of sacred spaces and further integrated religious beliefs into daily life.

✧ Literature and the Epic Tradition

Homer's "Iliad" and "Odyssey"

Homer's epic poems, the "Iliad" and the "Odyssey," stand as monumental works of Greek literature and are steeped in religious themes. The intervention of gods in mortal affairs, the concept of divine fate, and the reverence for the gods were central elements of these narratives. For instance, the "Iliad" explores the wrath of Achilles and the consequences of divine intervention during the Trojan War, while the "Odyssey" follows Odysseus' trials and tribulations on his journey home, emphasizing the significance of piety and divine favor.

Moral and Cultural Significance

Beyond their artistic and literary merits, these epics played a crucial role in shaping Greek cultural identity and ethical norms. They conveyed the ideals of bravery, loyalty, and honor, while also emphasizing the importance of honoring the gods and understanding one's place in the cosmic order.

✧ Drama and Religious Festivals

Theatrical Performances in Religious Context

Greek drama, particularly tragedies, emerged as an integral part of religious festivals in honor of gods like Dionysus. These performances showcased mythological stories, often exploring the complex relationship between mortals and gods and delving into philosophical questions of fate and human agency.

Philosophical and Moral Reflection

The tragedies of Aeschylus, Sophocles, and Euripides presented compelling characters facing moral dilemmas and confronting divine forces. Audiences were prompted to reflect on the human condition, the consequences of hubris, and the role of divine justice. In this way, ancient Greek drama facilitated discussions about the relationship between gods and mortals and the complexities of the human experience.

Conclusion

The representation of mythology in ancient Greek art, literature, and drama exemplified the enduring connection between religious beliefs and cultural expressions. These artistic endeavors not only celebrated the divine and heroic but also served as vehicles for conveying moral values and philosophical reflections. The integration of mythology into various forms of artistic expression was instrumental in preserving religious narratives, shaping cultural norms, and fostering a deeper understanding of the relationship between humans and the divine in ancient Greek society.

Democracy and Governance

In ancient Greece, religion permeated all aspects of society, and its influence extended beyond personal beliefs to shape the very fabric of civic life. This section explores the role of religion in the functioning of Greek city-states, highlighting how religious institutions, festivals, oracles, and priestly counsel impacted governance and civic virtue.

✧ Temples and Sanctuaries: Focal Points of Civic Life

Sacred Architecture and Civic Identity

Temples and sanctuaries were central to the civic life of ancient Greek city-states. These sacred spaces served as not only places of worship but also symbols of the city's identity and unity. The Parthenon in Athens, dedicated to the goddess Athena, stands as a prime example of how religious architecture was intertwined with civic pride.

Civic Functions of Religious Buildings

Beyond their religious significance, temples and sanctuaries also served practical civic functions. They housed the city's treasuries, records, and valuable offerings, making them centers of economic and administrative activity. Additionally, these sacred sites often hosted public gatherings and civic ceremonies, fostering a sense of community and shared purpose among the citizens.

✧ Religious Festivals: Fostering Unity and Collective Identity

The Significance of Religious Festivals

Religious festivals held in honor of various gods and goddesses were integral to Greek civic life. These festivals provided opportunities for communal celebrations, entertainment, and expressions of collective identity. Events such as the Olympic Games, dedicated to Zeus, brought together city-states in peaceful competition, strengthening diplomatic ties and promoting a sense of pan-Hellenic unity.

Civic Participation and Civic Pride

Participation in religious festivals was considered a civic duty, and attendance was expected from all citizens. Engaging in these events fostered a sense of civic pride and reinforced the importance of community cohesion in the well-being of the city-state.

✧ Political Decision-Making and Divine Guidance

Influence of Oracles

Oracles, such as the famous Oracle of Delphi, were highly regarded as sources of divine guidance. Political leaders and citizens sought counsel from the oracle before making important decisions, whether in matters of state, warfare, or colonization.

The pronouncements of the oracle were often interpreted and considered in shaping political strategies and policies.

The Role of Priests and Priestesses

Priests and priestesses held significant influence in the civic affairs of ancient Greece. They acted as intermediaries between the divine and mortal realms, presiding over religious ceremonies and rituals. Their counsel and insights were sought by political leaders and citizens alike, further blurring the line between religious and political spheres.

✦ Civic Virtue and Religious Duties

Piety and Civic Virtue

Ancient Greek religion emphasized the concept of civic virtue, where piety and reverence toward the gods were seen as essential qualities of a responsible citizen. Citizens were expected to actively participate in religious rites and uphold the religious traditions of the city-state.

Moral Responsibilities

Religious duties were intertwined with moral responsibilities, as the belief was that virtuous behavior and adherence to religious principles contributed to the welfare of the city-state. By fulfilling their religious obligations, citizens demonstrated their commitment to the community's well-being.

Conclusion

Religion played a central and multifaceted role in the civic life of ancient Greek city-states. From sacred architecture to religious festivals, oracles, and priestly counsel, religious institutions influenced governance and civic identity. The emphasis on civic virtue and the moral responsibilities of citizens in their religious duties further solidified the integration of religion into the fabric of civic life. This interplay between religion and governance contributed to the cohesiveness and enduring legacy of ancient Greek city-states.

✦ Ethics and Moral Philosophy

Ancient Greek religion served as a powerful vehicle for imparting ethical values and moral lessons through its myths and religious teachings. These narratives were replete with virtuous heroes, gods, and goddesses who demonstrated admirable conduct and principles for individuals and society to follow.

Virtuous Heroes as Moral Exemplars

Myths featuring virtuous heroes like Heracles (Hercules) showcased the triumph of courage, determination, and self-sacrifice. Heracles, renowned for his strength and bravery, symbolized the importance of courage and heroism in facing life's challenges. Other heroes like Odysseus exemplified cunning, intelligence, and resourcefulness, emphasizing the significance of wisdom and intellect in navigating life's complexities.

Exemplary Conduct of Gods and Goddesses

Ancient Greek religion also provided ethical models through the exemplary conduct of gods and goddesses. Athena, the goddess of wisdom and warfare, was revered for her strategic intellect and justice. Her adherence to fair judgment and wisdom highlighted the importance of righteousness and rationality. These divine role models not only represented ideals for individuals to emulate but also reinforced the significance of ethical conduct in the grand scheme of the cosmos.

✦ Influence on Ethical Philosophers

The ethical teachings embedded within ancient Greek religion had a lasting impact on the development of ethical philosophy. Philosophers from various schools of thought drew inspiration from these religious concepts and incorporated them into their ethical systems.

Stoicism: Living in Accordance with Divine Order

Stoicism, founded by philosophers like Zeno of Citium and expanded upon by thinkers like Epictetus and Marcus Aurelius, emphasized the importance of living in harmony with the divine order of the universe. Drawing from the religious notion of a rational and ordered cosmos governed by the gods, Stoicism promoted the cultivation of self-control, virtue, and moral rectitude. By aligning one's actions with the cosmic harmony, individuals could achieve eudaimonia, a state of inner peace and contentment.

Epicureanism: Pursuit of Tranquility and Happiness

Epicureanism, based on the teachings of Epicurus, encouraged the pursuit of happiness (ataraxia) and tranquility (aponia) through the avoidance of unnecessary desires and fears, including the fear of the gods. While Epicurus did not deny the existence of gods, he believed that the gods were not concerned with human affairs, thereby negating the need to fear divine punishment. By fostering an understanding of the natural world and detaching from irrational fears, individuals could attain a state of serenity and contentment.

Conclusion

Ancient Greek religion's profound influence on ethical thought and philosophy has left a lasting imprint on Western civilization. The myths and religious teachings, replete with virtuous heroes and exemplary gods, offered valuable moral exemplars for individuals and society. These ethical values became intertwined with the foundations of philosophical schools like Stoicism and Epicureanism, enriching their perspectives on self-control, virtue, happiness, and tranquility.

By delving into the ethical teachings of ancient Greek religion, students gain a deeper appreciation for the enduring legacy of these ancient beliefs in shaping Western culture. The insights from this rich tapestry of myths and religious teachings continue to resonate with modern thought, making the study of ancient Greek religion a pivotal subject for understanding the interconnectedness between religion, culture, and the evolution of human civilization.

The enduring legacy of Greek religious concepts in Western art, literature, and philosophy

The impact of ancient Greek religious concepts on Western civilization is profound and far-reaching. The rich tapestry of Greek mythology, religious beliefs, and philosophical ideas has left an indelible mark on Western art, literature, and philosophy. This section delves into the enduring legacy of Greek religious concepts, examining how they have influenced and shaped various aspects of Western culture over the centuries.

✧ Influence on Western Art

Ancient Greek religion's profound impact on Western art spans millennia, leaving an indelible mark on artistic expression and aesthetic sensibilities. The rich pantheon of Greek gods and goddesses, their heroic exploits, and the timeless themes embedded in mythology provided fertile ground for artists across the ages to draw inspiration and create masterpieces that continue to resonate with contemporary audiences.

Mythological Depictions in Ancient Art

In ancient times, Greek artists skillfully portrayed mythological stories on various mediums, including sculpture, pottery, and painting. Temples and sanctuaries were adorned with sculptures of gods and goddesses, showcasing their divine beauty and power. Pottery featured scenes from famous myths, serving both utilitarian and decorative purposes. Notably, the black-figure and red-figure pottery techniques allowed artists to intricately illustrate mythological narratives and heroic tales.

Renaissance Revival of Classical Themes

During the Renaissance, there was a revival of interest in classical antiquity, particularly Greek art and culture. Artists such as Michelangelo and Raphael drew inspiration from ancient Greek sculptures and reliefs to create lifelike and idealized depictions of the human form. Renaissance artworks often incorporated mythological themes, presenting gods and goddesses as archetypal embodiments of beauty, wisdom, and divine power.

Neoclassical Art and the Grandeur of Antiquity

In the 18th and 19th centuries, the Neoclassical movement rekindled enthusiasm for Greek mythology and its artistic representation. Artists like Jacques-Louis David embraced the principles of reason, order, and simplicity, mirroring the idealized aesthetics of ancient Greece. Neoclassical paintings frequently depicted scenes from Greek mythology and history, evoking a sense of grandeur and nobility.

Symbolism and Allegory

In more recent times, symbolism and allegory have played a prominent role in depicting ancient Greek religious themes. Artists like Gustave Moreau and Odilon Redon used mythological symbols and characters as allegorical representations of human emotions, desires, and spiritual quests. These symbolic depictions transcended literal interpretations and delved into the depths of the human psyche.

Contemporary Reinterpretations

Even in the modern era, ancient Greek religious themes continue to inspire contemporary artists. The fusion of classical elements with modern techniques gives rise to innovative and thought-provoking artworks. In sculpture, painting, and digital art, artists explore the interplay between the divine and mortal realms, challenging traditional notions and reimagining mythological narratives for today's audience.

❖ Exercises and Critical Thinking

Choose a famous ancient Greek myth and compare how it has been depicted in different artistic periods, such as ancient Greek, Renaissance, and contemporary art. Analyze how each artwork reflects the prevailing cultural and artistic values of its time.

Investigate the use of symbolism in Neoclassical art and its connection to ancient Greek religious themes. How did Neoclassical artists use symbols and allegory to convey deeper meanings in their works?

Research a contemporary artist who draws inspiration from ancient Greek religion in their art. Examine the artist's techniques, style, and the messages conveyed in their work. How do they reinterpret and engage with ancient myths in a modern context?

Discuss the ethical implications of using ancient religious themes in contemporary art. How can modern artists respectfully draw inspiration from ancient Greek religion without appropriating or misrepresenting its significance?

Conclusion

The influence of ancient Greek religion on Western art is undeniable, spanning centuries of artistic expression. From ancient Greek sculptures to Renaissance masterpieces, Neoclassical revival, symbolism, and contemporary reinterpretations, Greek religious themes have remained a timeless source of inspiration for artists across diverse periods and artistic movements. The enduring appeal of these mythological narratives and divine representations underscores the lasting significance of ancient Greek religion in shaping Western art and culture. By studying the evolution of artistic depictions, students gain a profound appreciation for the cultural and philosophical depth embedded within these artistic expressions, fostering critical thinking and discussions on the enduring legacy of ancient Greek religious themes in Western art.

✧ Influence on Western Philosophy

The profound impact of ancient Greek religion on Western philosophy is evident in the philosophical inquiries and contemplations of early thinkers, as well as in the development of philosophical schools that have shaped the course of Western intellectual history.

The Presocratics and Religious Inquiries

The period of Presocratic philosophy, which predates Socrates, marks a crucial juncture in the development of Western thought. These early thinkers were deeply engaged in both religious inquiries and cosmological speculations, seeking to understand the fundamental nature of the universe and humanity's place within it.

❖ Thales: The Pursuit of the Arche

Thales of Miletus is often hailed as the first philosopher in Western history. His philosophical inquiries were heavily influenced by the prevailing religious beliefs of ancient Greece, which emphasized the existence of gods and the idea of divine order in the cosmos. Thales sought to uncover a single fundamental principle or "arche" that underlies all of reality. He rejected mythological explanations and turned to rational inquiry to understand the world.

Thales' arche, according to various accounts, was water. He posited that water was the primal element from which everything else emerged. This concept can be seen as a reflection of the ancient Greek belief in the significance of water in creation myths and its life-giving properties. By identifying water as the arche, Thales connected the physical world to a foundational, divine principle, bridging the gap between the material and the spiritual.

❖ Anaximander: Cosmic Origins and the Divine

Anaximander, a student of Thales, continued the tradition of religious and cosmological exploration. His inquiries delved into the origin and structure of the universe, contemplating the divine nature of its creation. Anaximander proposed a theory of "apeiron," an infinite and boundless substance that is the source of all things.

The concept of the apeiron can be seen as an attempt to grasp the divine essence that governs the cosmos. By positing an infinite principle, Anaximander acknowledged the transcendent and incomprehensible nature of the ultimate reality. This religious undertone in his cosmological theory suggests an intricate connection between the divine and the material world.

❖ Pythagoras: Mathematics, Harmony, and the Divine

Pythagoras, renowned for his mathematical contributions, also delved into the mystical and religious aspects of numbers. His philosophical school, the Pythagorean Brotherhood, emphasized the profound significance of numbers in understanding the cosmos and human existence. Pythagoras saw numbers as the building blocks of reality, representing divine harmony and cosmic order.

In Pythagorean thought, numerical relationships reflected the structure of the universe and its divine proportions. The pursuit of mathematical knowledge was, therefore, not merely an intellectual endeavor but also a spiritual quest to comprehend the divine order inherent in the cosmos. This connection between mathematics and the divine demonstrates the religious underpinnings of Pythagorean philosophy.

Conclusion

The Presocratic philosophers, as early pioneers of Western thought, demonstrated a profound intertwinement of religious inquiries and cosmological speculations. Thales, Anaximander, and Pythagoras all sought to grasp the divine order and unity underlying the universe through their philosophical investigations. Thales' identification of water as the arche, Anaximander's proposal of the apeiron, and Pythagoras' exploration of numerical harmony exemplify the intricate connections between ancient Greek religious beliefs and the birth of philosophical thought. By studying these Presocratic thinkers, students gain insights into the formative period of Western philosophy and the enduring interplay between religion, cosmology, and the quest for understanding the fundamental nature of reality.

Socrates and the Examination of Religious Beliefs

The Socratic tradition, spearheaded by the influential philosopher Socrates and his disciple Plato, heralded a significant shift in philosophical inquiry. It not only delved into ethical concepts but also engaged with religious beliefs, exploring questions about the divine, the soul, and the moral dimensions of human existence.

❖ Socrates: "Know Thyself" and Introspection

Socrates' philosophy was centered around the famous dictum "know thyself." This principle encompassed a profound sense of introspection and self-awareness, urging individuals to critically examine their beliefs, values, and moral conduct. This aspect of Socratic thought was influenced by the religious ideal of self-knowledge, as understanding one's place in the cosmic order was considered essential in ancient Greek religious practices.

Socrates believed that through self-examination, individuals could discover their own ignorance, leading to a humble acknowledgment of their limitations. This philosophical humility echoed the ancient Greek religious virtue of modesty before the gods, recognizing human fallibility in contrast to divine wisdom. Socratic dialogues often revolved around the quest for wisdom, inviting interlocutors to reflect on their deeply held beliefs and their moral implications.

❖   Plato: Religious Themes and Metaphysical Questions

Plato, one of the most influential philosophers of antiquity, further expanded on the examination of religious beliefs and metaphysical questions. His philosophical dialogues not only delved into ethical concepts but also explored the nature of the gods and the immortality of the soul.

In his work "Phaedo," Plato discussed the soul's immortality, suggesting that the soul exists before and after life, transcending the material world. This notion of the soul's immortality aligned with the religious belief in an eternal essence beyond the physical realm. Plato's "Theory of Forms," which posited a realm of ideal and perfect forms, had metaphysical and religious implications, paralleling the divine realm of gods in ancient Greek religious thought.

Plato's "Allegory of the Cave" in "The Republic" conveyed the idea of enlightenment and the ascent to higher knowledge. This allegory presented a journey from ignorance to wisdom, mirroring the religious idea of spiritual transformation and illumination through contact with divine truths.

❖   Exercises and Critical Thinking

Analyze Socrates' dictum "know thyself" in the context of ancient Greek religious ideals of self-awareness and humility before the gods. Discuss how this principle reflects both philosophical introspection and religious practices.

Explore the relationship between Plato's "Theory of Forms" and ancient Greek religious beliefs in divine realms and ideal realities.

Discuss the significance of Plato's "Allegory of the Cave" as a metaphor for philosophical enlightenment and its connections to religious notions of spiritual transformation.

Conclusion

The Socratic tradition, with its emphasis on introspection, moral reflection, and the examination of religious beliefs, brought philosophical inquiry closer to the realm of ethics and spirituality. Socrates' call to "know thyself" encouraged individuals to engage in critical self-examination, drawing parallels with religious ideals of self-awareness and humility before the divine. Plato's philosophical dialogues delved into religious themes, such as the nature of the gods and the immortality of the soul, and explored metaphysical questions that resonated with ancient Greek religious beliefs.

By studying the Socratic tradition, students gain insight into the profound interplay between philosophy and religion in ancient Greek thought. The integration of religious concepts with philosophical inquiry enriched the understanding of ethics, metaphysics, and the human quest for wisdom. This examination of religious beliefs and ethical concepts remains a pivotal subject of study, encouraging critical thinking and discussions about the complexities of human existence and the pursuit of knowledge.

Aristotle's Integration of Theology and Philosophy

Aristotle, the esteemed student of Plato, is widely recognized for his profound contributions to various fields, including ethics, politics, biology, and logic. His philosophical inquiries were extensive and encompassed a diverse range of subjects, demonstrating a rigorous and systematic approach to understanding the world. However, within his extensive body of work, Aristotle also delved into the realms of metaphysics and theology, showcasing an integration of philosophical reasoning with theological contemplation.

❖   Metaphysics and the Unmoved Mover

In his renowned work "Metaphysics," Aristotle sought to explore the fundamental nature of reality beyond the physical world. Central to his metaphysical inquiries was the concept of the "Unmoved Mover" or the "First Cause." This idea posited the existence of a transcendent and eternal entity that served as the ultimate cause and source of motion for all things in the universe.

Aristotle's notion of the Unmoved Mover represented a convergence of philosophical reasoning and theological contemplation. He argued that everything in the world is in constant motion, and this motion must have an ultimate cause that itself remains unmoved. This Unmoved Mover, according to Aristotle, must be pure actuality, devoid of potentiality, and its contemplation serves as the highest form of intellectual activity. In this way, Aristotle integrated metaphysical concepts with theological implications, exploring the existence of a divine and transcendent entity as the ultimate foundation of reality.

❖   Theology and the Prime Mover as God

Aristotle's concept of the Unmoved Mover bore similarities to the notion of God in religious contexts. While Aristotle did not explicitly equate the Unmoved Mover with the divine beings worshiped by ancient Greeks, the parallels between his philosophical ideas and religious theology are evident.

For many interpreters, the Unmoved Mover is seen as a reflection of a higher divine being or God. Just like the gods in ancient Greek religion, the Unmoved Mover represents a source of order, stability, and perfection in the cosmos. Its role as the prime cause and the ultimate source of motion aligns with the attributes often associated with gods in religious beliefs.

Conclusion

Aristotle's integration of theology and philosophy in his exploration of the Unmoved Mover showcased the interconnectedness of these disciplines in ancient Greek thought. His metaphysical inquiries into the ultimate cause of motion and the existence of a transcendent entity reflected a profound convergence of philosophical reasoning and theological contemplation.

While Aristotle's Unmoved Mover did not directly correspond to the gods of ancient Greek religion, the similarities between his philosophical concepts and religious theological beliefs highlight the nuanced relationship between philosophy and theology in ancient Greek intellectual discourse. By studying Aristotle's integration of theology and philosophy, students gain insight into the complexities of ancient Greek thought and the deep interplay between rational inquiry and religious contemplation in shaping philosophical frameworks.

Hellenistic Philosophy and Religious Syncretism

The Hellenistic period, which began with the conquests of Alexander the Great in the 4th century BCE and continued until the rise of the Roman Empire, witnessed the widespread dissemination of Greek culture, language, and ideas across diverse regions. This period of cultural diffusion resulted in a dynamic exchange between Greek and local traditions, giving rise to religious syncretism and the blending of diverse religious beliefs and practices.

❖   Cultural and Philosophical Impact

As Greek influence expanded, Hellenistic cities emerged as vibrant centers of intellectual and philosophical activity. The cosmopolitan nature of these cities facilitated cross-cultural interactions, enabling the fusion of Greek philosophy with various local belief systems. This intermingling of cultures contributed to the emergence of novel philosophical schools that integrated elements of Greek religious thought into their ethical and metaphysical systems.

◆   Hellenistic Philosophers and Their Integration of Religious Beliefs

❖   The Stoics: Pursuit of Virtue and Divine Order

The Stoics, founded by Zeno of Citium, were prominent Hellenistic philosophers who developed a comprehensive ethical and metaphysical system that incorporated aspects of Greek religious thought. Central to Stoic philosophy was the pursuit of virtue (aretē) and the attainment of eudaimonia, translated as "happiness" or "flourishing," which was believed to arise from living in harmony with the divine order of the universe.

The Stoics viewed the cosmos as a rational and providential entity governed by a divine intelligence, referred to as the Logos. This divine Logos, according to Stoic belief, permeated the entire universe, guiding its course and maintaining cosmic order. By aligning their lives with this divine order and accepting its will, Stoics sought inner tranquility and contentment, transcending worldly attachments and desires.

❖   The Epicureans: Pleasure and Aponia

The Epicureans, founded by Epicurus, also emerged during the Hellenistic period and developed a philosophical system that encompassed both metaphysics and ethics. Contrary to Stoic beliefs, Epicureanism promoted a pursuit of pleasure as the ultimate aim of human life. However, this pursuit of pleasure was not to be confused with hedonism or excess, but rather, it was rooted in the attainment of ataraxia (freedom from disturbance) and aponia (freedom from physical pain).

While Epicureans did not explicitly emphasize religious elements, their philosophy provided an alternative ethical framework that diverged from traditional religious notions of virtue and divine order. Instead, they emphasized the importance of individual happiness and tranquility through the cultivation of wisdom and moderation.

Conclusion

The Hellenistic period was a pivotal era marked by the expansion of Greek culture and ideas. Hellenistic philosophers, such as the Stoics and the Epicureans, exemplified the integration of religious beliefs into their philosophical systems, emphasizing the pursuit of virtue, happiness, and harmony with the divine order. Their contributions to ethical and metaphysical discourse continue to resonate in Western philosophy, demonstrating the enduring influence of religious syncretism and the blending of diverse traditions during this transformative period in history.

The Influence of Neoplatonism

Neoplatonism, a philosophical system founded by Plotinus in the 3rd century CE, further integrated Greek religious and mystical elements into philosophical thought. Neoplatonism posited a hierarchical structure of reality, with the One as the ultimate source of all existence and emanation. This metaphysical framework drew heavily on religious notions of divine unity and the transcendent nature of reality.

Conclusion

The influence of ancient Greek religion on Western philosophy is profound and multifaceted. From the religious inquiries of the Presocratic philosophers to the ethical teachings of Socrates, Plato, and Aristotle, Greek religious thought laid the foundation for the development of Western philosophical traditions. The integration of religious concepts into philosophical systems, as seen in Hellenistic philosophy and Neoplatonism, further illustrates the enduring interplay between religion and philosophy in shaping Western intellectual history. By engaging in critical analysis and contemplation of these philosophical developments, students gain insights into the complexities of the relationship between ancient Greek religion and Western philosophical thought, fostering a deeper understanding of the cultural and intellectual heritage that underpins Western civilization.

✧ Integration into Western Cultural Values

The enduring legacy of ancient Greek religion has left an indelible mark on Western cultural values. The philosophical, artistic, and ethical contributions of ancient Greek religious thought continue to shape contemporary Western society. This section explores the ways in which Greek religious concepts have integrated into Western cultural values, permeating various aspects of art, literature, philosophy, and societal norms.

Influence on Art and Aesthetics

Ancient Greek mythology and religious themes have profoundly impacted Western art and aesthetics. From the classical sculptures of the Parthenon to Renaissance paintings depicting Greek myths, artistic representations of gods, heroes, and tragic tales serve as a testament to the enduring fascination with Greek religious narratives. The use of Greek architectural elements, such as columns and pediments, in Western buildings further reflects the integration of ancient Greek religious aesthetics into Western culture.

Impact on Literature and Language

Greek religious beliefs and myths have been woven into the fabric of Western literature. Works such as John Milton's "Paradise Lost" draw upon Greek religious themes to explore questions of good and evil and the nature of divine beings. Additionally, the English language is replete with words derived from Greek mythology, demonstrating the pervasive influence of ancient Greek religion on linguistic expression.

❖ Philosophical Continuity

The integration of Greek religious thought into Western cultural values is most evident in philosophy. The ethical teachings of Socrates, Plato, and Aristotle have permeated Western moral and ethical frameworks, emphasizing the pursuit of virtue, the importance of self-awareness, and the examination of one's beliefs and actions. Furthermore, the Stoics and the Epicureans, influenced by Greek religious ideals, have contributed to Western philosophical discourse on issues of happiness, the nature of the cosmos, and the human place within it.

❖ Societal Values and Governance

Greek religious concepts also influenced the development of societal values and governance in Western culture. The idea of civic virtue and the belief that piety and religious reverence contribute to the well-being of the state have had a lasting impact on Western notions of citizenship and civic responsibility. Moreover, the separation of religious and political authority, a concept rooted in ancient Greek religious practices, continues to shape Western democratic governance.

❖   Exercises and Critical Thinking

Analyze a contemporary work of art or literature that draws upon Greek religious themes. Discuss how the integration of these themes enhances the overall meaning and message of the work.

Compare and contrast the ethical teachings of the Stoics and the Epicureans with a contemporary ethical framework. Identify areas of convergence and divergence, considering how Greek religious ideals have influenced modern ethical thought.

Debate the significance of civic virtue and the role of religion in governance, exploring the historical roots of these concepts in ancient Greek religious practices and their relevance to modern political systems.

Conclusion

The integration of ancient Greek religious concepts into Western cultural values is evident in various domains of human expression and thought. From art and literature to philosophy and governance, the legacy of ancient Greek religion continues to resonate in contemporary Western society. The study of this integration allows us to better understand the rich tapestry of Western cultural values and the enduring impact of ancient Greek religious thought on shaping the foundations of Western civilization.

How ancient Greek religious themes continue to shape contemporary cultural expressions

The profound and enduring influence of ancient Greek religious themes on contemporary cultural expressions is a testament to the timeless significance of Greek mythology, beliefs, and rituals. Despite the passage of millennia, the rich tapestry of Greek religious concepts continues to resonate and inspire various fields, including art, literature, film, music, and even modern spiritual practices. This section explores the ways in which ancient Greek religious themes persistently influence and shape contemporary cultural expressions.

✧   Influence on Artistic Representations

Ancient Greek religion, with its rich pantheon of gods and goddesses, mythological stories, and religious rituals, has served as a profound source of inspiration for artistic expressions throughout history. From sculpture and pottery to painting and literature, Greek religious themes have been skillfully portrayed, celebrating the divine, heroic exploits, and tales of tragedy and triumph. This section delves into the influence of ancient Greek religion on artistic representations and explores how these representations have preserved religious narratives, conveyed moral lessons, and reflected cultural ideals.

Sculpture and Pottery

Ancient Greek sculpture and pottery offer significant insights into the influence of religion on artistic representations. Statues of gods and goddesses, such as Zeus, Athena, and Apollo, were sculpted with great attention to detail, capturing the idealized beauty and power of the divine beings. These sculptures often adorned temples and sanctuaries, symbolizing the presence of the gods and acting as focal points of religious devotion. The inclusion of mythological scenes on pottery, such as the adventures of Heracles or the myth of the birth of Aphrodite, further exemplifies how Greek religious narratives were integrated into artistic forms.

Painting and Mosaics

While ancient Greek paintings have been largely lost to time, the influence of Greek religious themes on this medium is evident in later Roman and Byzantine art. Frescoes and mosaics found in ancient Roman villas and Byzantine churches often depicted scenes from Greek mythology and religious stories. These artworks not only conveyed religious narratives but also conveyed moral messages and served as expressions of devotion to the gods.

Literature and Epic Tradition

The ancient Greek religious beliefs and myths found their way into epic poems, such as Homer's "Iliad" and "Odyssey." These literary masterpieces celebrated the heroics of mortals, such as Achilles and Odysseus, and showcased the interactions between gods and humans. The portrayal of gods intervening in mortal affairs and the reverence for divine fate highlighted the intertwining of religion and human destinies. These epic poems served as cultural touchstones, shaping ethical norms and conveying a shared sense of identity among ancient Greeks.

Theater and Dramatic Festivals

The dramatic festivals in honor of gods, particularly Dionysus, were instrumental in the development of Greek theater, where plays were infused with religious themes. The tragedies of Aeschylus, Sophocles, and Euripides explored the human condition and the divine-human relationship, prompting audiences to reflect on profound philosophical and moral questions. These plays served not only as religious performances but also as reflections of the complexities of the human experience.

Conclusion

The influence of ancient Greek religion on artistic representations has been profound and far-reaching. From sculpture and pottery to literature and theater, Greek religious themes have provided a wellspring of inspiration for artists across cultures and throughout history. These artistic representations not only preserved religious narratives but also conveyed moral lessons, cultural ideals, and philosophical reflections. By studying the integration of ancient Greek religious concepts into art, students gain a deeper appreciation for the interconnectedness between religion, culture, and the enduring impact of artistic expressions on human civilization.

✧ Influence on Contemporary Literature

Ancient Greek religion's enduring legacy has transcended the boundaries of time and space, leaving an indelible mark on various aspects of human civilization, including literature. The influence of Greek religious concepts, mythologies, and philosophical inquiries continues to resonate with contemporary writers, who draw inspiration from these ancient themes to explore human nature, ethical dilemmas, and the complexities of the human experience. This section delves into the ways in which ancient Greek religious ideas have found their way into modern literature, shaping and enriching contemporary literary expressions.

Mythological Retellings and Modern Adaptations

One of the most direct manifestations of Greek religious influence in contemporary literature is the retelling and adaptation of ancient myths. Writers often draw on Greek myths as a source of inspiration to craft new narratives, exploring the psychological depths of characters and infusing timeless themes of love, jealousy, betrayal, and heroism. For example, modern works such as Madeline Miller's "Circe" and "Song of Achilles" breathe new life into the tales of ancient Greek heroes and heroines, inviting readers to view these mythological figures from fresh perspectives.

Themes of Fate and Destiny

The ancient Greeks believed in the concept of fate, where the actions of individuals were bound by predetermined events. Contemporary authors have incorporated this notion of fate into their literary works, exploring the themes of destiny, free will, and the struggle against one's own predetermined path. Through these narratives, writers contemplate the complexities of human agency and the desire to defy the gods' predetermined outcomes. For example, in J.K. Rowling's "Harry Potter" series, prophecies and the struggle against destiny are prominent motifs that mirror the ancient Greek belief in the power of prophecy.

Examination of Ethical Dilemmas

Ancient Greek religion often emphasized ethical values and moral responsibilities. Contemporary literature continues this tradition by exploring ethical dilemmas faced by characters, prompting readers to reflect on moral choices and the consequences of actions. Works such as Cormac McCarthy's "The Road" and Kazuo Ishiguro's "Never Let Me Go" delve into the ethical implications of the human condition and challenge readers to consider the ethical complexities of human existence, much like the philosophical inquiries of ancient Greek thinkers.

Contemporary Philosophical Reflections

Greek philosophers engaged in profound debates on the nature of reality, the existence of gods, and the search for wisdom. Contemporary literature echoes these philosophical reflections by exploring metaphysical questions, the nature of consciousness, and the search for meaning in a rapidly changing world. Writers like Haruki Murakami and Ursula K. Le Guin use elements of magic realism and science fiction to delve into philosophical concepts, much like the speculative inquiries of ancient Greek philosophers.

Conclusion

The impact of ancient Greek religion on contemporary literature is a testament to the enduring power of these age-old themes and narratives. From mythological retellings to philosophical reflections, writers continue to draw on the rich tapestry of ancient Greek religious concepts to explore the complexities of the human experience. By examining the integration of Greek religious ideas into modern literature, students gain a deeper appreciation for the interconnectedness between ancient and contemporary cultures, as well as the timeless relevance of these profound themes in shaping human thought and expression.

✧ Influence on Music and Performing Arts

The influence of ancient Greek religion on music and the performing arts is profound and multifaceted. The rich tapestry of Greek mythology, cosmology, and philosophical inquiries has inspired countless composers, playwrights, choreographers, and performers throughout history. This section delves into the ways in which ancient Greek religious concepts continue to shape music and the performing arts, illustrating the enduring impact of these themes on human expression and creativity.

Musical Odes and Homeric Hymns

Ancient Greek religious practices often included musical performances, with odes and hymns serving as expressions of devotion to the gods. Contemporary composers and musicians have drawn inspiration from these ancient musical traditions, creating modern compositions that evoke the solemnity and reverence of ancient hymns. For instance, the English composer Gustav Holst's orchestral suite "The Planets" includes a movement titled "Jupiter, the Bringer of Jollity," which echoes the jubilant spirit of ancient odes celebrating the gods' benevolence.

Theatrical Reenactments and Modern Adaptations

The performing arts, especially theater, hold a profound connection to ancient Greek religious festivals and rituals. The Greek tragedies and comedies staged during religious festivals explored the human condition and the divine-human relationship, touching on themes of fate, morality, and the intervention of gods in mortal affairs. Modern theater often draws on these ancient traditions, with contemporary playwrights adapting ancient Greek plays to explore timeless themes and questions. For example, Jean-Paul Sartre's play "The Flies" reimagines the ancient Greek tragedy of Oresteia to comment on existentialist philosophy and human freedom.

Dance and Ritualistic Movement

Ancient Greek religious rituals often involved dance as a form of worship and celebration. This tradition has left a profound impact on contemporary dance, where choreographers incorporate symbolic movements and ritualistic elements to evoke the ancient Greek reverence for the gods. Dance performances may explore themes of divine interaction with mortals, human emotions, and the cosmic order, reflecting the intricate relationship between dance and religious expression in ancient times.

Sacred Music and Choral Works

The choral tradition in ancient Greek religious ceremonies has had a lasting impact on sacred music in Western culture. Modern choral works often draw on the grandeur and spirituality of ancient Greek choral odes, using vocal harmonies to evoke the transcendent and the divine. Composers like Johann Sebastian Bach and Wolfgang Amadeus Mozart integrated choral elements into their religious compositions, reflecting the reverence for the divine found in ancient Greek religious practices.

Conclusion

The enduring resonance of ancient Greek religious themes in music and performing arts is a testament to the timeless power of these age-old narratives and philosophical inquiries. From musical odes to theatrical reenactments, contemporary artists continue to draw on the profound legacy of ancient Greek religious expressions, infusing their works with a sense of reverence, spirituality, and philosophical contemplation. By exploring the integration of ancient Greek religious concepts into music and the performing arts, students gain a deeper understanding of the profound impact of these themes on human creativity and expression across time and cultures.

✧ Influence on Modern Spirituality

The legacy of ancient Greek religion extends far beyond the confines of its historical context, permeating various facets of modern spirituality. The profound philosophical inquiries, the rich tapestry of mythological narratives, and the exploration of human connections to the divine in ancient Greece continue to shape contemporary spiritual practices and beliefs. This section delves into the ways in which ancient Greek religious concepts have left an indelible mark on modern spirituality, fostering a deeper understanding of the enduring influence of these ancient ideas on the human quest for meaning and transcendence.

Neo-Paganism and Revivalist Movements

The resurgence of neo-paganism in the modern era has drawn inspiration from ancient Greek religious traditions. Neo-pagan practitioners often incorporate elements of ancient Greek mythology, rituals, and symbolism into their spiritual practices. For instance, the worship of ancient Greek deities such as Zeus, Aphrodite, and Apollo is revived, with contemporary adherents seeking a connection to these divine figures as expressions of nature's forces and archetypal energies.

Ecospirituality and Nature Worship

Ancient Greek religion had a deep reverence for nature and its interconnectedness with the divine. This ecological worldview continues to influence modern ecospirituality, where spiritual seekers embrace the intrinsic value of the natural world and seek spiritual insights through nature-based practices. Drawing parallels with ancient Greek beliefs, ecospirituality emphasizes the importance of living in harmony with the environment and recognizing the sacredness of the natural world.

Modern Hermeticism and Alchemy

Hermeticism, an esoteric tradition rooted in ancient Egyptian and Greek teachings, explores the relationship between the divine and the material world. The concept of Hermes Trismegistus, the legendary figure associated with the fusion of Egyptian and Greek wisdom, has inspired modern Hermeticists and alchemists seeking spiritual transformation and the union of the soul with the divine. These mystical traditions often draw on ancient Greek concepts of divine wisdom and the transmutation of the soul.

Conclusion

The enduring influence of ancient Greek religion on modern spirituality is a testament to the universality and timelessness of the human quest for meaning and transcendence. From neo-paganism's revival of ancient deities to ecospirituality's reverence for nature and Hermeticism's exploration of divine wisdom, these modern spiritual movements draw on the profound legacy of ancient Greek religious concepts. By examining the integration of ancient Greek ideas into contemporary spiritual practices, students gain a deeper appreciation for the ongoing dialogue between past and present, and the way in which ancient wisdom continues to inform and enrich our spiritual pursuits in the modern world.

Insights into Human Spirituality and Nature

The exploration of human spirituality and its interconnectedness with nature has been a perennial pursuit across cultures and civilizations throughout history. The ancient Greeks, in particular, developed a profound and multifaceted understanding of the relationship between humanity and the natural world, a perspective that continues to resonate with modern seekers of spiritual insight. This section delves into the insights offered by ancient Greek religious and philosophical traditions concerning human spirituality and nature, fostering a deeper appreciation for the timeless relevance of these ideas in contemporary discourse.

The Divine in Nature: Awe and Reverence

Ancient Greek religious thought recognized the inherent divinity present in the natural world. The personification of natural phenomena as gods and goddesses attested to the Greeks' perception of nature's power and agency. For example, the mighty Zeus embodied the force of thunder and lightning, while the nurturing Demeter represented the fertile earth. The ancient Greeks' awe and reverence for nature as expressions of the divine continue to inspire modern ecological spirituality and environmental ethics, prompting individuals to consider the intrinsic value of the natural world.

Mythology and Archetypal Symbolism

Greek mythology abounds with stories that explore the human experience and our relationship with nature. The myths of Persephone's cyclical journey between the underworld and the surface, for instance, mirror the changing seasons and the cyclicality of life. These archetypal symbols offer profound insights into the human condition, resonating with modern individuals who seek to understand their place in the grand tapestry of existence.

Philosophy and the Cosmos

The ancient Greek philosophers, too, grappled with questions about human spirituality and nature. The Presocratic thinkers contemplated the fundamental principles of the cosmos, seeking to understand the underlying unity of all things. Later philosophers, such as Plato and Aristotle, explored the metaphysical aspects of divinity and the human soul's connection to the cosmos. Their philosophical musings continue to ignite contemporary discussions on the nature of consciousness and the universe.

Conclusion

The insights into human spirituality and nature gleaned from ancient Greek religious and philosophical traditions have left an indelible mark on the collective consciousness of humanity. The Greeks' awe and reverence for nature as a manifestation of the divine, the enduring archetypal symbolism found in their mythology, and their philosophical contemplations of the cosmos continue to inspire and inform contemporary seekers of spiritual understanding. By engaging with these ancient ideas, students are invited to explore their own spiritual inclinations and foster a deeper appreciation for the profound interconnection between humanity and the natural world. The exploration of human spirituality and nature is a timeless endeavor, one that enriches our understanding of the human experience and offers valuable insights into the multifaceted tapestry of existence.

Analyzing the Greeks' relationship with nature and their understanding of the divine

The ancient Greeks' relationship with nature was deeply ingrained in their religious, philosophical, and cultural beliefs. Their understanding of the natural world was characterized by a sense of awe, reverence, and interconnectedness with the divine. This section examines the multifaceted aspects of the Greeks' relationship with nature, offering insights into their spiritual and philosophical perspectives.

Divine Personification of Nature
In ancient Greek religion, natural phenomena were personified as gods and goddesses, imbuing the natural world with divine agency and significance. For example, Poseidon personified the vast and powerful sea, while Artemis embodied the untamed wilderness and wild animals. This divine personification not only reflected the Greeks' belief in the power of nature but also reinforced the idea that the natural world was intrinsically linked to the divine order.

Nature's Sacred Spaces

The ancient Greeks established sacred spaces in nature, such as groves, grottoes, and mountains, as sites of religious significance. These sanctuaries were dedicated to specific deities and served as places of worship and communion with the divine. For instance, the Oracle of Delphi was located on the slopes of Mount Parnassus, where the god Apollo's priestess would deliver prophetic messages. The Greeks' reverence for these natural sanctuaries highlighted their belief in the sacredness of nature.

Environmental Ethics and Ecological Consciousness

The Greeks' relationship with nature was marked by a sense of environmental ethics and ecological consciousness. Their agricultural practices, such as offering the first fruits to the gods, demonstrated a recognition of the interdependence between human prosperity and the natural world's fertility. Additionally, ancient Greek mythology contained moral lessons about the consequences of disrespecting nature, as seen in the myths of punishment inflicted by gods on mortals who violated sacred places or harmed animals.

Philosophical Contemplation of Nature

Philosophers like the Presocratics and Aristotle engaged in deep contemplation of the natural world, seeking to understand its underlying principles and order. Thales' belief in water as the fundamental substance and Anaximander's exploration of cosmological theories both reflected their attempt to discern the unity and order within nature. Aristotle's concept of the "unmoved mover" as the ultimate cause of all things further integrated philosophical reasoning with the divine order present in nature.

Relationship with Animals and Wildlife

The Greeks' relationship with nature extended to their interactions with animals and wildlife. Certain animals were considered sacred to specific deities, while others held symbolic significance. For instance, the owl was associated with the goddess Athena, symbolizing wisdom and protection. Additionally, the Greeks had rituals and festivals dedicated to the protection and appreciation of wildlife, showcasing their harmonious coexistence with the natural world.

Conclusion

The ancient Greeks' relationship with nature was multifaceted, characterized by a profound sense of awe, reverence, and interconnectedness with the divine. Their religious practices, philosophical contemplations, and ethical considerations all contributed to a comprehensive understanding of the natural world as a manifestation of the divine order. This perspective continues to inspire contemporary discussions on ecological consciousness, environmental ethics, and spiritual connections with nature. By examining the Greeks' relationship with nature, students gain valuable insights into the timeless significance of human beings' interaction with the natural world and the enduring impact of ancient Greek thought on contemporary environmental philosophy.

Comparing ancient Greek spirituality with modern ecospirituality and environmental concerns

Ancient Greek spirituality and modern ecospirituality both center around the relationship between humans and the natural world, but they do so in distinct ways. While ancient Greek spirituality was rooted in the worship of anthropomorphic gods and the personification of natural phenomena, modern ecospirituality is characterized by a more holistic and interconnected view of nature. This section delves into the key differences and similarities between these two spiritual perspectives and explores their implications for contemporary environmental concerns.

Anthropomorphic Gods vs. Divine Immanence

In ancient Greek spirituality, the gods were anthropomorphic, possessing human-like qualities, emotions, and interactions with mortals. For instance, Zeus, the king of the gods, was depicted with human attributes and emotions, ruling over the heavens from Mount Olympus. In contrast, modern ecospirituality tends to embrace the concept of divine immanence, seeing the sacred or divine as permeating all of nature. This view emphasizes the interconnectedness of all living beings and the recognition of the sacredness of the Earth as a whole.

Nature as a Realm of Divinity vs. Nature as Sacred

In ancient Greek spirituality, nature was considered the realm of divinity, with specific gods and goddesses presiding over natural elements and phenomena. For example, Demeter was associated with agriculture and the harvest, while Poseidon was the god of the seas. This view assigned a divine purpose to various aspects of the natural world. In contrast, modern ecospirituality emphasizes the sacredness of nature as a whole, viewing the entire Earth as a living and interconnected entity worthy of reverence and protection.

Environmental Ethics and Stewardship

Both ancient Greek spirituality and modern ecospirituality have ethical implications regarding the relationship between humans and the environment. In ancient Greece, religious practices often involved rituals and offerings to appease the gods and maintain harmony with nature. Similarly, modern ecospirituality advocates for environmental stewardship and a sense of responsibility towards the Earth. This entails promoting sustainable practices, conservation efforts, and a deep respect for all life forms.

Influence on Environmental Concerns

While ancient Greek spirituality shaped the Greeks' perception of nature and influenced their ethical considerations, modern ecospirituality plays a significant role in contemporary environmental concerns. The ecological crises facing the planet, such as climate change, deforestation, and species extinction, have led many individuals and communities to embrace ecospiritual perspectives. Ecospirituality encourages a sense of interconnectedness and responsibility towards the Earth, motivating environmental activism and sustainable practices.

Relevance in Contemporary Society

Ancient Greek spirituality and modern ecospirituality are both relevant in contemporary society, albeit in different ways. The study of ancient Greek spirituality provides valuable insights into historical perspectives on nature and the divine, offering a foundation for understanding the cultural and philosophical roots of Western civilization. On the other hand, modern ecospirituality offers a holistic and ecologically conscious framework for addressing pressing environmental challenges, encouraging individuals and communities to cultivate a deeper connection with nature and to take active steps to protect the planet.

Conclusion

The comparison between ancient Greek spirituality and modern ecospirituality reveals the evolution of human perspectives on nature and the divine. While ancient Greek spirituality was characterized by anthropomorphic gods and the worship of nature as a realm of divinity, modern ecospirituality embraces the interconnectedness of all living beings and the sacredness of the Earth. Both perspectives offer valuable insights into humanity's spiritual and ethical relationship with the natural world, informing discussions on contemporary environmental concerns and the need for responsible stewardship of the planet. By exploring these two spiritual traditions, students gain a deeper understanding of the diverse ways in which human spirituality and environmental consciousness have evolved over time.

Divination and Mystical Practices

Divination and mystical practices have played a significant role in human history, encompassing a diverse array of traditions across cultures and civilizations. These practices involve seeking insights into the unknown, glimpsing hidden truths, and connecting with the divine or spiritual realms. Divination, in particular, has been a crucial method employed by individuals and communities to gain knowledge of the future, understand the present, or seek guidance from higher powers. This section provides an in-depth exploration of divination and mystical practices, their historical significance, cultural contexts, and enduring relevance in contemporary society.

✧ The Nature and Purpose of Divination

Defining Divination

Divination is the art of obtaining knowledge or insight about future events or hidden truths through supernatural means or symbolic interpretation. It is rooted in the belief that the universe operates under certain patterns and interconnected forces, and by deciphering these patterns, practitioners can discern information beyond the realm of ordinary human perception.

The Purpose of Divination

Divination serves various purposes, depending on the cultural and historical context in which it is practiced. For some, it is a means to gain foresight into potential challenges and opportunities, aiding in decision-making and future planning. For others, divination may be employed to seek divine guidance in matters of personal, communal, or political significance. It can also serve therapeutic purposes, providing individuals with spiritual healing and psychological solace during times of uncertainty or distress.

Mystical Practices and Their Significance

Defining Mystical Practices

Mystical practices are spiritual or religious experiences that involve the direct encounter with the transcendent or divine. These practices often entail altered states of consciousness, meditative techniques, and rituals aimed at achieving unity with the sacred. Mysticism seeks to deepen one's understanding of existence and the mysteries of the cosmos beyond ordinary sensory perception.

The Significance of Mystical Practices

Mystical practices have been integral to the development of spiritual and philosophical traditions worldwide. The pursuit of mystical experiences is often associated with the desire for enlightenment, spiritual awakening, and a deeper connection with the divine or universal consciousness. Such practices are found in numerous belief systems, including Hinduism, Buddhism, Sufism, Christian mysticism, and various indigenous spiritual traditions.

✦ Cultural Context and Diversity of Divination and Mystical Practices

Cross-Cultural Perspectives

Divination and mystical practices have manifested in diverse ways across cultures, reflecting the unique beliefs, cosmologies, and mythologies of each society. For example, the Oracle of Delphi in ancient Greece played a crucial role in advising rulers and offering prophetic insights, while the Yoruba tradition in Nigeria utilized divination through the Ifá oracle to communicate with deities and ancestors.

Regional Variations

Different regions and historical periods have witnessed distinct forms of divination and mystical practices. In the Americas, indigenous peoples engaged in shamanic rituals to access spiritual realms and provide healing, while in the medieval period, European cultures employed methods such as scrying and astrology to foresee future events.

✧ The Role of Divination and Mystical Practices in Contemporary Society

Contemporary Relevance

Despite significant advancements in science and technology, divination and mystical practices continue to hold relevance in contemporary society. For many individuals, these practices offer a means to explore spirituality, gain personal insight, and cope with the complexities of modern life. In a world characterized by uncertainty, divination can provide a sense of comfort and direction, while mystical experiences offer seekers a deeper connection to their inner selves and the cosmos.

Skepticism and Criticism

It is important to note that divination and mystical practices have faced skepticism and criticism from various quarters. Skeptics argue that these practices lack empirical evidence and are rooted in subjective interpretations. As such, they may be perceived as mere superstitions or illusions, devoid of any substantive value.

Conclusion

Divination and mystical practices have captivated human imagination and curiosity for millennia. These practices offer unique insights into the human quest for knowledge, spiritual enlightenment, and connection with the divine. As students delve into the intricacies of divination and mystical experiences, they gain a deeper appreciation for the diverse ways in which humans have sought meaning, guidance, and transcendence throughout history. By studying these practices with a critical and open mind, students engage in discussions about the complexities of belief systems, the nature of human spirituality, and the enduring impact of divination and mystical practices on individuals and societies across time and cultures.

The role of oracles, divination, and prophecy in ancient Greek religious life

In the religious landscape of ancient Greece, the practice of seeking divine guidance through oracles, divination, and prophecy held a prominent and influential position. These forms of communication with the divine were deeply woven into the fabric of Greek society, shaping political decisions, personal choices, and communal beliefs. This section delves into the significance of oracles, divination, and prophecy in ancient Greek religious life, exploring their methods, cultural context, and enduring impact.

✧ Oracles: Intermediaries Between Mortals and Gods

Definition and Function

Oracles were revered as the mouthpieces of the gods, serving as intermediaries through whom divine messages and guidance were delivered to mortals. People sought oracles to inquire about a range of matters, including state affairs, military campaigns, personal decisions, and even weather predictions. Oracular responses were believed to offer insights into the will of the gods, shaping the course of human actions and events.

Notable Oracles

The Oracle of Delphi, dedicated to Apollo, was among the most renowned oracles in ancient Greece. Located at the sanctuary of Pytho, the Pythia, a priestess of Apollo, delivered prophecies in a trance-like state, often in cryptic and symbolic language. Other notable oracles included the Oracle of Dodona, associated with Zeus, and the Oracle of Ammon in Egypt, which attracted Greek seekers.

✧ Divination: Seeking Clarity Through Signs and Symbols

Divination Methods

Divination encompassed diverse practices through which individuals sought guidance by interpreting signs and symbols believed to carry hidden meanings. Methods of divination included casting lots, reading the patterns of animal entrails (haruspicy), observing the flight of birds (augury), and interpreting celestial phenomena (astrology). These practices provided a means to gain insight into future events and divine intentions.

Social Significance

Divination permeated all aspects of ancient Greek society, from private households to state affairs. Before embarking on significant ventures, such as military campaigns or colonial expeditions, city-states often consulted diviners to assess the favorability of the gods. Similarly, individuals sought divinatory guidance to navigate personal challenges and important life decisions.

✧ Prophecy: Foretelling the Future Through Inspired Insight

The Nature of Prophecy

Prophecy involved individuals known as prophets or seers who claimed to possess the ability to foresee the future or gain insights into divine will through inspired visions or dreams. Prophets were revered figures, and their counsel was sought by individuals and rulers alike. Some prominent prophets, such as Cassandra, were gifted with foresight but cursed to have their predictions disbelieved.

The Intersection of Prophecy and Politics

Prophecy played a crucial role in political life, influencing the decisions of leaders and shaping the fate of cities. For instance, before the Battle of Salamis, a prophecy inspired the Athenians to seek protection behind their "wooden walls," which was interpreted to refer to their naval fleet. This prophetic guidance ultimately led to their victory over the Persians.

✧ Critical Analysis: Skepticism and Interpretation

Skepticism Towards Divination and Prophecy

Despite their widespread practice, divination and prophecy faced skepticism from some segments of ancient Greek society. Philosophers like Xenophanes and Euripides expressed doubts about the reliability of divinatory practices, arguing that interpretations could be manipulated or misunderstood.

Interpretation and Influence

Interpreting oracular responses, divinatory signs, and prophetic visions required skill and often left room for subjective interpretation. The influence of these practices on decision-making processes highlights the power attributed to divine guidance and the complex interplay between human agency and the divine will.

Conclusion

Oracles, divination, and prophecy were integral to the religious and cultural life of ancient Greece, providing a means for individuals and communities to seek divine guidance, comprehend the unknown, and navigate the complexities of existence. The enduring legacy of these practices lies in their influence on historical events, their significance in shaping belief systems, and their resonance with human curiosity and quest for understanding. By studying the role of oracles, divination, and prophecy in ancient Greek religious life, students gain insights into the multifaceted nature of spirituality and the interplay between human agency and the mystical realms throughout history.

Exploring modern practices like tarot reading, astrology, and their historical connections

In the contemporary world, ancient divinatory practices like tarot reading and astrology have experienced a resurgence in popularity. These practices, rooted in ancient beliefs and spiritual traditions, continue to captivate individuals seeking guidance, self-discovery, and a deeper understanding of their lives. This section delves into the historical origins of tarot reading and astrology, their evolution over time, and their enduring relevance in modern spirituality.

✧ Tarot Reading: A Journey through Archetypal Symbols

Historical Context

The origins of tarot reading can be traced back to the 15th century, with early decks used for card games and later adapted for divination purposes. The symbolism of tarot cards draws upon various esoteric and spiritual traditions, incorporating elements from ancient Egypt, Jewish Kabbalah, and Western occultism.

Structure and Interpretation

Tarot decks consist of 78 cards, divided into the Major Arcana (22 cards representing significant life themes) and the Minor Arcana (56 cards reflecting everyday experiences and challenges). Tarot readers interpret the cards' imagery, archetypal symbols, and their position in a spread to provide insights into personal journeys, relationships, and future possibilities.

Modern Tarot Practice

Tarot reading has evolved into a modern practice embraced by individuals seeking guidance, introspection, and spiritual growth. Contemporary tarot practitioners often combine traditional interpretations with their intuition and empathic abilities to offer personalized readings.

✧ Astrology: Mapping the Cosmic Influences

Ancient Origins

Astrology, the study of celestial bodies' positions and their influence on human affairs, has ancient roots dating back to Mesopotamia, Egypt, and ancient Greece. Astrologers believed that the positions of planets and stars influenced human traits, behaviors, and destiny.

The Zodiac and Horoscopes

Astrology's central concept is the zodiac, a band of constellations through which the sun, moon, and planets appear to move in the sky. Each zodiac sign is associated with specific personality traits and characteristics. Horoscopes, based on an individual's birth chart, provide astrological predictions and guidance based on the alignment of celestial bodies at the time of birth.

Contemporary Astrology

Astrology has experienced a revival in contemporary times, with many turning to their horoscopes for self-reflection, relationship insights, and life guidance. Online platforms and popular astrology apps offer personalized horoscopes, making astrology easily accessible to a broader audience.

✧ Historical Connections: Tracing the Threads

Ancient Divinatory Roots

Both tarot reading and astrology have deep connections to ancient divinatory practices. Tarot's use of archetypal symbols and its focus on personal journeys and transformation can be linked to the ancient Greek concept of the hero's journey and the symbolic imagery found in religious art and myths.

Cosmic Interpretations

The belief that celestial bodies influence human destiny resonates with ancient Greek astrological traditions and the idea of a cosmic order. The Greeks observed planetary movements, considering them omens for significant events and the guidance of gods.

Conclusion

The revival of ancient divinatory practices like tarot reading and astrology reflects the enduring appeal of seeking guidance, meaning, and connection in the modern world. As individuals turn to these practices for introspection and insight, they participate in a centuries-old tradition of seeking wisdom from the cosmos and exploring the deeper mysteries of the human experience. By exploring the historical connections of tarot reading and astrology, students gain a nuanced understanding of the evolution of human spirituality and the timeless quest for self-discovery and divination.

Magic and the Occult in Ancient Greece

The ancient Greek civilization, renowned for its contributions to philosophy, art, and governance, also had a rich and complex relationship with magic and the occult. Magic, in the context of ancient Greece, encompassed a diverse range of practices, rituals, and beliefs aimed at harnessing supernatural powers for various purposes. This section explores the multifaceted nature of magic and the occult in ancient Greek society, delving into its historical development, prevalent beliefs, and significance within religious and cultural contexts.

✦ Historical Background: Magic in the Ancient World

Pre-Classical Origins

The roots of Greek magic can be traced back to pre-classical times, with the influence of neighboring civilizations like Egypt and Mesopotamia. These cultures held deeply ingrained beliefs in the power of spells, charms, and incantations to influence the natural world and the divine.

The Role of Magicians and Practitioners

Magicians, known as magoi or goetes, were individuals skilled in the art of magic and the invocation of supernatural forces. They held a unique position in ancient Greek society, as they were both revered and feared for their abilities to connect with the otherworldly realms.

✧ Religious Context: The Intersection of Magic and Mythology

Magical Practices in Religious Rituals

Magic and religious practices were closely intertwined in ancient Greece. In religious festivals and ceremonies, magicians and practitioners performed rituals, seeking divine favor, protection, or assistance. Offerings, libations, and incantations were common components of these magical rites.

Mythological Connections

Many magical practices found their roots in ancient Greek mythology. The stories of gods and heroes provided a wealth of inspiration for magical rituals and incantations. For example, invoking the name of a specific deity might be believed to grant specific powers or protection.

✧ The Occult and Divination: Seeking Knowledge of the Unknown

Divination and Oracle Consultations

Divination, the practice of seeking knowledge of the future or unknown through supernatural means, played a significant role in ancient Greek culture. Oracle consultations at sacred sites, such as the Oracle of Delphi, were highly revered, and individuals sought guidance from the gods on matters of personal and communal importance.

The Occult Sciences

Ancient Greeks also engaged in occult sciences, such as astrology and alchemy. Astrology involved the study of celestial bodies' movements to predict human destinies and events, while alchemy sought to transmute substances and discover the elixir of life.

✧ Ethical Considerations: The Boundaries of Magic and Religion

Magic and the occult in ancient Greece were met with a combination of acceptance and skepticism. While many embraced magical practices as an essential aspect of their religious and cultural identity, others, particularly philosophers like Plato, expressed reservations about the potential dangers of magic and its manipulation of divine forces.

Conclusion

The study of magic and the occult in ancient Greece offers invaluable insights into the complexities of human spirituality and the cultural expressions of ancient societies. The interplay between religion, mythology, and magical practices illuminates the ancient Greeks' quest for meaning, knowledge, and divine intervention. By delving into the world of ancient Greek magic, students gain a deeper understanding of the human fascination with the unknown and the enduring allure of the mystical and the supernatural throughout history.

Unraveling the concepts of magic and witchcraft in Greek society

In ancient Greek society, the concepts of magic and witchcraft held multifaceted and intriguing roles that went beyond mere supernatural beliefs. The distinction between magic and witchcraft was not always clear-cut, and both practices were intertwined with religious, cultural, and social aspects of Greek life. This section delves into the complexities of magic and witchcraft in ancient Greece, exploring their definitions, practitioners, beliefs, and significance within the broader cultural context.

✧ Defining Magic and Witchcraft

Magic: Manipulation of Supernatural Forces

Magic in ancient Greece referred to the art and practice of harnessing supernatural forces to achieve specific outcomes. These practices encompassed various rituals, spells, charms, and incantations, all believed to influence the natural and divine realms. Magicians, known as magoi, were skilled practitioners who performed these magical rites.

Witchcraft: The Role of Witches in Greek Society

Witchcraft, on the other hand, was often associated with individuals, predominantly women, who were believed to possess innate supernatural powers. Witches, known as pharmakeis or goeteis, were thought to have the ability to curse or bless others, manipulate fate, and cause harm or healing.

✧ The Intersection of Magic and Religion

Magical Rituals in Religious Contexts

Magic was deeply intertwined with religious practices in ancient Greece. It played a significant role in religious ceremonies, festivals, and rituals. For instance, practitioners used magical incantations to seek divine favor, protection, or assistance during religious events.

Temples and Oracle Consultations

Temples acted as focal points for magical activities, with priests and priestesses performing rituals to invoke the gods' favor. Oracle consultations were a common form of divination, involving the seeking of guidance from deities on matters of personal and communal importance.

✧ Societal Perceptions of Magic and Witchcraft

Acceptance and Distrust

While magic and witchcraft were an integral part of ancient Greek life, they were not universally accepted. Some individuals embraced these practices as essential aspects of their cultural and religious identity. However, others, particularly philosophers like Plato, expressed skepticism about the legitimacy and potential dangers of magic and witchcraft.

Legal and Social Implications

The practice of magic and witchcraft was not immune to legal scrutiny. Some magical practices were viewed as harmful and punishable by law. Accusations of witchcraft could lead to social ostracism or even persecution.

✧ Counterarguments and Dissenting Opinions

Philosophers such as Plato and his student Aristotle voiced reservations about magic and witchcraft. They argued that these practices relied on superstition and irrational beliefs, challenging the ethical implications of manipulating divine powers for personal gain.

Conclusion

The concepts of magic and witchcraft in ancient Greek society were nuanced and integral to the cultural and religious fabric of the time. Understanding these practices sheds light on the complexities of ancient Greek spirituality, beliefs, and societal norms. As students explore the intricate relationship between magic, witchcraft, and Greek culture, they gain valuable insights into the dynamics of human belief systems and the enduring fascination with the supernatural throughout history.

Comparing magical practices in ancient Greece with contemporary Wicca and neopaganism

The study of magical practices in ancient Greece provides a fascinating lens through which to examine the development and evolution of contemporary Wicca and neopaganism. While separated by millennia and cultural contexts, these belief systems share some common threads, reflecting humanity's enduring fascination with the supernatural, spiritual connections with nature, and the pursuit of mystical knowledge. This section explores the similarities and differences between magical practices in ancient Greece and modern Wicca and neopaganism, highlighting the ways in which ancient beliefs have influenced and shaped contemporary spiritual expressions.

✧ Nature-Centric Spirituality

Ancient Greek Practices

In ancient Greece, the veneration of natural elements and deities associated with nature was an integral part of magical practices. Rituals aimed at invoking the powers of the earth, sea, and sky were performed to seek blessings, protection, and divine guidance. The belief in the interconnectedness of all living beings with the natural world contributed to a reverence for the environment.

Contemporary Wicca and Neopaganism

Modern Wicca and neopaganism also emphasize a nature-centric spirituality. Practitioners often revere nature as sacred and find spiritual significance in the changing seasons, the cycles of the moon, and the interconnectedness of all living beings. Nature-based rituals and ceremonies are common in Wiccan and neopagan practices, fostering a sense of harmony and oneness with the natural world.

✧ Rituals, Spells, and Incantations

Ancient Greek Practices

In ancient Greece, magical rituals, spells, and incantations were used to influence the natural and divine realms. These practices aimed to gain favor from the gods, invoke blessings, or protect against malevolent forces. Magicians and practitioners of magic played a significant role in performing these rites.

Contemporary Wicca and Neopaganism

Similarly, modern Wicca and neopaganism involve the use of rituals, spells, and incantations to manifest intentions, connect with spiritual energies, and promote personal growth. These practices are often seen as a means of tapping into the inherent power within oneself and the natural world, aligning with the belief in a universal energy or life force.

✧ Mysticism and Personal Transformation

Ancient Greek Practices

Magical practices in ancient Greece were often intertwined with mysticism, seeking hidden knowledge, and achieving personal transformation. Initiatory rites and mystical experiences were sought by those desiring a deeper understanding of the divine and the mysteries of existence.

Contemporary Wicca and Neopaganism

Modern Wicca and neopaganism also value mysticism and personal transformation. Many practitioners seek to develop a deeper spiritual connection, engage in initiatory processes, and explore esoteric teachings that lead to self-discovery and inner growth.

✧ Deities and Pantheons

Ancient Greek Practices

In ancient Greece, magical practices were closely tied to the worship of a diverse pantheon of gods and goddesses. Different deities were invoked for specific purposes, and temples served as sacred spaces for performing rituals.

Contemporary Wicca and Neopaganism

While contemporary Wicca and neopaganism draw inspiration from various ancient pantheons, they often embrace a more eclectic approach to deity worship. Many Wiccans and neopagans honor deities from different cultural traditions, incorporating them into their practices based on personal affinities and spiritual connections.

Conclusion

The comparison between magical practices in ancient Greece and contemporary Wicca and neopaganism reveals a dynamic interplay of spirituality, nature reverence, mystical pursuits, and the exploration of human consciousness. While the cultural contexts differ, the enduring themes of magic, spirituality, and connection with the divine underscore the universal human quest for meaning, understanding, and personal transformation. By critically examining these practices, students gain insights into the rich tapestry of human spiritual expressions across time and cultures.

The Significance of Ancient Greek Religion in Modern Academia

The study of ancient Greek religion holds profound significance in modern academia, transcending the boundaries of historical inquiry to encompass a wide range of interdisciplinary fields. Its influence extends not only to religious studies but also to philosophy, literature, art, politics, and cultural studies. This section explores the multifaceted importance of ancient Greek religion in contemporary scholarship, shedding light on its enduring impact on various academic disciplines.

✧ Religious Studies and Comparative Religion

Understanding the Roots of Western Religions

The examination of ancient Greek religion provides a foundation for understanding the development of Western religious traditions. Scholars often draw parallels between Greek religious beliefs and practices and those of other ancient civilizations, such as Mesopotamia and Egypt. This comparative approach enriches our comprehension of the universal themes and motifs that underpin human spirituality and the human-divine relationship.

Mythology and Symbolism

The vast corpus of Greek myths and religious narratives offers a wealth of material for the study of religious symbolism, rituals, and cosmology. By analyzing these myths, scholars gain insights into the ways in which ancient Greeks perceived the world, the divine, and the human condition. This exploration serves as a valuable resource for comparative mythological studies and the interpretation of symbols in various religious contexts.

✧ Philosophy and Metaphysics

Theological Concepts in Ancient Philosophy

Ancient Greek religious thought had a profound impact on the development of Western philosophy. Early philosophers, such as the Presocratics, grappled with questions about the nature of the divine, the cosmos, and the metaphysical foundations of reality. The integration of religious concepts into philosophical discourse laid the groundwork for subsequent philosophical inquiries into the existence of gods, morality, and the nature of knowledge.

Moral and Ethical Considerations

The ethical teachings embedded in Greek religious narratives also contributed to the formation of ethical philosophies in ancient Greece. Socratic dialogues, for instance, often contemplated questions of virtue, justice, and human responsibility in relation to the divine. The exploration of moral principles in the context of ancient Greek religion remains pertinent in contemporary ethical discussions.

✧ Literature and Arts

Literary and Artistic Expressions

The influence of ancient Greek religion on literature and the arts is indelible. From epic poetry like Homer's "Iliad" and "Odyssey" to the tragedies of Aeschylus, Sophocles, and Euripides, religious themes and the portrayal of gods and mythical figures pervade Greek literary works. In visual arts, depictions of gods and goddesses, heroic narratives, and religious rituals are emblematic of the religious significance attributed to artistic expression in ancient Greek culture.

Inspiration for Modern Creations

The enduring allure of Greek mythology and religious tales continues to inspire contemporary literature, poetry, and art. Countless novels, plays, films, and visual artworks draw from these ancient sources, providing a bridge between the past and the present and reflecting the timeless appeal of Greek religious narratives.

✧ Cultural Studies and Identity

Shaping Western Cultural Identity

Ancient Greek religion played a pivotal role in shaping the cultural identity of Western societies. The enduring legacy of Greek religious concepts, symbols, and philosophical ideas is evident in contemporary Western thought and cultural expressions. By examining ancient Greek religion, scholars gain insight into the cultural foundations that underpin Western civilization.

Diversity and Plurality

The study of Greek religious practices also highlights the diversity and plurality of religious expressions in antiquity. This inclusivity encourages students and scholars to appreciate the complexities of human spirituality and the multiplicity of religious beliefs and practices across different historical periods and cultures.

Conclusion

The significance of ancient Greek religion in modern academia is far-reaching, permeating multiple disciplines and enriching our understanding of human spirituality, cultural heritage, and the enduring interplay between the divine and the mortal. As scholars and students engage with the complexities of ancient Greek religious thought and practices, they embark on a journey of critical thinking and interdisciplinary exploration, fostering a deeper appreciation for the profound and enduring impact of Greek religion on contemporary scholarship and cultural expressions.

The value of studying ancient Greek religion in understanding human history and culture

The study of ancient Greek religion holds immense value in comprehending the complexities of human history and culture. By delving into the religious beliefs, rituals, and practices of ancient Greeks, scholars gain profound insights into the fundamental aspects of human experience, societal structures, and the interplay between the sacred and the secular. This section explores the significance of studying ancient Greek religion in understanding the historical and cultural dimensions of human civilization.

✧ Historical Context and Cultural Heritage

Foundation of Western Civilization

Ancient Greece is considered one of the cradles of Western civilization, and its religious beliefs played a pivotal role in shaping the foundations of Western thought. The study of Greek religion allows us to explore the roots of Western cultural and intellectual heritage, including the development of philosophy, literature, art, and politics.

Historical Narratives and Mythology

Greek mythology offers a window into the historical narratives and collective memory of ancient societies. By analyzing these myths, historians unravel the cultural values, aspirations, and challenges faced by the ancient Greeks. Myths serve as a repository of cultural memory and reflect the worldview and identity of a civilization.

✧ Human Spirituality and the Divine Connection

Exploration of Human Spirituality

Ancient Greek religion provides a unique perspective on human spirituality, offering a rich tapestry of beliefs and practices concerning the divine and the afterlife. The study of Greek religious experiences and rituals allows scholars to understand the deep-rooted desire of human beings to connect with the sacred and seek meaning in their existence.

The Divine-Human Relationship

The interplay between gods and mortals in Greek religious narratives sheds light on the dynamics of the divine-human relationship. The portrayal of gods intervening in human affairs and mortal reverence for the divine fate underscores the complexities of this relationship and its impact on human conduct and values.

✧ Social Structure and Civic Life

Religious Institutions and Governance

Religion played a significant role in ancient Greek society, permeating various aspects of civic life. Temples and sanctuaries served as focal points of community gathering and worship, while religious festivals fostered a sense of unity and collective identity. The study of Greek religious institutions allows us to explore the interaction between religion and governance in ancient city-states.

Civic Virtue and Ethical Values

Ancient Greek religion emphasized civic virtue and moral responsibility, encouraging citizens to actively participate in religious rituals and ceremonies. The belief that piety contributed to the well-being of the state highlights the interconnectedness of religious practices and ethical values in shaping societal norms.

✧ Art, Literature, and Cultural Expressions

Artistic Representations and Symbolism

Greek religious beliefs provided a rich source of inspiration for artistic expression. Sculpture, pottery, and painting skillfully portrayed mythological stories, divine beings, and religious rituals, preserving cultural narratives and conveying moral lessons. The analysis of these artistic representations enriches our understanding of the religious and cultural values of ancient Greeks.

Literary Themes and Moral Lessons

Greek religious themes permeated epic poems, tragedies, and philosophical dialogues, reflecting the fusion of religious and literary traditions. The examination of these texts deepens our comprehension of ethical dilemmas, human virtues, and the search for wisdom in ancient Greek thought.

Conclusion

The study of ancient Greek religion offers a unique and multidimensional perspective on human history and culture. By analyzing the religious beliefs, practices, and cultural expressions of ancient Greeks, scholars gain profound insights into the foundations of Western civilization, the complexities of human spirituality, and the intertwining of the divine and the mortal. The value of studying ancient Greek religion lies in its capacity to enrich our understanding of the human experience, cultural heritage, and the enduring legacy of Greek thought in shaping contemporary intellectual and artistic expressions.

Ethical considerations in the study of ancient religions and cultural appropriation

The academic examination of ancient religions is a complex endeavor that necessitates careful ethical considerations. As scholars delve into the beliefs, practices, and cultural expressions of ancient civilizations, they are faced with the challenge of navigating ethical dilemmas, particularly regarding cultural appropriation. This section delves into the ethical aspects of studying ancient religions and the nuanced issue of cultural appropriation, highlighting the need for sensitivity, respect, and critical reflection in academic pursuits.

✧ The Ethics of Academic Inquiry

Respect for Cultural Heritage

When studying ancient religions, scholars must approach their research with a profound respect for the cultural heritage of the communities under examination. These religions were fundamental to the identity, worldview, and social fabric of ancient societies. As such, the study of their religious practices, symbols, and sacred texts demands a nuanced and conscientious approach.

Avoiding Presentism and Anachronism

One ethical concern in the study of ancient religions is the risk of imposing contemporary values, biases, and interpretations onto past beliefs and practices. Scholars must be cautious not to engage in presentism, which involves interpreting the past through the lens of present-day perspectives. Likewise, anachronism, the introduction of modern ideas and concepts into historical contexts, should be meticulously avoided.

✧ Cultural Appropriation: A Controversial Issue

Definition and Complexity

Cultural appropriation is a contentious concept that refers to the borrowing, adoption, or use of elements from one culture by members of another culture, often without appropriate understanding, appreciation, or acknowledgment. In the context of the study of ancient religions, cultural appropriation can arise when contemporary individuals or groups appropriate religious symbols, rituals, or practices without recognizing their historical and cultural significance.

Cultural Exchange vs. Appropriation

One of the challenges in addressing cultural appropriation is discerning between cultural exchange and outright appropriation. Cultural exchange involves mutual sharing, dialogue, and understanding between cultures, fostering cross-cultural learning and appreciation. In contrast, cultural appropriation can perpetuate harmful stereotypes, commodify sacred practices, and undermine the integrity of the culture being appropriated.

✧ Ethical Engagement with Ancient Religions

Contextualization and Interpretation

Scholars must contextualize their research within historical, social, and cultural frameworks to gain a comprehensive understanding of ancient religions. Interpreting religious beliefs and practices demands sensitivity to the unique cultural contexts in which they originated and evolved.

Engaging Descendant Communities

Ethical engagement also involves reaching out to descendant communities and involving them in the research process. This collaboration allows for shared knowledge, mutual respect, and a more inclusive understanding of ancient religious traditions.

✦ Addressing Counterarguments

Academic Freedom and Objectivity

Some argue that strict ethical guidelines may hinder academic freedom and objectivity in the study of ancient religions. They posit that scholars should have the liberty to explore different perspectives and interpretations, even if they might be controversial or challenging.

Unintentional Appropriation

Critics of cultural appropriation discourse contend that some cases of borrowing from ancient religions may be unintentional, with individuals unaware of the cultural implications of their actions.

Conclusion

The study of ancient religions is a crucial academic pursuit that offers valuable insights into human history and cultural diversity. However, ethical considerations must underpin scholarly endeavors to ensure respectful engagement, contextualized interpretation, and sensitivity to the legacy of the past. Cultural appropriation remains a complex issue, calling for critical reflection, dialogue, and a conscious effort to navigate the boundaries between academic exploration and responsible research. As students delve into the study of ancient religions, they must grapple with these ethical complexities to promote a more inclusive, informed, and empathetic understanding of our shared human heritage.

Part 2 - Origins and Evolution

The study of ancient Greek religion unveils a fascinating journey of human spirituality, from its prehistoric origins to the sophisticated pantheon of gods and goddesses that came to define classical Greek culture. Part 2 delves into the roots of Greek religious practices and the gradual evolution that shaped the belief systems of this ancient civilization. This section explores the prehistoric religious practices in Greece, the transition from Mycenaean religion to the Greek pantheon, and the profound influence of Minoan and Mycenaean cultures on Greek religious thought.

Prehistoric Religious Practices in Greece

The origins of Greek religious beliefs lie in the depths of prehistory, in a time shrouded in mystery and the absence of written records. Long before the establishment of city-states and the grand temples, the early inhabitants of Greece engaged in religious practices that reflected their intimate connection with the natural world. This section uncovers the archaeological evidence and remnants of prehistoric rituals, including cult objects, votive offerings, and sacred sites, shedding light on the spiritual consciousness of ancient Greeks before the advent of recorded history.

Mycenaean Religion and Transition to the Greek Pantheon

With the rise of the Mycenaean civilization, the religious landscape of Greece experienced a transformative period. Drawing upon the influences of earlier cultures, the Mycenaeans developed a complex religious system that involved the worship of deities associated with nature, fertility, and celestial bodies. The palatial centers and tholos tombs found in Mycenaean archaeological sites offer invaluable insights into the religious practices and beliefs of this era. This section examines the religious motifs and ritualistic practices of the Mycenaeans, marking the transition from prehistoric religiosity to the emergence of the Greek pantheon.

The Influence of Minoan and Mycenaean Cultures on Greek Religion

The Minoan and Mycenaean cultures, flourishing in the Aegean region, profoundly influenced the development of ancient Greek religion. The maritime prowess and trade connections of the Minoans brought a rich tapestry of religious symbols and practices that left an indelible mark on subsequent Greek religious expressions. The Mycenaeans, in turn, absorbed and integrated aspects of Minoan religion, forging a synthesis that laid the groundwork for the pantheon of gods revered in classical Greek mythology. This section explores the cross-cultural exchanges between these ancient civilizations, illuminating the dynamic interplay that shaped the religious consciousness of the Greek people.

Conclusion

Part 2 embarks on a captivating exploration of the origins and evolution of Greek religious practices. From the enigmatic prehistoric era to the assimilation of diverse cultural influences, the religious landscape of ancient Greece reflects a dynamic process of growth and transformation. By delving into the archaeological evidence and cultural interactions, students will gain a deeper appreciation for the rich tapestry of beliefs and rituals that shaped the spiritual identity of one of the most influential civilizations in history. As we journey through this transformative period, we uncover the intricate threads that weave the fabric of Greek religion, offering profound insights into the human quest for meaning, transcendence, and connection with the divine.

Chapter 5: Prehistoric Religious Practices in Greece

As we delve deeper into the prehistoric periods of Greece, we venture into a realm where archaeology, comparative ethnography, and cautious conjecture converge. This chapter embarks upon an exploration of the religious practices that permeated the fabric of society during the prehistoric eras of Greece, illuminating the dawn of spiritual cognizance that would, in time, evolve into the rich tapestry of classical Greek religion.

Religion, inherently woven into the societal, economic, and cultural aspects of life, provides crucial insights into our understanding of prehistoric communities. However, as we embark on this journey, it is pertinent to remember that our understanding of prehistoric religious practices is necessarily inferential. In the absence of written records, we are left to interpret and speculate based on the mute testimony of archaeological artifacts, the vestiges of ancient rites, and the whispers of tradition embedded within later historical and mythological narratives.

In the realm of prehistoric Greece, we navigate a broad temporal span that includes the Neolithic period, the Bronze Age, inclusive of the Minoan and Mycenaean civilizations, and the so-called Dark Age. Each of these periods, each with its unique religious manifestations, will be meticulously examined, revealing a complex matrix of beliefs, rituals, and deities that waxed, waned, and transformed over millennia.

In the Neolithic era, our understanding is shaped primarily by archaeological findings, which suggest rudimentary forms of animism, ancestor veneration, and fertility cults. Intriguingly, evidence from this period already hints at the recognition of both male and female divine figures, an element that becomes a cornerstone of later Greek religious thought.

Transitioning into the Bronze Age, we encounter the sophisticated religious practices of the Minoan and Mycenaean civilizations. The presence of grand palaces and frescoes in Minoan Crete provides tantalizing glimpses of ritual practices, including the famous 'bull-leaping' ritual. In contrast, the Mycenaean civilization, with its Linear B tablets, provides the earliest written evidence of a pantheon that includes deities who would later become central to classical Greek religion.

As we venture into the Dark Ages, we confront a period where the grandeur of the past receded into societal memory, leaving traces in the form of heroic legends and nascent mythologies. These would later crystallize into the epic tradition, eventually contributing to the formation of classical Greek religious thought.

This chapter invites the reader not merely to absorb historical data but also to engage in the task of interpretation, questioning, and critical reflection. It challenges us to understand how prehistoric communities perceived the divine and the supernatural, how they sought to mediate their relationship with these forces, and how these practices laid the foundation for the robust religious tradition of Classical Greece. We must acknowledge the uncertainties and gaps in our understanding, even as we strive to decipher the religious ethos of a world that predates written history. Yet, it is precisely within these uncertainties that the allure of studying prehistoric religious practices lies, an allure that beckons us to continue exploring, questioning, and learning.

Overview of prehistoric era in Greece

The prehistoric era in Greece is a vast temporal stretch commencing from the Neolithic period and encompassing the Bronze Age, inclusive of the Minoan and Mycenaean civilizations, concluding with the Dark Ages. This expanse of time, spanning several millennia, presents a fascinating tableau of the gradual evolution and sophistication of societies, as evidenced in their technological, artistic, architectural, and, of course, religious advancements.

The Neolithic period, beginning around 7000 BCE, marks the transition from a predominantly hunter-gatherer lifestyle to settled agriculture. This period, characterized by the development of farming, pottery production, and the building of permanent settlements, provides us with our earliest glimpses into the religious practices in Greece. Archaeological findings from this era, such as figurines and burial practices, suggest the existence of animistic beliefs, veneration of ancestors, and a focus on fertility rites.

Transitioning into the Early and Middle Bronze Age (circa 3000-1600 BCE), we encounter the Minoan civilization on Crete. Known for its impressive palace complexes, frescoes, and complex trade networks, the Minoan civilization provides evidence of a highly developed society with intricate religious practices. Snake goddess figurines, bull iconography, and possible communal ritual spaces indicate a religion that encompassed animal symbolism, possibly fertility rites, and potentially even ritualistic performances.

The Mycenaean civilization, emerging around 1600 BCE and persisting until roughly 1100 BCE, represents the zenith of the Bronze Age in mainland Greece. The

Mycenaeans are well known for their martial prowess, architectural grandeur, and administrative sophistication, which is evidenced by the Linear B tablets. These tablets, a form of early Greek script, offer tantalizing insights into the Mycenaean pantheon, which already includes many names familiar from later Greek mythology. The Mycenaean civilization seems to have integrated aspects of Minoan religion while also developing distinct religious practices of its own.

Following the collapse of the Mycenaean civilization, Greece entered a period known as the Dark Ages (circa 1100-800 BCE). This period is characterized by a decline in population, the disappearance of the writing system, and a return to simpler forms of living, all of which are reflected in the archaeological record. Yet, the religious practices of this period are believed to have been instrumental in preserving and transmitting cultural memories of the earlier Mycenaean civilization, ultimately influencing the development of the religious systems of Archaic and Classical Greece.

The prehistoric era in Greece, therefore, presents a rich and diverse spectrum of religious practices and beliefs, marked by continuity, adaptation, and transformation. As we delve into the study of these periods, we must remember that our interpretation and understanding are contingent on the archaeological and epigraphic data available to us. We are peering into a distant past through the fragmented lens of material culture, striving to reconstruct a holistic picture of the spiritual life of these early societies.

Importance of studying prehistoric religious practices

The study of prehistoric religious practices offers a compelling narrative of the human quest for understanding and interacting with the cosmos, and our perpetual endeavor to perceive and personify the forces of nature. Studying prehistoric religious practices is akin to delving into the earliest layers of human thought and philosophy. It unearths the roots of human culture and societal development, elucidating the foundational beliefs and rituals that shaped ancient societies and, in turn, our contemporary world.

Religion, in its myriad forms, fulfills a multitude of roles within a society. It presents a cosmological framework that elucidates the nature of the universe and the human place within it. It imparts moral and ethical codes of conduct, shaping social interactions and promoting cohesion within a community. Religion also provides a mechanism for expressing awe, wonder, and fear in the face of the unknown, thereby offering solace and coping strategies in times of crisis.

Studying prehistoric religious practices is therefore a study of humanity's earliest attempts to confront and explain the fundamental questions of existence, the mysteries of birth and death, the forces of nature, and the ethical quandaries of social life. It uncovers the underpinnings of societal structure and governance, economy, gender roles, and the concept of the self and the other. Moreover, the exploration of religious symbols, rituals, and deities reveal the societal values and concerns of these ancient cultures.

Furthermore, the examination of prehistoric religious practices provides vital context for understanding subsequent religious developments. The continuity and changes in religious practices across different eras elucidate the processes of cultural exchange, synthesis, and innovation. For example, the religious practices of the Mycenaeans can be traced both backward to Minoan influences and forward to the pantheon and rituals of Classical Greece. This underscores the interconnectivity of different epochs and civilizations.

Understanding prehistoric religious practices is also a reminder of the diversity and plurality of human belief systems. It challenges any notion of a linear, monolithic progression of religious thought and underscores the complexity and multiplicity of human spiritual experiences.

Finally, the study of prehistoric religious practices enriches other fields of research such as archaeology, anthropology, sociology, psychology, and history. The multi-disciplinary approach employed in such a study results in a comprehensive, nuanced understanding of ancient societies, enhancing our knowledge and broadening our perspective on our collective past.

As we delve into the exploration of prehistoric religious practices, we must tread with respect and humility, aware of the limitations and biases inherent in our interpretations, yet inspired by the potential for insight and understanding. The study of prehistoric religious practices, therefore, is not just an academic pursuit; it is a journey of discovery and connection, revealing the shared threads of our collective human experience.

Challenges and methods in reconstructing prehistoric beliefs

Reconstructing prehistoric religious beliefs and practices poses significant challenges for the scholar. These stem largely from the nature of the evidence available. Prehistoric cultures, by definition, predate written records. Therefore, the main sources of evidence for prehistoric religious beliefs are material in nature, derived from archaeology. These include structures that may have served a ritual purpose, figurines and other artefacts that may represent deities or spirits, and burial practices that suggest beliefs about the afterlife.

The first challenge, then, lies in the interpretation of this material evidence. Unlike written texts, which can often be straightforward in conveying information (though not without their own complexities), material artefacts are mute. They do not inherently 'speak' of their purpose or meaning. Thus, they require interpretation, which is necessarily subjective and may vary according to the perspectives and biases of different interpreters.

For example, a small figurine of a woman with exaggerated sexual features might be interpreted as a fertility goddess, a charm for individual women, or a child's toy. Without any accompanying text or oral tradition to provide context, it is difficult to definitively establish its meaning. Furthermore, beliefs may have been regional, changing over time, or held only by certain segments of society, further complicating the matter.

Another challenge is the fact that much of the evidence for prehistoric religious practices is likely to have been perishable and thus not preserved. Religious rituals may have involved dances, songs, oracular pronouncements, or the consumption of special foods. These would leave no trace in the archaeological record. Even those artefacts or structures that are preserved are often discovered by chance and represent only a fraction of the culture's material output. Thus, we must approach any attempt at reconstruction with the awareness that we are seeing only a partial picture.

Despite these challenges, scholars have developed several strategies for the reconstruction of prehistoric beliefs. One of these is the comparative method, which involves comparing the beliefs and practices of the culture under study with those of culturally or historically related societies. This method, however, must be employed with caution. It is easy to overstate the similarities between different cultures, and one must be wary of imposing the structures and meanings of one culture onto another.

Another approach is to apply theories from anthropology and sociology, using these as a framework for interpreting the evidence. For example, theories about the role of religion in society, or the psychology of religious belief, can provide valuable insights. Yet again, caution is needed to avoid overgeneralizing or ignoring the unique aspects of the culture under study.

Finally, there is the evidence from later historical periods, including myths, legends, and religious texts. These can sometimes provide clues to earlier beliefs, particularly if there are elements within them that seem archaic or out of place in their later context. But such evidence must be handled with care, recognizing that later societies may have reinterpreted or modified earlier beliefs to fit their own cultural contexts.

In sum, while reconstructing prehistoric religious beliefs is a complex and challenging task, it is not an impossible one. With careful, critical analysis, and by employing a range of interdisciplinary methods, we can gain valuable insights into the spiritual world of our distant ancestors. In doing so, we further our understanding of the diverse ways in which humans have sought to understand and engage with the world around them.

Neolithic Period: The Foundations of Prehistoric Religion

The Neolithic period, extending approximately from 7000 to 3000 BCE in the region of Greece, is an epoch of profound cultural and spiritual transformations. The shift from mobile hunting and gathering to settled agriculture brought with it significant changes in societal organization, material culture, and—pertinent to our study—religious beliefs and practices.

Foremost among these transformations was the development of a sedentary lifestyle, in which communities were built around fixed agricultural sites. This transition likely brought about significant shifts in the spiritual realm. If, as is commonly believed, the religious beliefs of hunter-gatherers were characterized by animism—the attribution of souls or spirits to animals, plants, and natural phenomena—it is plausible that the shift to farming entailed a parallel shift towards agricultural deities or spirits. Deities of fertility, earth, and grain, for instance, might have gained increased importance.

Archaeological evidence from this period reveals the presence of anthropomorphic figurines, frequently female, whose ample hips and breasts suggest associations with fertility. These have often been interpreted as 'goddesses', although they may also represent human priestesses or serve as talismans for individual women. The association of femininity with fertility, and hence with the earth and its produce, is a recurring theme in many agricultural societies, providing some support for this interpretation.

The Neolithic period also witnessed the construction of the first large-scale structures, which have often been interpreted as having a religious or ritual purpose. These include 'megalithic' constructions, such as the stone circles found across Europe. These structures' exact function remains uncertain, but their size and the effort required to build them suggest they were significant communal projects, perhaps serving as places of gathering, ritual, and social cohesion.

The inclusion of grave goods—objects buried with the deceased—indicates beliefs about an afterlife and perhaps a desire to ensure the deceased's welfare in that afterlife. Alternatively, they might represent the status of the deceased or the mourning of the living. The fact that graves are often found within or near human habitations suggests that the ancestors may have been venerated and felt to be an ongoing presence in the lives of the community.

Although our understanding of Neolithic religious beliefs is necessarily fragmentary and speculative, it seems clear that this period laid the foundations for many aspects of later religious thought and practice. The development of agricultural deities, the construction of communal ritual spaces, the association of femininity with fertility and the earth, and the veneration of ancestors are all themes that recur in various forms throughout the history of religion. As such, the Neolithic period represents a crucial stage in the evolution of human religious thought and practice.

Problem for discussion: Reflect on the influence of the shift from a nomadic lifestyle to a settled, agricultural lifestyle on the religious practices of the period. What parallels can you draw with other historical shifts in societal organization and their impacts on religious beliefs and practices?

Exercise: Analyze an artifact from the Neolithic period, such as a Venus figurine or a megalithic structure. Discuss its potential religious significance, referencing archaeological context, form, and potential function.

Neolithic settlements and their religious significance

Neolithic settlements, characterized by their permanence and the accompanying shift to agrarian lifestyles, brought forth not just a change in human habitation but also in religious expression. The permanence of settlements, coupled with the increasingly intricate societal structures, allowed for the emergence of places with specific spiritual connotations, which we may understand as early precursors to temples or sanctuaries.

The locations of settlements themselves likely bore religious significance. Many Neolithic settlements were situated near bodies of water or elevated sites, which were often perceived as liminal or sacred spaces in later religious traditions. Such locations would have been conducive to fishing and navigation, facilitating trade and communication. In addition, these locations were perhaps also selected for their symbolic meanings; the meeting of land and water, for example, is often a place of creation or transformation in mythologies around the world.

The arrangement of dwellings within these settlements also appears to reflect religious beliefs. Some sites reveal clusters of homes around a central space, often interpreted as communal or ceremonial areas. These spaces, devoid of the typical debris of daily life, could have served as gathering spots for religious ceremonies, communal feasting, or the enactment of societal rituals. The positioning of such spaces at the center of settlements underscores the integral role of religion in structuring Neolithic life.

Additionally, the discovery of extensive burial sites within or near the settlements indicates a deep reverence for ancestors, hinting at possible ancestor worship. The inclusion of grave goods further emphasizes beliefs regarding the afterlife and the continued spiritual presence of the deceased within the community.

Furthermore, the presence of figurines and other ritual objects in domestic contexts suggests that religious practice permeated everyday life, rather than being confined to particular times or places. This integration of the sacred and the mundane is a defining characteristic of many prehistoric and traditional religions and underscores the deeply embedded nature of religion in Neolithic societies.

In summary, Neolithic settlements provide a window into the religious beliefs and practices of the time, revealing a world in which the spiritual was intimately intertwined with the practicalities of daily life. The study of these settlements enables us to discern the early foundations of religious thought, as humanity made the critical transition from a nomadic to a settled lifestyle.

Problem for Discussion: Reflect on the impact of settled life on the religious practices of Neolithic societies. How did permanence in settlement influence the creation of sacred spaces?

Exercise: Compare the religious significance of Neolithic settlements with that of settlements in later historical periods (e.g., Classical Greece or Medieval Europe). Consider factors such as the location of the settlement, the arrangement of its buildings, and the presence of dedicated religious structures.

Ritual practices and cult objects

In any study of religious practices, it is important to consider not only the beliefs but also the actions and objects that embody them. Prehistoric Greece, like other ancient societies, utilized a variety of ritual practices and cult objects to express and manifest religious devotion.

Ritual Practices

The ritual practices of prehistoric Greece often mirrored the necessities and events of daily life. The predominance of agricultural societies during this period is reflected in the cyclical nature of many of these practices, which often correlated with seasonal changes and agricultural cycles. The ceremonial sowing of seeds, for instance, might have been performed to invoke divine favor for a bountiful harvest. Similarly, harvest festivals could have served both to thank the divine for a successful crop and to propitiate the gods for the next growing season.

Ritual practices also played a significant role in the marking of life stages. Births, marriages, and deaths were significant events that likely incorporated religious rites. For instance, burial practices and associated grave goods suggest beliefs about the afterlife and ancestor veneration.

Cult Objects

Cult objects serve as material expressions of religious beliefs and are integral to ritual practices. In prehistoric Greece, these objects took on various forms, including statues, figurines, vessels, and other artifacts.

Figurines, often anthropomorphic or zoomorphic, are among the most prevalent types of cult objects. Many of these figurines likely represented deities, while others might have been used in sympathetic magic, a practice in which an object is used to influence a person or event that it resembles.

Ceramic vessels and other utilitarian objects, when found in a ritual context, might have served specific roles in ceremonies, perhaps to hold offerings or to perform ritual ablutions. The presence of such objects in graves could suggest their continued use in the afterlife or their function as offerings to the deceased or chthonic deities.

Finally, certain structures and locations themselves can be considered cult objects. Stone circles, megaliths, and other features of the landscape might have served as sacred sites where rituals were performed. Similarly, the arrangement of dwellings around central spaces within Neolithic settlements suggests the existence of communal areas for religious ceremonies.

In conclusion, ritual practices and cult objects provide crucial insights into the religious life of prehistoric Greece. They serve as tangible manifestations of the community's shared beliefs and offer glimpses into their communal rites and personal devotions.

Problems for Discussion: Consider the role of cult objects in prehistoric religious practice. How might the interpretation of these objects be influenced by their archaeological context?

Exercise: Compare the ritual practices and cult objects of prehistoric Greece with those of another ancient society, such as Ancient Egypt or the Indus Valley civilization. Consider the similarities and differences in their religious expressions and the possible reasons for these.

Ancestor worship and connections to the natural world

Ancestor Worship

Veneration of ancestors has been a widespread phenomenon across diverse cultures and temporalities, and the societies of prehistoric Greece were no exception. The respect and reverence shown towards ancestors was often based on a belief in the ongoing connection between the living and the deceased and the potential influence that the latter could exert on the living world. Ancestor worship, therefore, could be seen as a strategy for managing this potentially beneficial or destructive post-mortem agency.

Burial practices provide some of the most compelling evidence for ancestor worship. The treatment of the deceased body, the construction and location of graves, and the selection and arrangement of grave goods can all shed light on beliefs about death and the afterlife. The recurring practice of including personal belongings and ritual objects in burials suggests that the deceased were expected to maintain an active existence after death.

Burial sites might also have served as places for ongoing ritual engagement with the deceased. Regular visits to graves, the leaving of offerings, and the performance of commemorative feasts are all practices that have been documented in various cultural contexts and could have formed part of the ancestor worship in prehistoric Greece.

Connections to the Natural World

The natural world held immense significance for prehistoric societies, and its influence permeated religious beliefs and practices. The rhythms of the natural world, including the changing of seasons, the movement of celestial bodies, and the cycles of plant and animal life, would have provided a framework for understanding the passage of time and the processes of change and renewal.

Sacred landscapes played a crucial role in connecting prehistoric communities with the natural world. Features such as mountains, rivers, caves, and springs could be imbued with spiritual significance, serving as points of contact with the divine or the supernatural. These natural features might also have been perceived as the abodes of gods, spirits, or ancestors.

The recognition of natural elements within the pantheon of deities further reflects the deep connection between prehistoric religious practices and the natural world. Deities associated with natural forces, such as the earth, the sky, the sun, and the sea, feature prominently in the reconstructed pantheons of prehistoric Greece.

In conclusion, the religious practices of prehistoric Greece reveal a profound interconnectedness between the human, the natural, and the divine. Ancestor worship and the veneration of the natural world both served to articulate and manage the relationships between these realms, contributing to the maintenance of social and cosmic order.

Problems for Discussion: Reflect on the role of the natural world in shaping the religious beliefs and practices of prehistoric Greece. How might changing environmental conditions have influenced these religious practices?

Exercise: Compare the practices of ancestor worship and nature veneration in prehistoric Greece with those of another prehistoric society, such as the Neolithic communities of the British Isles or the Jomon culture of Japan. Identify similarities and differences, and consider possible explanations for these.

Early Bronze Age: Spiritual Beliefs and Symbolism

The advent of the Early Bronze Age in Greece, approximately 3200–2000 BC, ushered in a period of significant cultural and technological development, which in turn likely affected the spiritual beliefs and practices of the time. This epoch, corresponding to the Helladic period in mainland Greece, is notable for the development of urban centers, the emergence of social hierarchies, and technological innovations such as the introduction of metallurgy. These transformations inevitably influenced the way communities interacted with the world and perceived the divine.

Religious Practices and Spiritual Beliefs

In the absence of written texts, our understanding of the religious practices and spiritual beliefs of the Early Bronze Age is largely derived from archaeological evidence, including ritual objects, burial practices, and sacred architecture. It is evident that the religious sphere was not isolated from the broader cultural changes taking place during this period. For instance, the emergence of social hierarchies is mirrored in the complexity of burial practices, with wealthier individuals often receiving more elaborate funerary rites.

Despite these societal changes, continuity with earlier religious traditions is evident. Ancestor worship, the veneration of the natural world, and the use of symbol-laden ritual objects remained integral aspects of spiritual practice. It is also likely that a pantheon of deities existed, reflecting various aspects of the natural and human world. Though their exact nature remains shrouded in time, these deities likely represented elemental forces and aspects of daily life that were vital for survival and societal growth.

Symbolism in Early Bronze Age

Symbols played a vital role in Early Bronze Age religious practices. Archaeological findings reveal the use of a rich visual language incorporating both abstract and representational elements. These symbolic elements would have been imbued with meanings understood within the cultural context, serving as a medium for communication with the divine.

One of the most prevalent symbols in Early Bronze Age art is the spiral. Its exact meaning remains a topic of debate, but possible interpretations suggest associations with cycles of life and death, the movement of celestial bodies, and the idea of journey or transformation.

Furthermore, the frequent use of anthropomorphic and zoomorphic symbols in ritual objects, such as figurines and seals, suggests a belief in the power of these forms to connect with or represent divine entities. These artifacts also provide an insight into the reciprocal relationship between humans and the divine, which was likely mediated through ritual activities and symbolic communication.

The Early Bronze Age thus witnessed a dynamic interaction between continuity and change in the religious sphere. As communities grew and societal structures became more complex, old beliefs were adapted and new ones emerged, forming a spiritual framework that reflected the multifaceted realities of the time.

Problems for Discussion: Discuss how societal changes might have influenced spiritual beliefs and practices during the Early Bronze Age. What impact might the development of metallurgy have had on these beliefs and practices?

Exercise: Compare the symbolism of the Early Bronze Age with that of another contemporary culture, such as the Early Dynastic Period in Egypt. Identify commonalities and differences and suggest possible explanations for these.

Early Bronze Age cultures and religious expressions

As we venture further into the Early Bronze Age, around 3200 to 2000 BC, a thorough examination of distinct regional cultures provides us with nuanced understanding of religious beliefs and practices that unfolded during this significant era. Notably, the Helladic culture of mainland Greece, the Cycladic culture of the Aegean Islands, and the Minoan culture of Crete each had unique expressions of spirituality, influenced by their specific geographical and social contexts.

The Helladic Culture

The Helladic culture, named after Hellas, the Greek name for Greece, is particularly noteworthy for the proliferation of fortified settlements on hilltops. In these settlements, religious expression appears to have been intimately tied to the social and political landscape. One sees a correlation between architectural developments and societal hierarchy, likely indicative of religious stratification as well.

While definitive sacred structures are lacking from this period, archaeologists have uncovered a variety of "cultic" objects, including clay figurines and seal stones. These objects, often found in burial contexts, suggest a continued belief in afterlife rituals and perhaps even an emerging idea of divine intervention or protection in the journey after death.

The Cycladic Culture

Turning to the Cycladic culture of the Aegean Islands, we encounter a unique form of religious expression most famously represented by marble figurines. These stylized human figures, often interpreted as idols, embody a sense of spiritual abstraction quite distinct from the more representational depictions found elsewhere.

The enigmatic nature of these figurines, along with the fact that they are often found in burial contexts, has led to theories that they were intended to ensure the deceased's safe passage into the afterlife or perhaps serve as a form of ancestor worship. The emphasis on the human form in Cycladic artistry might also suggest a theology centered around anthropomorphic deities or spiritual beings.

The Minoan Culture

Finally, the Minoan civilization of Crete during the Early Bronze Age, commonly referred to as the Prepalatial period, set the stage for the island's subsequent emergence as a major cultural and religious center. Early Minoan culture shows evidence of complex rituals, often involving offerings and sacrifices in cave sanctuaries or peak sanctuaries, which were usually located on mountaintops. Such practices indicate a strong connection to the natural world in Minoan spirituality, with these sacred sites perhaps serving as portals to the divine realm.

Conclusion

In sum, the Early Bronze Age of Greece saw the development of unique regional expressions of religion, shaped by local cultures and geographical contexts. These religious beliefs and practices, whether centered around the journey to the afterlife, the veneration of deities, or the sacredness of the natural world, formed a crucial component of societal structures and cultural identities. As such, they offer invaluable insights into the spiritual lives of ancient peoples and their attempts to understand and navigate the complexities of existence.

Problems for Discussion: How do geographical and cultural factors influence religious expression? Why might societies with similar technological capabilities, like those of the Early Bronze Age, develop different religious practices?

Exercise: Choose one artifact from each of the Helladic, Cycladic, and Minoan cultures. Discuss its potential religious significance and the role it may have played in rituals or spiritual beliefs. Consider its symbolic representations, the context in which it was found, and its relation to societal structures and cultural values.

Sacred sites and the cult of the dead

An exploration of sacred sites during the Early Bronze Age in Greece reveals an intricate web of spiritual beliefs and practices, weaving together threads of awe, reverence, mortality, and the quest for the divine. These sacred sites, whether in the form of natural sanctuaries or man-made structures, were often the stage upon which the cult of the dead played out, a testimony to the intricate relationship between life, death, and the sacred in the ancient world.

The Profound Significance of Natural Sanctuaries

Natural sanctuaries, particularly those found in Crete, are key to understanding prehistoric religious practices. Caves and peaks were perceived as liminal spaces where the human and the divine realms converged. Caves, with their subterranean character, may have been linked to chthonic deities or underworld spirits, making them apt settings for rites associated with death and the afterlife. Peak sanctuaries, by contrast, being closer to the sky, might have been sites to venerate celestial deities.

Artefacts found at such sanctuaries include a variety of offerings, such as figurines and vessels, attesting to rituals that likely sought divine protection or favors. The act of making offerings, and the careful selection of objects for this purpose, testifies to the significant role of material culture in mediating the relationship between humans and their deities.

The Emergence of Tholos Tombs and Their Significance

Another type of sacred site that emerged in the Early Bronze Age were tholos tombs. These beehive-shaped structures, predominantly found in the southern and central regions of mainland Greece, indicate the development of more complex funerary practices. Tholos tombs, often used for multiple interments over an extended period, suggest an evolving concept of communal identity that extended into the realm of the dead. The construction of such monumental tombs required significant communal effort and resources, implying a societal reverence towards the dead and possibly the veneration of ancestors.

The presence of ritual objects within tholos tombs further demonstrates the intertwining of religious practices with death. These include offerings, grave goods, and so-called "Psi" and "Phi" figurines, which are named after the Greek letters they resemble. While interpretations of these figurines vary, it is generally agreed that they hold a religious significance, potentially as funerary deities, psychopomps (guides of souls to the afterlife), or symbols of rebirth.

In conclusion, the sacred sites of the Early Bronze Age are monumental testaments to the profound religious significance of death in prehistoric Greek societies. They show how beliefs about the afterlife, veneration of the dead, and rituals for divine communion were spatially enacted, materialized, and integrated into the social fabric. As such, they offer invaluable insights into the worldview of these ancient peoples and their strategies for negotiating the eternal human confrontation with mortality.

Problems for Discussion: How do sacred sites reflect societal attitudes towards death and the divine? How do the artefacts found at these sites contribute to our understanding of prehistoric religious practices?

Exercise: Compare and contrast the roles of natural sanctuaries and tholos tombs in Early Bronze Age religious practices. Consider their spatial and architectural characteristics, the types of artefacts found within them, and the likely rituals associated with these sites. What do these differences and similarities tell us about the diverse ways in which prehistoric societies approached the divine and the afterlife?

Religious symbolism in pottery and artifacts

The archaeological record is rich with pottery and artifacts from the Early Bronze Age in Greece. These materials not only provide a window into the artistic prowess of prehistoric societies but also into their religious and spiritual worldviews. By analyzing the symbolism within these objects, we can glean insights into the gods, goddesses, spirits, and cosmic principles that these ancient peoples revered.

The Importance of Pottery

Pottery, as one of the most durable forms of material culture, forms a substantial part of the archaeological record. Throughout the Early Bronze Age, pottery evolved from utilitarian ware into an expressive medium. As potters became adept at manipulating clay and controlling firing conditions, the shapes, sizes, and surface decorations of pots became more varied and complex. These transformations likely reflected not only aesthetic preferences but also religious and symbolic significances.

One of the characteristic pottery types of the Early Bronze Age in Greece is the sauceboat, found extensively at both settlement and burial sites. Sauceboats, characterized by their elongated shape and single handle, are thought to have been used in libation rituals. By pouring liquids in honor of the gods or the dead, individuals and communities affirmed their relationships with these powerful beings and the cosmic order they represented.

Religious Symbolism in Artifacts

Aside from pottery, other artifacts, such as figurines, seals, and jewelry, also bear religious symbols. Figurines, often crafted in the shape of humans or animals, might have served as votive offerings, talismans, or representations of deities. The 'Phi' and 'Psi' figurines, named after their resemblance to these Greek letters, are particularly intriguing. Their stylized forms suggest a symbolic rather than realistic representation, possibly embodying concepts of fertility, protection, or the afterlife.

Seals and sealings, commonly made of stone, bone, or clay, were also important carriers of religious symbolism. These items were used to mark goods or secure containers, doors, and other objects, which could signify the owner's identity, status, or property rights. However, the motifs engraved on these seals — which often included animals, humans, or mythological creatures — could reflect religious beliefs. For example, the depiction of bull-leaping scenes on seals from Minoan Crete might point to the significance of bulls in their religious rituals or mythologies.

Jewelry, too, served both functional and symbolic roles. The frequent occurrence of amulets, such as the bulla (a hollow pendant) or the double-axe pendant, indicates a widespread belief in the protective or beneficent power of certain symbols or materials.

In conclusion, the pottery and artifacts of the Early Bronze Age in Greece offer compelling evidence of a complex spiritual landscape. These objects speak to an intricate interplay of human, divine, and natural forces, as perceived and negotiated by prehistoric societies through their material culture.

Problems for Discussion: How does the religious symbolism in pottery and artifacts reflect the spiritual concerns and aspirations of prehistoric societies? How might these symbolic expressions have mediated the relationship between individuals, communities, and the divine?

Exercise: Choose an artifact type (e.g., pottery, figurines, seals, or jewelry) from the Early Bronze Age in Greece. Analyze its form, decoration, and archaeological context, and speculate on its possible religious symbolism. Consider how this artifact could have functioned as an object of worship, a protective talisman, a votive offering, or a medium for divine communication.

Middle Bronze Age: The Emergence of Complex Rituals

The Middle Bronze Age (c. 2000-1600 BCE) was a period of significant social, political, and cultural transformation in the Aegean region. This era, defined by burgeoning trade networks, the emergence of complex societies, and the intensification of metallurgical activities, also witnessed the development of intricate religious rituals. These complex rituals were not only instrumental in the negotiation of societal relationships and cosmic orders but also constituted crucial elements in the creation and maintenance of the emerging Bronze Age societies.

Understanding Ritual Complexity

The term 'ritual complexity' refers to the multidimensional nature of rituals, encompassing their organizational structure, symbolic repertoire, and performative aspects. Complex rituals are often distinguished by their elaborate procedures, extensive participation, and profound symbolic meanings. They typically involve multiple stages or phases, each with its specific roles, actions, and symbols, and require significant investments of time, effort, and resources. Such rituals can serve various functions, from cementing social hierarchies to mitigating existential anxieties, and from mediating human-divine interactions to effecting cosmic regeneration.

Evidences of Complex Rituals in the Middle Bronze Age

A primary source of evidence for complex rituals in the Middle Bronze Age is the archaeological remains of ritual sites, particularly those associated with burial and cult practices. These include tholos tombs, such as the ones found in Mycenae and other sites in mainland Greece, as well as peak sanctuaries, cave shrines, and other sacred places in Minoan Crete.

Tholos tombs, with their monumental architecture and rich grave goods, attest to elaborate burial rituals that possibly involved processions, feasts, and offerings. The physical layout of these tombs, featuring a dromos (entrance passage), stomion (doorway), and circular burial chamber, might have symbolized a journey to the underworld, a metaphorical transformation, or a cosmic reenactment. The diversity and value of the grave goods, ranging from pottery and weapons to jewelry and luxury items, indicate differential access to the ritual and possibly reflect the social status of the deceased or the donors.

Peak sanctuaries, cave shrines, and other sacred places in Minoan Crete provide evidence for complex cult practices. These sites often yield a plethora of artifacts, such as clay figurines, stone vases, and animal bones, suggesting offerings, sacrifices, and other ritual actions. The spatial configuration and landscape setting of these sites, usually marked by natural features or constructed altars, shrines, or enclosures, might have been significant in the ritual performances and their symbolic interpretations.

The Emergence of Complex Rituals: Implications and Interpretations

The emergence of complex rituals in the Middle Bronze Age is inseparable from the concurrent societal changes. As societies became more differentiated and hierarchical, rituals could function as arenas for social competition, identity negotiation, or power legitimation. Furthermore, as communities faced new challenges or uncertainties, such as environmental changes, population movements, or intercultural encounters, rituals could provide means for crisis management, risk mitigation, or social integration.

Moreover, complex rituals might reflect evolving cosmologies or theologies. They could embody intricate mythologies, intricate deities, or moral principles, symbolize intricate relationships between humans, gods, and nature, or manipulate intricate forces of life, death, and rebirth. Thus, studying complex rituals can offer profound insights into the spiritual imaginations, ethical sensitivities, and aesthetic sensibilities of the Middle Bronze Age societies.

Problem for Discussion: How can we interpret the emergence of complex rituals in the Middle Bronze Age in relation to the societal, environmental, and cultural dynamics of this period?

Exercise: Choose a ritual site (e.g., a tholos tomb or a peak sanctuary) from the Middle Bronze Age in Greece. Analyze its architectural, artifactual, and spatial aspects, and reconstruct a possible sequence of ritual actions. Consider how this complex ritual might have functioned in its historical and cultural contexts, and what it might have meant to its participants or observers.

Megalithic structures and their religious functions

Megalithic structures, literally meaning "large stone," constitute some of the most enduring and enigmatic vestiges of prehistoric human activity. Originating in the Neolithic and extending into the Bronze Age, these grand architectural edifices punctuate landscapes across the globe, from the iconic stone circles of Stonehenge in England to the elaborate passage graves of Newgrange in Ireland and Carnac's alignment in France. The purpose and significance of these monumental structures have been the subject of intensive scholarly debate, especially concerning their religious or ritualistic functions.

Architectural Forms and Their Associated Rituals

Megalithic architecture, despite its geographic ubiquity, showcases a plethora of structural designs. These range from menhirs (single upright stones), dolmens (stone tables), and cromlechs (stone circles), to more elaborate configurations like passage graves and henges. The varying structural features of these megalithic monuments provide crucial clues to their potential religious and ceremonial purposes.

Passage Graves and Burial Rituals: Passage graves are perhaps the most overtly ceremonial megalithic structures. Comprising a narrow passage leading to a burial chamber, often covered with a large mound of earth or stones, these monuments suggest a robust ritualistic association with the dead. Archaeological findings of human remains and grave goods within such structures reinforce the belief that passage graves were sites of elaborate funerary rites and ancestor veneration, representing a nexus between the living and the dead, and perhaps even serving as portals to an envisioned afterlife.

Stone Circles and Astronomical Alignments: Megalithic stone circles, like Stonehenge or Avebury in England, showcase the intriguing incorporation of astronomical observations into their design. The precise alignment of these structures with solstices, equinoxes, and lunar cycles underscores their role as prehistoric observatories or "timekeepers." These alignments suggest that megalithic structures facilitated rituals tied to celestial bodies, the passage of time, or seasonal changes, potentially supporting agricultural cycles or other natural rhythms, thus embodying an early form of "ecospirituality."

Symbolic Meanings and Social Functions

The colossal size and energy invested in creating megalithic structures denote their societal importance and symbolic potency. From a religious perspective, megalithic monuments can be perceived as sacred landscapes, symbolizing the cosmos, encoding mythologies, or enshrining spiritual powers. Their impressive scale could reflect the community's desire to communicate with divine entities or the spirit world, express reverence towards their ancestors, or establish a sacred space for communal rituals.

Furthermore, the construction and usage of megalithic structures likely required organized communal effort and social stratification, providing opportunities for social cohesion, power display, or status competition. Thus, their religious functions were intertwined with their social and political dimensions.

Dissenting Opinions and Interpretative Challenges

However, these interpretations remain conjectural due to the paucity of direct evidence and the long temporal span of megalithic culture. Some scholars argue for a more mundane interpretation of megalithic structures, attributing their construction to utilitarian purposes like territorial marking or shelter construction. The diversity of megalithic structures across different cultural and geographical contexts also complicates any attempt at a universal interpretation of their religious functions.

Discussion Question: Given the archaeological evidence and various interpretative theories, how can we construct a balanced understanding of the religious functions of megalithic structures?

Exercise: Select a specific megalithic structure or site. Investigate its architectural features, associated artifacts, and cultural contexts. Develop an argument about its potential religious functions, considering both the supporting evidence and the potential challenges or counterarguments.

Religious ceremonies and communal gatherings

The societal life of early human communities was deeply intertwined with their religious and spiritual beliefs. Ceremonies and communal gatherings formed the backbone of this interconnection, serving as arenas for the communal expression of faith, the transmission of cultural values, and the strengthening of social bonds. This section aims to provide an in-depth analysis of the nature and significance of such religious ceremonies and communal gatherings in early societies.

Function and Purpose of Ceremonies and Gatherings

Religious ceremonies in early societies were multifaceted phenomena that served a variety of purposes:

Cosmological Narration: Ceremonies often enacted cosmological narratives, providing a performative illustration of the community's worldview and beliefs. For instance, the ritualistic dances of many indigenous cultures often tell stories about the creation of the world, the actions of deities, or the relationships between humans, animals, and the natural world.

Societal Cohesion: Regular communal gatherings and ceremonies facilitated societal bonding. Shared participation in rituals and festivals provided a sense of communal identity and fostered unity, facilitating the maintenance of social order.

Seasons and Agricultural Cycles: Many early religious ceremonies were tied to the rhythm of the seasons or agricultural cycles. The purpose of such rituals could be to seek divine favor for a successful harvest, celebrate the arrival of a new season, or thank the deities for their bounty.

Transitions and Milestones: Ceremonies often marked significant life events or transitions, such as birth, coming-of-age, marriage, and death. These rites of passage served to acknowledge and sanctify these crucial moments, guiding individuals through the different stages of life.

Religious Artifacts and Sacred Spaces

Religious ceremonies often involved the use of particular artifacts, which were believed to embody spiritual power or serve as conduits to the divine. Such cult objects could range from simple stone idols to elaborate ceremonial regalia. The nature and use of such objects provide vital clues about the religious beliefs and practices of early societies.

Similarly, sacred spaces - be it natural locations such as groves and springs, or built structures like temples and megaliths - played a crucial role in hosting these ceremonies. The choice of these sacred spaces was often imbued with symbolic meaning and could influence the nature and conduct of the ceremony.

Counter Perspectives and Interpretative Challenges

While the existence of religious ceremonies and communal gatherings is well-documented across various early societies, their precise nature, significance, and impact are harder to ascertain. The lack of written records, the cultural and temporal diversity, and the potential for archaeological misinterpretation pose significant challenges. Some scholars warn against overemphasizing the religious aspect of these gatherings, suggesting that they could have equally served secular or social purposes.

Discussion Question: How can archaeological evidence and ethnographic analogies aid us in reconstructing the nature and significance of early religious ceremonies and communal gatherings?

Exercise: Select a specific early society or culture. Based on the available archaeological evidence and cultural context, outline what a typical religious ceremony or communal gathering might have looked like in that society, and discuss its potential significance and functions.

Spiritual beliefs surrounding fertility and agricultural practices

The intricate relationship between fertility, agriculture, and spirituality permeates the fabric of early societies. Not merely an aspect of material survival, agriculture was often imbued with profound spiritual significance, resonating with the life-giving and cyclical nature of the earth. This section will delve into the spiritual beliefs surrounding fertility and agricultural practices across various early societies.

The Fertility of the Earth: Symbolism and Personification

Fertility was a paramount concern for agrarian societies, the yield of the earth being crucial to their survival. Consequently, the earth's fertility was often personified and worshipped as a divine entity. The earth goddesses, such as Gaia of ancient Greece, the Roman Ceres, and Demeter, or the Incan Pachamama, exemplify this ubiquitous pattern. These deities personified the fecundity of the earth and were invoked for bountiful crops.

Agricultural cycles and Fertility Rites

The agricultural cycle, mirroring the cycle of life and death, found resonance in numerous religious rituals. These rites, commonly held at pivotal moments in the agricultural year - planting, harvesting, the onset of winter - sought to ensure the earth's fertility and abundance.

For instance, ancient Greeks held the Thesmophoria, a festival in honor of Demeter, to ensure the fertility of the sown seed. Similarly, the ancient Celts celebrated Beltane, marking the beginning of the summer grazing season with rituals involving fire, believed to promote the land's fertility.

Sacred Plants and Animals

Agriculture also brought about a spiritual focus on particular plants and animals deemed significant due to their nutritional value or roles within the ecosystem. From the sacred maize of Native American tribes to the revered cows of ancient India, these beings were often seen as gifts from the divine, their consumption either regulated by religious laws or accompanied by ritualistic practices.

Challenges and Counterarguments

While the link between fertility, agriculture, and spirituality seems clear-cut, it is essential to note the potential pitfalls in this analysis. Firstly, while the agricultural focus is evident in many spiritual practices, it should not overshadow other aspects of these societies' complex spiritual landscapes. Furthermore, the interpretation of archaeological evidence related to agricultural practices and fertility rites is often fraught with difficulties, necessitating cautious interpretation.

Discussion Questions: What might be the psychological and social effects of spiritualizing agricultural practices in early societies?

Exercise: Consider the spiritual practices surrounding agriculture in a contemporary society. Are there parallels to the ancient practices outlined above? How have these practices evolved, and what factors might account for their endurance or transformation?

Critical Thinking Challenge: Much of the focus in studies of ancient religions is on fertility related to the earth and agriculture. However, what about societies where fertility in other contexts, such as human fertility, might have been more pressing? Explore this alternative focus and its implications.

Late Bronze Age: The Influence of Minoan Culture

One cannot discuss the genesis and evolution of Greek religion without paying significant attention to the Minoan civilization, which left an indelible mark on the religious landscape of the Aegean during the Late Bronze Age. This civilization, named after the legendary King Minos, blossomed on the island of Crete from about 2000 to 1450 BCE.

A distinguishing feature of Minoan religion was the prominence accorded to goddesses, a fact inferred from the preponderance of female figures in Minoan religious iconography. Goddesses were often depicted as commanding nature's forces, suggesting a possible early Greek tradition that worshipped a mother earth deity or a number of earth deities. This reverence for the female divine, reflected in artifacts such as the Snake Goddess figurines and the terracotta figurines from the peak sanctuaries, significantly influenced Greek religious beliefs and practices.

Minoan religious practice was also characterized by the presence of sacred spaces beyond formal temple structures, including peak sanctuaries, cave sanctuaries, and sacred groves. These spaces resonate with a form of nature worship that was incorporated into Greek religion in various ways, including the designation of sacred groves to specific deities, like the olive grove of Athena at the Acropolis in Athens.

Minoan religious rituals incorporated a variety of elements such as dance, music, feasting, and possibly even drug use, as suggested by the depiction of opium poppies on a ceremonial rhyton from Zakros. The physicality and ecstasy of these rituals bear similarities with Greek religious practices such as the Dionysian mysteries, where ecstatic dances and the consumption of wine played a central role.

The Minoan culture also seems to have influenced the concept of sacred animals in Greek religion. The ubiquitous presence of bulls in Minoan iconography, as seen in the renowned fresco of the "Bull-Leaping," likely played a part in the significance attributed to the bull in Greek myths and rituals. These symbols were woven into later Greek culture, as is evident in the story of the Cretan Bull in the Labors of Heracles and the Minotaur myth.

In summary, the Minoan civilization provided a fertile ground from which many facets of Greek religious practices and beliefs emerged. From the reverence for the goddesses to the sacred rituals and the veneration of animals, the Minoan influence played a crucial role in shaping the religious consciousness of ancient Greece. This deep-seated influence underscores the importance of studying the Minoan civilization to fully comprehend the complexity and richness of Greek religion.

Minoan trade and cultural exchanges with mainland Greece

The Bronze Age in the Aegean region heralded a period of intense intercultural interactions and exchange, and the Minoan civilization, with its strategic location and maritime prowess, was a central player in this vibrant network of trade and cultural communication. This section aims to explore the extent and implications of Minoan trade and cultural exchanges with mainland Greece, particularly the Mycenaean civilization.

During the Middle and Late Bronze Age, the Minoans developed a maritime trade network that extended across the Aegean, the Eastern Mediterranean, and beyond. Excavations have revealed Minoan pottery in sites across mainland Greece, evidencing the wide reach of Minoan merchants. Conversely, Mycenaean pottery has been found in Crete, indicating a two-way exchange of goods. In addition to the exchange of material goods, these trading relationships facilitated cultural, technological, and religious exchanges.

Indeed, the influence of Minoan culture on the mainland is profound, particularly during the Middle and Late Minoan periods. The spread of Minoan architectural styles, fresco techniques, pottery styles, and administrative practices to mainland Greece are well attested. For instance, the presence of Minoan architectural elements, such as light wells and columned hallways, in Mycenaean palaces like Pylos and Mycenae, bespeak of Minoan influence. Moreover, Minoan-style frescoes have been discovered in Mycenaean palaces, reflecting a cultural assimilation of Minoan art forms.

The realm of religion, too, was significantly affected by these exchanges. As mentioned earlier, the preponderance of goddess worship and sacred natural spaces in Minoan culture left a lasting imprint on Greek religious traditions. The bull, an animal of great importance in Minoan religious iconography, also permeated Greek myth and ritual, further evidencing the diffusion of religious symbols and practices from Crete to mainland Greece.

On the other hand, it is critical not to perceive this as a one-sided process of cultural diffusion. Recent scholarship has emphasized the reciprocal nature of Minoan-Mycenaean interactions. The Mycenaeans, with their mastery of bronze-working techniques and military prowess, would also have contributed to these cultural exchanges, affecting the course of Minoan civilization.

To conclude, the Minoan trade and cultural exchanges with mainland Greece during the Bronze Age were multifaceted and far-reaching. They entailed not only the exchange of material goods but also the transmission and adaptation of cultural practices, technologies, artistic styles, and religious beliefs. This period of active engagement between Minoan Crete and Mycenaean Greece significantly shaped the cultural and religious landscapes of both regions, leaving a legacy that would reverberate through the ages.

Minoan religious motifs and symbols

The religious sphere of the Minoan civilization, much like the intricate frescoes adorning the palace walls of Knossos, is replete with a rich tapestry of symbols and motifs. This section will delve into the analysis of the key Minoan religious motifs and symbols and their possible interpretations, with the aim of enhancing our understanding of the spiritual worldview of this ancient civilization.

One of the salient characteristics of Minoan religion is the prominence of naturalistic motifs and symbols. The Minoan pantheon appears to be closely interwoven with the natural world, reflecting perhaps an animistic worldview. This is exemplified by the recurrent images of flora and fauna in Minoan religious iconography. Sacred trees, birds, and animals, such as bulls, are recurring elements in Minoan art, likely symbolizing divine entities or attributes.

The bull holds a particularly significant place in Minoan religious symbolism. The spectacular ritual of 'bull-leaping,' depicted in several frescoes and seals, seems to underscore the spiritual importance of the bull. While interpretations vary, this practice could be a ritualistic demonstration of human mastery over nature or a form of bull worship.

Another pervasive symbol in Minoan religion is the double axe or 'labrys.' The labrys, often associated with the goddess, was possibly a symbol of divine power or a tool used in religious rituals. The presence of the labrys in 'lustral basins' and 'pillar crypts,' both presumed to be sacred spaces, corroborates its religious significance.

Additionally, the Minoan religion is marked by the prevalence of female deities or priestesses, often represented with open arms, serpents, or sacral knots. The 'Snake Goddess' figurines unearthed at Knossos, portraying women holding snakes with a feline atop their heads, are compelling evidence of the importance of female figures in Minoan worship. These figures might represent a mother goddess or priestesses embodying the goddess.

Minoan religion also manifests in the form of sacred landscapes and architectural symbols. Peak sanctuaries, cave shrines, and palatial complexes with complex labyrinths are integral to Minoan religious life, suggesting a veneration of nature and sacred spaces. These places were likely seen as liminal spaces where the mortal and divine realms intersected.

In conclusion, the exploration of Minoan religious motifs and symbols reveals a complex spiritual landscape that revered the natural world, embodied by a myriad of deities and rituals. These symbols not only offer a glimpse into the spiritual life of the Minoans but also elucidate the cultural exchanges with and influences on the subsequent Mycenaean and Greek religious practices. Nevertheless, the interpretation of these symbols remains a matter of scholarly debate, underscoring the nuanced and multifaceted nature of Minoan religion.

Integration of Minoan religious practices into mainland Greece

The Minoan civilization, with its vibrant culture and sophisticated maritime network, played a pivotal role in the evolution of religious practices in mainland Greece. This chapter will analyze the integration of Minoan religious practices into the culture of the Mycenaean civilization and their enduring impact on the subsequent evolution of Greek religion.

To begin with, it is essential to highlight the complex interaction between Minoan Crete and Mycenaean Greece. The archeological record demonstrates clear evidence of Minoan influence on Mycenaean material culture, particularly during the Late Bronze Age. This influence is also discernible in the religious realm, with Minoan religious symbols and rituals finding resonance in the Mycenaean context.

One of the most potent symbols of this cultural exchange is the presence of Minoan religious motifs in the Mycenaean palace complex at Pylos. The frescoes discovered at Pylos depict scenes that bear strong resemblance to the 'bull-leaping' ritual, a practice intimately associated with Minoan religious life. This suggests the possibility that the Mycenaeans adopted or adapted Minoan religious rituals, integrating them into their own spiritual practices.

Another notable instance of Minoan influence on Mycenaean religious practices is the depiction of female figures in religious iconography. The prevalence of female deities or priestesses in Minoan religion, exemplified by the iconic 'Snake Goddess' figurines, finds a parallel in Mycenaean frescoes and figurines. This suggests a possible integration of the Minoan reverence for the feminine divine into Mycenaean religious culture.

Furthermore, the integration of Minoan religious practices can also be discerned in the context of sacred architecture. Mycenaean tholos tombs and the 'megaron' (great hall) in the palace complexes display architectural elements that echo Minoan religious structures. The presence of 'lustral basins' and 'pillar crypts,' akin to those found in Minoan palaces, suggest the adoption and adaptation of Minoan architectural symbolism in Mycenaean sacred spaces.

The influence of Minoan religious practices also extends to the realm of Mycenaean burial customs. The rich grave goods, diverse burial practices, and complex mortuary architecture in Mycenaean society show parallels with Minoan funerary traditions, indicating a potential integration of Minoan beliefs regarding death and the afterlife.

In conclusion, the integration of Minoan religious practices into mainland Greece presents a compelling narrative of cultural interaction and exchange during the Late Bronze Age. The Minoan religious symbols, rituals, and sacred spaces not only enriched the spiritual landscape of Mycenaean society but also contributed to the shaping of the religious traditions in classical Greece. However, the interpretation of these cultural exchanges remains open to scholarly discussion, reflecting the complex and multifaceted nature of ancient religious practices.

Conclusion

Our exploration of the religious practices of the Minoan and Mycenaean civilizations in the Late Bronze Age has revealed a rich tapestry of beliefs and rituals that formed the bedrock of later Hellenic spirituality. The Minoans, with their advanced maritime culture, celebrated the feminine divine, indulged in intricate rituals such as bull-leaping, and adorned their sacred spaces with vibrant frescoes that encapsulated their spiritual worldview. On the other hand, the Mycenaeans, with their militaristic ethos and sophisticated palace complexes, demonstrated an amalgamation of indigenous practices and borrowed elements from Minoan culture. The religious practices of these societies, while distinct, were nonetheless intertwined, forming a complex web of cultural and religious exchange that would shape the spiritual landscape of ancient Greece.

Reflection on the Significance of Prehistoric Beliefs for Understanding Ancient Greek Culture and Spirituality

The significance of understanding these prehistoric beliefs cannot be overstated, particularly for students of ancient Greek culture and spirituality. These early religious practices provide crucial insights into the cosmological perspectives of ancient Greek societies. They reflect the multifaceted nature of the human-divine relationship in these cultures, emphasizing the centrality of religion in social organization, politics, economics, and art. Furthermore, the syncretic nature of these religious practices—evident in the integration of Minoan motifs and rituals into Mycenaean culture—underscores the dynamic nature of religious beliefs and their propensity for adaptation and evolution in response to cultural exchanges.

Implications of Prehistoric Religion for the Development of the Greek Pantheon in Later Periods

The prehistoric religious practices of the Minoans and Mycenaeans also have significant implications for the development of the Greek pantheon in later periods. The reverence for female deities in Minoan religion, for instance, finds echoes in the exalted status of goddesses like Athena, Artemis, and Demeter in the later Greek pantheon. Similarly, the importance of funerary rituals and afterlife beliefs in Mycenaean culture can be seen in the complex rituals of hero-cults and the eschatological narratives in Hellenic mythology.

Moreover, the prehistoric religious practices also provide a foundation for understanding the incorporation of magic and divination in later Greek religious life. The ritual use of natural elements in Minoan religion, for instance, can be linked to the later Greek practices of herbalism and ecospirituality. Similarly, the Mycenaean emphasis on prophecy and oracles hints at the significant role divination would play in classical Greek religion.

In conclusion, the study of prehistoric religious practices in Greece not only illuminates the spiritual landscape of the Minoan and Mycenaean civilizations but also provides a foundational understanding of the complexities of ancient Greek culture and spirituality. It allows us to appreciate the long temporal arc of religious evolution, revealing how ancient beliefs and practices informed, shaped, and were transformed by the historical, cultural, and spiritual currents that flowed through the Hellenic world.

Chapter 6: Mycenaean Religion and Transition to the Greek Pantheon

Chapter 6 of this textbook explores the intriguing period of Mycenaean religion and the significant transition that marked the emergence of the Greek pantheon. The Mycenaean civilization, flourishing from approximately 1600 BCE to 1100 BCE, occupies a crucial place in the historical trajectory of ancient Greece. The religious practices and beliefs of the Mycenaean people offer valuable insights into the early religious landscape of the region, serving as a foundation for the development of Greek mythology and pantheon.

✧   **Understanding the Mycenaean Civilization:**

The Mycenaean civilization, known for its fortified palaces, warrior elite, and rich artistic legacy, represents one of the first advanced civilizations in mainland Greece. Archaeological discoveries, including the decipherment of the Linear B script, have shed light on various aspects of Mycenaean culture, including their religious practices.

✧   **Mycenaean Religious Practices and Rituals:**

Archaeological evidence points to the centrality of religious practices in Mycenaean society. The presence of religious artifacts, dedicatory offerings, and religious structures indicates that rituals played a vital role in their daily lives, governance, and interactions with the divine.

✧   **Unraveling Mycenaean Beliefs:**

The religious beliefs of the Mycenaeans were deeply intertwined with the natural world, where divine forces and supernatural entities played significant roles in shaping human experiences. The study of religious iconography and symbolism helps in understanding their perception of the divine.

✧   **The Mycenaean Pantheon:**

The pantheon of gods and goddesses worshipped by the Mycenaeans formed the backbone of their religious system. The deities were associated with various aspects of life, such as fertility, warfare, and craftsmanship. Examining the roles and relationships between these deities offers insights into Mycenaean religious narratives.

✧ **The Transition to the Greek Pantheon:**

As the Mycenaean civilization declined, it left an indelible mark on the development of Greek religious thought. The transition from Mycenaean religion to the Greek pantheon involved the assimilation of Mycenaean deities into the emerging Greek religious framework.

✧ **Legacy of Mycenaean Religion:**

The influence of Mycenaean religion can be traced through later Greek literature, particularly in the context of heroic narratives and mythological traditions. This chapter will explore the connections between Mycenaean myths and their integration into the broader tapestry of Greek mythology.

✧ **Challenges in Reconstructing Mycenaean Religion:**

Studying Mycenaean religion comes with inherent challenges due to the fragmentary nature of the available evidence. Scholars must navigate these limitations and engage in interpretative debates to arrive at a comprehensive understanding of Mycenaean religious practices.

✧ **Significance and Relevance:**

Understanding Mycenaean religion is crucial for comprehending the evolution of ancient Greek culture and the foundation of their religious identity. The religious practices and beliefs of the Mycenaeans provide valuable insights into the historical and cultural context that laid the groundwork for the subsequent development of Greek civilization.

In conclusion, delving into the world of Mycenaean religion opens a window into the early spiritual landscape of ancient Greece. This chapter aims to illuminate the religious practices, beliefs, and mythological narratives of the Mycenaean civilization while exploring their enduring impact on the formation of Greek religious traditions and cultural identity.

Overview of the Mycenaean civilization

The Mycenaean civilization, flourishing from approximately 1600 BCE to 1100 BCE, occupies a significant place in the history of ancient Greece. Named after the fortified city of Mycenae, this Bronze Age civilization left a lasting impact on the development of Greek culture, religion, and society. This overview aims to provide a comprehensive understanding of the key aspects of the Mycenaean civilization, including its political organization, economy, art, architecture, and religious practices.

✧ **Historical Context and Archaeological Discoveries:**

The emergence of the Mycenaean civilization during the late Bronze Age in mainland Greece marked a crucial phase in the region's history. It succeeded the influential Minoan civilization of Crete, which had a significant impact on the development of early Greek culture. Understanding the historical context and the archaeological discoveries related to the Mycenaean civilization provides valuable insights into the complex social, political, and cultural dynamics of this ancient society.

◆ The Late Bronze Age in Mainland Greece:

The late Bronze Age in mainland Greece, often referred to as the Mycenaean period, was a time of significant historical developments and cultural achievements. Spanning approximately from 1600 BCE to 1100 BCE, this era witnessed the emergence and flourishing of the Mycenaean civilization, which left a lasting impact on the region's history and culture.

➤ Sociopolitical Changes:

During the Late Bronze Age, the political landscape of mainland Greece underwent notable changes. The society transitioned from small-scale chiefdoms to more complex hierarchical structures, with powerful leaders ruling over fortified citadels. These leaders, often referred to as "wanax" (lords) or "basileus" (kings), controlled territories that included surrounding towns and villages.

➤ Economic Growth and Trade:

The Mycenaean civilization experienced economic growth and prosperity, facilitated by increased trade and commerce. The mainland Greeks engaged in maritime activities and established trade routes that connected them to other Mediterranean cultures, including the Minoans of Crete, the Egyptians, and civilizations in the Near East. This trade network enabled the exchange of goods, ideas, and cultural influences.

> ➤ Cultural Exchange with the Minoans:

The Minoans, based on the island of Crete, played a vital role in shaping the early Greek world during the Late Bronze Age. They were renowned for their seafaring expertise and commercial ventures, which allowed them to establish far-reaching trade networks. The interaction between the Minoans and the Mycenaeans led to a significant exchange of cultural and artistic elements.

> ➤ Transmission of Cultural Influences:

The cultural exchange between the Minoans and the Mycenaeans is evident in various aspects of Mycenaean culture. For instance, Mycenaean pottery often displayed Minoan-inspired motifs and artistic styles. Minoan religious practices and iconography also influenced the religious beliefs of the Mycenaeans. Additionally, architectural features, such as the construction of monumental palaces and the use of frescoes, showed traces of Minoan influence.

> ➤ Adaptation and Syncretism:

While the Mycenaeans absorbed certain aspects of Minoan culture, they also adapted and transformed these influences to suit their own needs and beliefs. This process of syncretism resulted in a distinct Mycenaean cultural identity, characterized by its unique blend of influences from various neighboring civilizations.

> ➤ Decline and Collapse:

The Late Bronze Age in mainland Greece eventually came to an end, marked by a period of decline and upheaval. Around 1200 BCE, the Mycenaean civilization faced numerous challenges, including the breakdown of trade networks, internal conflicts, and external invasions. The exact reasons for the collapse of the Mycenaean centers are a subject of scholarly debate, and several factors likely contributed to their downfall.

In conclusion, the Late Bronze Age in mainland Greece was a transformative period characterized by the rise of the Mycenaean civilization and its interactions with the Minoan culture of Crete. The exchange of ideas, trade, and cultural influences between these two civilizations shaped the early Greek world and laid the foundations for the rich and diverse cultural heritage of ancient Greece. Despite the eventual decline and collapse of the Mycenaean centers, their impact on subsequent Greek civilization endured, leaving behind a lasting legacy that continues to be studied and admired by scholars and enthusiasts alike.

◆ Minoan-Mycenaean Interaction:

The Minoan civilization, flourishing on the island of Crete during the Late Bronze Age, exerted a profound influence on the development of the early Greek world. The Minoans were a seafaring people known for their advanced maritime skills and extensive trade networks, which facilitated contact with neighboring regions, including mainland Greece. This cross-cultural interaction between the Minoans and the mainland Greeks played a pivotal role in shaping various aspects of Mycenaean culture, art, and religious practices.

➢ Maritime Trade and Commerce:

The Minoans' mastery of navigation and their sophisticated ships enabled them to establish extensive trade routes throughout the Mediterranean Sea. They engaged in the exchange of commodities such as textiles, metals, ceramics, and luxury goods with other prominent civilizations of the time, including Egypt and the Near East. Their maritime prowess allowed them to venture beyond Crete's shores and establish trade contacts with the inhabitants of the Greek mainland.

➢ Influence on Mycenaean Architecture:

One of the most significant outcomes of Minoan-Mycenaean interaction was the architectural influence of the Minoans on the Mycenaeans. Mycenaean palaces, such as the renowned citadels of Mycenae, Tiryns, and Pylos, bore striking similarities to Minoan palatial complexes in terms of layout and construction techniques. The Mycenaeans adapted and incorporated Minoan architectural elements, such as the construction of monumental entranceways, central courtyards, and the use of columns, into their own building practices.

➢ Pottery and Artistic Influences:

Minoan pottery and artistic styles made a lasting impression on Mycenaean culture. Mycenaean pottery often featured Minoan-inspired motifs, such as marine life, floral patterns, and intricate designs. This is evident in the development of a distinctive Mycenaean pottery style known as "Kamares ware," characterized by its vibrant colors and intricate decorations, inspired by Minoan ceramics.

➢ Religious Syncretism:

The interaction with the Minoans also had a significant impact on Mycenaean religious practices. The Minoan pantheon of deities and religious iconography influenced the Mycenaean religious beliefs. For example, certain Minoan goddesses, such as the "Mistress of the Animals," seem to have been incorporated into the Mycenaean religious framework. This syncretism resulted in the emergence of new religious traditions that reflected a blend of Minoan and Mycenaean elements.

➤ Technological and Cultural Exchange:

Apart from art and religion, the Minoans' technological knowledge and cultural practices also influenced the Mycenaeans. The Mycenaeans adopted various aspects of Minoan culture, including writing systems, administrative practices, and burial customs. The adaptation of Linear A, the script of the Minoans, into Linear B, a script used by the Mycenaeans for administrative and accounting purposes, attests to this cultural exchange.

In conclusion, the interaction between the Minoans and the mainland Greeks during the Late Bronze Age was a dynamic and multifaceted process that profoundly impacted the development of Mycenaean civilization. The Minoans' expertise in trade, seafaring, art, and architecture left a lasting impression on the Mycenaeans, leading to the assimilation and adaptation of various cultural elements. This rich cross-cultural exchange played a critical role in shaping the early Greek world and laid the foundation for the subsequent cultural achievements of ancient Greece.

◆ Mycenae: Center of Mycenaean Power:

The city of Mycenae, situated in the northeastern Peloponnese of ancient Greece, stands as a testament to the magnificence and significance of the Mycenaean civilization. With its fortified citadel and impressive cyclopean walls, Mycenae emerged as the dominant center of Mycenaean power during the Late Bronze Age. This city-state played a pivotal role in shaping the political, cultural, and economic landscape of the Mycenaean world.

➤ Strategic Location and Fortifications:

Mycenae's strategic location atop a hill allowed it to overlook the surrounding plains, providing a vantage point for defense and surveillance. The city's fortified citadel, enclosed by massive cyclopean walls constructed from enormous limestone blocks, showcased the engineering prowess of the Mycenaeans. These walls, renowned for their immense size and precise construction, not only protected the city from external threats but also symbolized the power and authority of the ruling elite within.

➢ Political and Administrative Center:

Mycenae served as the political and administrative heart of the Mycenaean civilization. The city-state was governed by a centralized authority, likely comprising a monarch or a ruling elite who exercised authority over an extensive territory. Mycenaean palaces, such as the one found within the citadel, were the administrative hubs of the civilization. These palaces served as centers of governance, where economic transactions, record-keeping, and distribution of resources took place.

➢ Economic Prosperity and Trade:

Mycenae's control over a vast territory facilitated economic prosperity and trade. The city-state's extensive territorial influence allowed for the exploitation and distribution of valuable resources, such as metals, agricultural products, and luxury goods. Mycenaean traders engaged in maritime commerce with other Mediterranean cultures, establishing connections with civilizations like the Minoans of Crete and the Egyptians. The wealth derived from trade further solidified Mycenae's position as a prominent power in the region.

➢ Artistic and Cultural Influence:

The city of Mycenae was not only a political and economic powerhouse but also a center of artistic and cultural expression. The Mycenaeans excelled in various art forms, including pottery, metalwork, and sculpture. Intricately decorated ceramics and finely crafted metal objects discovered in Mycenaean tombs attest to the artistic sophistication of the civilization. The presence of tholos tombs, such as the famous "Treasury of Atreus," showcases the Mycenaeans' architectural achievements and their reverence for their ancestors.

➢ Military Might and Hegemony:

Mycenae's imposing citadel, along with its military strength, allowed the city-state to assert hegemony over neighboring regions. The Mycenaeans were formidable warriors, as depicted in their epic poetry, such as the Homeric epics, where Mycenae plays a central role. The city's military might was instrumental in maintaining control over its territory and exerting influence over other Mycenaean palatial centers.

➢ Decline and Legacy:

Despite its prominence, the Mycenaean civilization faced challenges and eventually declined. The exact reasons for its downfall are complex and still subject to scholarly debate. Some theories suggest that internal strife, climate change, or invasions by external forces might have contributed to its collapse. Nevertheless, the legacy of Mycenae endured in later Greek history and mythology. The myths and legends surrounding Mycenae and its legendary rulers, such as Agamemnon and the House of Atreus, continued to inspire Greek literature and cultural identity throughout the ages.

In conclusion, the city of Mycenae stands as a remarkable testament to the power, influence, and cultural achievements of the Mycenaean civilization. Its fortified citadel, political centrality, economic prosperity, artistic expression, and military prowess solidified Mycenae's position as the dominant center of Mycenaean power. While the civilization eventually experienced a decline, its legacy persisted, leaving an indelible mark on the history and culture of ancient Greece.

◆ Archaeological Excavations:

The study of the Mycenaean civilization would be incomplete without acknowledging the pivotal role of archaeological excavations. The diligent work of archaeologists, such as Heinrich Schliemann at Mycenae and Arthur Evans in Crete for the Minoans, has been instrumental in shedding light on the enigmatic and fascinating world of the Mycenaeans. Through their pioneering efforts, these early archaeologists paved the way for a deeper understanding of the Mycenaean culture, revealing the complexities of their society, art, and religious practices.

➢ Heinrich Schliemann and Mycenae:

Heinrich Schliemann, a German archaeologist, made significant contributions to the study of ancient Greece and the Mycenaean civilization. His excavations at the hill of Mycenae in the late 19th century were groundbreaking, as he sought to uncover the mythical city of Agamemnon and his legendary wealth. Schliemann's methods were controversial, characterized by the use of dynamite to clear large areas quickly. Nonetheless, his efforts unearthed the imposing Lion Gate, the royal tombs, and numerous precious artifacts, including the famous "Mask of Agamemnon." Although some aspects of his work were criticized for their lack of precision, Schliemann's discoveries laid the foundation for the study of Mycenaean archaeology.

➢ Arthur Evans and the Minoans:

Arthur Evans, a British archaeologist, focused on the study of the Minoan civilization on the island of Crete. His excavation of the ancient site of Knossos revealed a complex and sophisticated civilization that predated the Mycenaeans. Evans coined the term "Minoan" after the mythical King Minos of Crete. His meticulous recording and preservation of artifacts and wall paintings at Knossos were pioneering steps in archaeological methodology. Evans' work not only brought to light the Minoan civilization but also provided crucial context for understanding the interactions and influences between the Minoans and Mycenaeans.

> ➢ Contributions to Mycenaean Studies:

The archaeological excavations conducted by Schliemann and Evans, among others, have provided valuable insights into the material culture and social structures of the Mycenaean civilization. The uncovering of palaces, tombs, pottery, frescoes, and other artifacts has enabled scholars to reconstruct the daily life, religious practices, and economic activities of the Mycenaeans. These discoveries have also shed light on the network of trade and cultural exchange between the Mycenaeans and other ancient Mediterranean societies.

Archaeological Excavations Exercise:

Imagine you are an archaeologist participating in a new excavation at a Mycenaean site. What are the key research questions you hope to answer, and what specific excavation techniques would you employ to gather the necessary evidence?

Compare and contrast the methods and approaches used by Heinrich Schliemann and Arthur Evans in their respective excavations. Assess the strengths and limitations of their methodologies and their impact on the field of archaeology.

Examine the significance of the "Mask of Agamemnon" discovered by Heinrich Schliemann at Mycenae. Discuss its possible function and symbolism in Mycenaean society and funerary practices.

In conclusion, archaeological excavations at Mycenaean sites, spearheaded by pioneering archaeologists like Heinrich Schliemann and Arthur Evans, have been paramount in illuminating the ancient Mycenaean world. Their discoveries have enriched our understanding of this sophisticated civilization, offering glimpses into their art, religious beliefs, and social structures. The meticulous documentation of artifacts and structures has provided valuable data for scholars to reconstruct the past, further deepening our appreciation of the rich cultural heritage of the Mycenaean civilization.

◆ Unearthing Fascinating Artifacts:

The archaeological excavations at Mycenae, Tiryns, Pylos, and other significant Mycenaean sites have yielded a rich assemblage of artifacts, spanning a wide array of objects that provide valuable glimpses into the craftsmanship, trade networks, and social structure of the Mycenaean civilization. These artifacts offer a tangible connection to the past, allowing us to better understand the material culture and the daily lives of the Mycenaean people.

➢ Pottery and its Cultural Significance:

Mycenaean pottery is among the most notable and ubiquitous artifacts uncovered during excavations. The Mycenaeans produced a variety of pottery styles, including the iconic "stirrup jars" and "kraters" used for storage and libations. The intricate designs and motifs found on these vessels provide evidence of the Mycenaean artistic sensibility and aesthetic preferences. Archaeologists have noted the influence of Minoan and other eastern Mediterranean cultures on Mycenaean pottery, revealing the interconnectedness of ancient civilizations through trade and cultural exchanges.

Exercise: Analyze the decoration on a Mycenaean stirrup jar and speculate on its possible symbolic significance in Mycenaean religious practices or daily rituals.

➢ Jewelry and Personal Adornments:

The Mycenaeans were skilled metalworkers, crafting exquisite gold and silver jewelry adorned with intricate patterns and motifs. These artifacts not only exemplify the technical prowess of Mycenaean artisans but also offer insights into the social hierarchy and the display of wealth and status. Some of the most stunning finds include gold diadems, earrings, and ornate necklaces, often discovered in royal tombs. The presence of such lavish grave goods in burials underscores the belief in an afterlife and the importance of elaborate rituals associated with death and burial practices.

Exercise: Examine the design and symbolism of a Mycenaean gold diadem. Discuss its potential use in religious ceremonies or as a status symbol for elite members of society.

➢ Tools and Weapons:

Mycenaean excavations have unearthed a plethora of tools and weapons, crafted from bronze, iron, and other materials. These artifacts provide evidence of the Mycenaeans' agricultural practices, craftsmanship, and military prowess. Bronze tools such as sickles and plowshares indicate their agricultural reliance, while weapons like swords, spears, and armor highlight the importance of warfare and defense in Mycenaean society. The presence of both utilitarian and martial artifacts attests to the multifaceted nature of their civilization..

➢ Elaborate Grave Goods:

One of the most captivating aspects of Mycenaean archaeology is the discovery of elaborate grave goods in royal tombs. These tombs, often known as "shaft graves," contained a wealth of artifacts buried with the deceased, including pottery, weapons, jewelry, and chariots. The presence of such valuable offerings suggests the belief in an afterlife and the notion of an aristocratic ruling class. The opulence of these burials also indicates the existence of social hierarchies, with a clear distinction between the elite and common people.

In conclusion, the excavations at Mycenae, Tiryns, Pylos, and other Mycenaean sites have uncovered an array of fascinating artifacts that offer valuable insights into the craftsmanship, trade networks, and social structures of this ancient civilization. The pottery, jewelry, tools, weapons, and grave goods provide a tangible link to the past, enriching our understanding of the material culture and complexities of Mycenaean society. These artifacts continue to be a testament to the ingenuity and cultural legacy of the Mycenaean people, prompting further research and scholarly exploration into the ancient world.

◆ Architectural Marvels:

The Mycenaean civilization, flourishing during the Late Bronze Age, left behind a legacy of remarkable architectural achievements that stand as a testament to the sophistication and ingenuity of its builders. The palaces and structures they constructed showcased not only their engineering prowess but also their artistic sensibilities. Among the most notable architectural marvels of the Mycenaean world are the fortified citadels and monumental entrances, with the iconic Lion Gate at Mycenae serving as a striking example.

➢ Mycenaean Palaces:

At the heart of Mycenaean centers, including Mycenae, Tiryns, and Pylos, were grand palaces. These palaces served as the administrative and political hubs of the civilization. They were centers of governance and likely the residences of the ruling elite. The architecture of Mycenaean palaces was characterized by grandiosity and functional design. The palaces were constructed using massive limestone blocks known as cyclopean masonry, named after the mythical Cyclops. These massive stones, some weighing several tons, were skillfully fitted together without the use of mortar, creating walls of immense strength and durability.

➢ Monumental Entrances:

Mycenaean palaces were typically accessed through monumental entrances that were designed to impress and intimidate. The entrances were fortified with gateways and massive doorways, often adorned with decorative elements. The most famous example is the Lion Gate at Mycenae, which remains an iconic symbol of the Mycenaean civilization. The Lion Gate features a massive lintel stone with a sculpted relief of two lionesses flanking a column. This symbolic representation of lions served as a powerful expression of the Mycenaean rulers' authority and strength.

➢ Megaron Halls:

One of the defining architectural features of Mycenaean palaces was the megaron hall. The megaron was a large, rectangular hall with a central hearth and a throne located at the far end, serving as the seat of the ruling authority. This architectural design can be seen in the Throne Room at Pylos and the Megaron at Mycenae. The megaron halls were not only functional spaces for administrative and ceremonial purposes but also impressive structures showcasing the architectural prowess of the Mycenaean builders.

➢ Cultural and Religious Significance:

The architecture of Mycenaean palaces and structures carried significant cultural and religious connotations. The elaborate entrances, imposing walls, and megaron halls reflected the hierarchical social structure and centralized power of the civilization. Moreover, the decoration of these structures with symbolic elements, such as the lion relief at the Lion Gate, hinted at the religious and mythological beliefs of the Mycenaean people.

Architectural Marvels Exercise:

Compare and contrast the architectural features of Mycenaean palaces with those of other contemporary civilizations, such as the Minoans and Egyptians.

Analyze the possible symbolic meanings behind the use of lions in the Lion Gate relief and discuss their significance in Mycenaean religion and ideology.

Imagine you are an architect in the Mycenaean civilization tasked with designing a new palace. Describe the key features and elements you would incorporate to reflect the power and authority of the ruling elite.

In conclusion, the architecture of the Mycenaean civilization, with its monumental entrances, megaron halls, and elaborate palaces, stands as a testament to the advanced engineering skills and artistic sensibilities of the Mycenaean builders. The Lion Gate at Mycenae, with its iconic lion relief, remains a powerful symbol of the civilization's strength and authority. The study of these architectural marvels offers valuable insights into the culture, society, and religious beliefs of the ancient Mycenaean world.

◆ Linear B Script and Administrative Records:

One of the most significant archaeological discoveries related to the Mycenaean civilization is the decipherment of the Linear B script. This early form of Greek writing was used for administrative purposes, and the clay tablets inscribed with Linear B have revealed details about economic transactions, land holdings, and the distribution of resources within Mycenaean society.

◆ Influence of Minoan Culture:

The archaeological evidence has highlighted the influence of Minoan culture on Mycenaean religious practices, art motifs, and architectural styles. The adoption of certain Minoan deities and artistic conventions in Mycenaean contexts reflects the interconnectedness of these two civilizations.

In conclusion, the historical context and archaeological discoveries related to the Mycenaean civilization provide a window into the dynamic and complex world of ancient Greece during the late Bronze Age. The interactions between the Mycenaeans and the Minoans, as well as the architectural achievements and material culture uncovered through excavations, showcase the richness and significance of the Mycenaean civilization in the context of ancient Mediterranean history. Through ongoing archaeological research, our understanding of the Mycenaean world continues to evolve, revealing new facets of this fascinating ancient society.

✧ Political Structure and Governance:

The Mycenaean civilization was characterized by a hierarchical political structure centered around powerful warrior elites. The existence of fortified palaces, such as those found in Mycenae and Pylos, suggests a centralized authority governing over extensive territories.

✧   **Economy and Trade:**

Mycenaean society was primarily agrarian, with agriculture forming the backbone of its economy. The Mycenaeans engaged in extensive trade networks, exchanging goods such as olive oil, pottery, metals, and textiles with neighboring cultures and beyond.

✧   Mycenaean Art and Architecture:

The Mycenaeans were skilled artisans, and their artistic expressions are evident in the intricate pottery, frescoes, and decorative elements found in palaces and tombs. The iconic "Mycenaean Lion Gate" at Mycenae stands as a remarkable example of their monumental architecture.

✧   Writing System: Linear B Script:

The decipherment of the Linear B script has been crucial in understanding the Mycenaean language and administrative records. This writing system was used for official and economic purposes, providing valuable insights into the administrative structure of Mycenaean society.

✧   Religious Practices and Beliefs:

Religion played a significant role in Mycenaean life, with a pantheon of deities closely associated with various aspects of human existence. Religious practices included offerings, rituals, and ceremonies conducted in sacred spaces like temples and sanctuaries.

✧   Social Organization and Daily Life:

The Mycenaean society was structured into distinct social classes, with the elite ruling class occupying positions of power and influence. Examining the everyday life of Mycenaean people, including their domestic habits, burial customs, and leisure activities, offers a glimpse into their social dynamics.

✧   Decline and Legacy:

The Mycenaean civilization experienced a gradual decline, likely influenced by a combination of factors such as political instability, external pressures, and internal conflicts. The decline of the Mycenaean centers marked the transition towards the Greek Dark Ages, setting the stage for the subsequent development of Greek culture and civilization.

In conclusion, the Mycenaean civilization stands as a critical phase in the ancient history of Greece, serving as a bridge between the Minoan civilization and the emergence of classical Greek culture. The study of the Mycenaean civilization provides valuable insights into the early foundations of Greek society, religion, and art, contributing to our understanding of the rich and diverse tapestry of ancient Greek civilization.

Importance of studying Mycenaean religious practices

The study of Mycenaean religious practices holds immense significance as it provides a unique window into the belief systems, rituals, and spiritual ideologies of an ancient civilization that laid the groundwork for the development of Greek religion and culture. Delving into Mycenaean religious practices not only deepens our understanding of the complexities of this early society but also sheds light on the origins and evolution of religious thought in the Mediterranean region.

✧   Understanding the Foundations of Greek Religion:

The Mycenaean civilization predates the classical period of ancient Greece, and its religious practices laid the foundation for the development of later Greek religious beliefs and rituals. By exploring the religious landscape of Mycenaean society, scholars can trace the origins of deities, religious symbols, and ceremonial practices that would later be integrated into the pantheon and religious customs of classical Greece. This historical context is crucial for comprehending the continuity and evolution of religious thought throughout Greek history.

Exercise: Compare the deities and religious practices of the Mycenaeans to those of classical Greece, identifying similarities and differences that highlight the evolution of Greek religion.

✧   Unveiling Mycenaean Rituals and Ceremonies:

The study of Mycenaean religious practices allows scholars to gain insight into the various rituals and ceremonies performed by the ancient Greeks. Through analysis of artifacts and inscriptions, we can discern the nature of religious offerings, sacrifices, and festivals. By understanding these rituals, researchers can explore how the Mycenaeans sought to interact with the divine, express gratitude, and seek divine intervention in their daily lives.

Exercise: Examine the iconography of Mycenaean religious artifacts and speculate on the potential significance of specific rituals depicted, considering their roles in addressing human concerns and expressing devotion to the gods.

✧   Tracing Cultural Interactions and Syncretism:

The Mycenaean civilization flourished in a region marked by cultural interactions and exchanges. Studying their religious practices enables us to discern the influence of neighboring civilizations, such as the Minoans and other eastern Mediterranean cultures, on Mycenaean religion. Such interactions fostered syncretism, the blending of religious beliefs and practices, which had a profound impact on the development of Greek spirituality.

Exercise: Investigate the influences of Minoan religious motifs and iconography on Mycenaean religious artifacts, discussing the implications of cultural syncretism in the evolution of Mycenaean religion.

✧   Social and Political Implications:

Religion played a pivotal role in shaping social and political structures in ancient societies, and the Mycenaeans were no exception. By examining their religious practices, scholars can gain insights into the social hierarchy, the role of religious specialists, and the significance of religious institutions in governance and decision-making processes. The study of Mycenaean religious practices contributes to a broader understanding of the complex interplay between religion and political authority in the ancient world.

Exercise: Analyze the inscriptions on Mycenaean religious objects, discussing the potential involvement of religious authorities and their relationship with political elites.

In conclusion, the study of Mycenaean religious practices offers a wealth of information about the origins of Greek religion, the nature of ancient rituals, the impact of cultural interactions, and the social and political implications of religious beliefs. By exploring these aspects of Mycenaean spirituality, scholars can enrich our understanding of ancient civilizations and their profound influence on the development of human history and culture. It provides a fascinating avenue for critical thinking and academic discussion, encouraging students to explore the complexities of ancient belief systems and their enduring legacy.

The role of Mycenaean religion in shaping the Greek pantheon

The Mycenaean civilization, flourishing during the Late Bronze Age in mainland Greece, significantly influenced the development of the Greek pantheon, which would later become a cornerstone of ancient Greek religion. The religious beliefs and deities of the Mycenaeans not only formed an integral part of their own spiritual practices but also laid the groundwork for the evolution of religious thought and divine representations in subsequent Greek cultures.

✧   The Mycenaean Pantheon and Deities:

The Mycenaeans had a rich pantheon of deities, although the names of many of these gods and goddesses remain obscure due to the linear B script's limitations in deciphering their full identities. The Mycenaean deities were anthropomorphic and governed various aspects of life, reflecting the ancient Greeks' inclination to ascribe divine attributes to natural phenomena and human experiences. Some of the prominent Mycenaean deities included a mother goddess, associated with fertility and nature, and a storm god, symbolizing the forces of nature.

✧   The Transition from Mycenaean to Classical Greek Pantheon:

As the Mycenaean civilization declined, its religious practices and deities underwent significant transformations, eventually merging with the beliefs and pantheon of the incoming Indo-European tribes, including the Dorians. This transition is known as the "Mycenaean-into-Classical" phase, where the religious elements of the Mycenaeans blended with those of the Dorians, leading to the formation of a cohesive Greek pantheon that played a central role in the lives of classical Greeks.

✧   Mycenaean Influence on Divine Representations:

The Mycenaean artistic expressions, especially in their elaborate grave goods and pottery, offer glimpses into the iconography of their deities. Although much of the artistic evidence is fragmentary, certain motifs and symbols found in Mycenaean artifacts show striking resemblances to later representations of gods and goddesses in Greek art. For instance, the Mycenaean figure known as the "Mistress of Animals" bears similarities to Artemis, the Greek goddess associated with the wilderness and wildlife.

✧   Continuity and Evolution of Religious Concepts:

The study of Mycenaean religion illuminates the enduring themes and concepts that persisted in Greek religious thought. Concepts such as divine intervention, ritual offerings, and the veneration of powerful deities are evident in both Mycenaean and later Greek religious practices. By examining the Mycenaean roots of these beliefs, students can explore the continuity and evolution of religious concepts across different historical periods.

In conclusion, Mycenaean religion played a vital role in shaping the Greek pantheon and religious traditions. By examining the religious beliefs and deities of the Mycenaeans, scholars can gain valuable insights into the origins and development of Greek religious thought and the enduring impact of the Mycenaean civilization on subsequent Greek culture. This exploration encourages critical thinking and nuanced discussions about the complexities of ancient belief systems and their role in shaping human history and spirituality.

Mycenaean Civilization: Historical and Archaeological Context

The Mycenaean civilization, which emerged during the Late Bronze Age in mainland Greece, represents a remarkable period of cultural and historical development. This section will delve into the historical and archaeological context of the Mycenaean civilization, examining its rise to prominence, its interactions with neighboring cultures, and the key archaeological discoveries that have provided valuable insights into this ancient society.

The Late Bronze Age in Mainland Greece:

The Late Bronze Age in mainland Greece, spanning from approximately 1600 BCE to 1100 BCE, was characterized by significant societal and cultural changes. During this period, the Mycenaean civilization rose to prominence, succeeding the Minoan civilization of Crete. The Late Bronze Age saw increased interaction and cultural exchange among various Mediterranean civilizations, shaping the trajectory of the Mycenaean society.

Minoan-Mycenaean Interaction:

The interaction between the Mycenaeans and the Minoans, centered on the island of Crete, played a crucial role in shaping the early Greek world. The Minoans, renowned for their advanced maritime trade and artistic achievements, had a profound influence on the Mycenaeans. This exchange is evident in the architectural styles, pottery, and religious practices adopted by the Mycenaeans, which bear striking resemblances to those of the Minoans.

Mycenae: Center of Mycenaean Power:

The city of Mycenae, located in the northeastern Peloponnese, became the dominant center of the Mycenaean civilization. Its fortified citadel, surrounded by massive cyclopean walls, served as the political and cultural heart of the civilization. The ruling elite of Mycenae controlled extensive territories and engaged in trade with other Mediterranean cultures, establishing Mycenae as a formidable power in the region.

Unearthing Fascinating Artifacts:

Archaeological excavations at Mycenaean sites, such as Mycenae, Tiryns, and Pylos, have yielded a wealth of artifacts that provide invaluable insights into Mycenaean craftsmanship, trade networks, and social hierarchies. Pottery, jewelry, tools, weapons, and elaborate grave goods all shed light on the daily life, religious practices, and cultural expressions of the Mycenaean people.

Importance of Studying Mycenaean Religious Practices:

The study of Mycenaean religious practices is of paramount importance in comprehending the roots of Greek mythology and religious traditions. The Mycenaeans' pantheon and religious beliefs laid the foundation for the evolution of the Greek pantheon and religious practices in subsequent Greek cultures.

In conclusion, the historical and archaeological context of the Mycenaean civilization offers students a glimpse into a vibrant ancient society that significantly shaped the course of Greek history and culture. By exploring the interactions between the Mycenaeans and neighboring civilizations, as well as the archaeological discoveries from Mycenaean sites, students can gain a deeper understanding of this fascinating period in ancient Greek history and its lasting impact on subsequent societies.

The rise of the Mycenaean civilization

In the annals of ancient history, few civilizations possess the captivating allure of the Mycenaeans. As successors to the Minoans and progenitors to the Classical

Greeks, the Mycenaean civilization marked an epoch of expansion, consolidation, and cultural synthesis in the Eastern Mediterranean from around 1600 to 1100 BCE.

The Emergence of Mycenaean Power

The Mycenaean civilization emerged during the Late Helladic period on the Greek mainland, when power shifted from the Minoan civilization on Crete. Historians believe that Mycenae, the namesake of this civilization, was not its original center. However, it was from this palace-state that the Mycenaeans projected their dominance across the Aegean.

Early Mycenaean society reflected a stratified hierarchy, with a wanax (king) at the helm. Evidence of this structure can be found in the Linear B script, a writing system adapted from the Minoan Linear A, which was primarily used for record-keeping. While Linear B did not contain extensive historical narratives like the later Greek alphabet, its tablets provided valuable insights into Mycenaean economy, religious practice, and social order.

Mycenaean Cultural Expression and Religion

The Mycenaean culture was richly diverse, incorporating elements of both the indigenous Helladic and the Minoan civilizations. Mycenaean art, architecture, and religion bear testament to this amalgamation. An examination of the grandiose palace complexes, such as those at Pylos, Tiryns, and Mycenae, reveals a blend of Minoan architectural elements with distinct local styles. Tholos or beehive tombs, monumental circular burial sites enclosed by stone, underscore this combination and stand as enduring symbols of Mycenaean funerary traditions.

Religion played a significant role in Mycenaean society, as attested by numerous references to deities and religious rituals in Linear B tablets. Many of the deities, including Zeus, Hera, and Poseidon, would later become mainstays in the pantheon of Classical Greek mythology, albeit in more developed forms.

Mycenaean Commerce and Interaction

Trade was a vital aspect of Mycenaean society. The distribution of Mycenaean pottery across the Mediterranean region and Near East attests to extensive maritime trade networks. Furthermore, precious objects made from gold, ivory, and imported stones found in Mycenaean tombs highlight their ability to acquire exotic goods from afar.

Moreover, the Mycenaeans had diplomatic and possibly even military interactions with other contemporary civilizations, as suggested by references to "Ahhiyawa" in Hittite texts - a term thought to refer to the Mycenaeans. However, the nature and extent of these relations remain debated among historians.

The Decline of Mycenaean Civilization

The Mycenaean civilization came to an abrupt end around 1100 BCE, ushering in the so-called "Greek Dark Ages." This collapse is often attributed to multiple factors, including natural disasters, internal strife, and invasions by the mysterious "Sea Peoples." Yet, the exact causes are still the subject of ongoing scholarly debate.

Regardless of the reasons for its decline, the influence of the Mycenaean civilization on subsequent Greek culture is unquestionable. Their legacy is imbued in the epic poems of Homer, in the religious pantheon of the Classical Greeks, and in the archaeological remnants that continue to fascinate scholars and laypersons alike.

Exercises:

Translate a passage from Linear B script to understand the intricacies of Mycenaean administrative records.

Evaluate the artistic and architectural elements in a Mycenaean palace complex or tomb.

Research and present a case study on the Mycenaean trade networks based on archaeological evidence such as pottery distribution or exotic material artifacts.

Key archaeological sites and artifacts related to Mycenaean religion

Delving into the religious practices of the Mycenaeans presents an intriguing tableau of how these ancient peoples interacted with the divine. We derive most of our understanding from the archaeological sites and artifacts they left behind, which provide valuable clues to their spiritual practices.

Sacred Sites and Sanctuaries

One of the crucial aspects of Mycenaean religion was the presence of sanctuaries, often located in natural settings like caves, mountaintops, and springs, which were believed to possess numinous qualities. Some were near palace centers, while others were in remote regions, indicating a complex web of local and regional cult practices.

The sanctuary at Phylakopi on the island of Melos offers a compelling illustration. Here, archaeologists discovered a series of rooms containing ritual pottery and figurines, dating from the Late Helladic period. The use of terracotta figurines in religious practice became widespread during this period, often depicting deities, worshippers, or animals.

Another significant sanctuary is the one at Ayia Irini on the island of Kea. It was a peak sanctuary, a sacred site located on the top of a mountain, which held sway over the entire island and beyond. It was in continuous use from the Middle Helladic to the Late Helladic periods, with abundant archaeological findings that include ceramic animal figurines, typically offered to deities.

Sacred Objects and Iconography

Archaeologists have unearthed a variety of objects, including pottery, figurines, frescoes, and seals, that offer invaluable insights into the religious practices and iconography of the Mycenaeans. The famous "Gold Rings of Mycenae," for instance, bear depictions of divine epiphanies, ritual practices, and mythological scenes, shedding light on the complex religious beliefs and rites of this civilization.

Among the most iconic artifacts are the terracotta figurines, notably the "phi" and "psi" types, named for their resemblance to the Greek letters. These figurines, usually female and associated with fertility, are believed to represent goddesses or their worshippers and were likely used in religious rituals.

Frescoes also provide visual narratives of Mycenaean religious practices. The "Cult Scene Fresco" from Pylos, for instance, depicts a procession of female figures carrying offerings to a deity, illustrating the important role of women in Mycenaean religious activities.

Linear B Tablets and Deities

The Linear B tablets, predominantly from Pylos and Knossos, offer the most explicit evidence of Mycenaean religion. These tablets record offerings to various deities, including recognizable names such as Zeus, Hera, and Poseidon, demonstrating continuity with later Classical Greek religion.

Also listed are a number of deities who do not appear in later Greek religion. For instance, the "Mistress of the Labyrinth," potentially linked with the Minoan "palace goddess," provides a fascinating insight into the syncretism between Minoan and Mycenaean religious practices.

Discussion:

Evaluate the role of natural settings in Mycenaean religious practice. How do sanctuaries like Phylakopi and Ayia Irini reflect the Mycenaeans' spiritual connection with nature?

Analyze the significance of various religious artifacts (e.g., "Gold Rings of Mycenae," "phi" and "psi" figurines) in understanding Mycenaean religion.

Discuss the depiction of women in Mycenaean religious practices based on the evidence from frescoes and figurines.

Assess the continuity and divergence between Mycenaean and Classical Greek religion using the Linear B tablets as a primary source.

Exercises:

Choose an artifact related to Mycenaean religion and prepare a presentation analyzing its symbolism, usage, and significance.

Examine the religious iconography in the "Cult Scene Fresco" from Pylos. Discuss its implications for understanding the role of women and the nature of ritual practices in Mycenaean society.

Translate and interpret a Linear B tablet recording religious offerings. Identify the deities mentioned and discuss their potential roles and attributes in Mycenaean religion.

Mycenaean religious centers and their significance

The Mycenaean civilization, like many ancient societies, was deeply imbued with religious fervor. This chapter explores the key religious centers of the Mycenaean world and their significant roles in the sociocultural fabric of the society.

Palatial Religious Centers

The Mycenaean palaces were not only administrative and economic hubs but also significant religious centers. Within these palatial complexes, distinct spaces were reserved for religious activities, as evidenced by architectural features, ritual paraphernalia, and iconographic representations.

The Palace of Pylos offers one of the most vivid examples of a palatial religious center. Within this complex, the Throne Room, adorned with frescoes depicting religious rituals, played a key role in religious ceremonies. The presence of a central hearth, a typical feature of Mycenaean megarons (great halls), may also point to its ritual significance.

The Palace of Knossos, originally a Minoan center that was later co-opted by the Mycenaeans, exhibits a similar intertwining of religious and secular spaces. The West Wing, with its numerous lustral basins and shrines, served as the primary locus of religious activity.

Rural and Natural Sanctuaries

Mycenaean religion was not confined to palatial settings; it also flourished in rural and natural sanctuaries. These sanctuaries were typically located in caves, atop mountains, or near springs — places believed to be imbued with divine presence.

The Hagia Triada cave in the Peloponnese provides a prominent example of a cave sanctuary. Inside the cave, archaeologists discovered a large number of terracotta figurines, suggesting that this was a popular place of pilgrimage and offering. Similarly, the peak sanctuary on Mount Juktas, overlooking the Palace of Knossos, shows evidence of extensive ritual activity, including animal sacrifice and the deposition of votive offerings.

Cultic Activities

Each religious center had its own set of cultic activities, often involving offerings, sacrifices, and feasting. For instance, the Linear B tablets from Pylos record various offerings made to deities, from livestock and agricultural produce to textiles and perfumed oil.

Feasting was another crucial aspect of Mycenaean religious practices. Archaeological evidence from palatial centers and rural sanctuaries alike reveals the remains of large-scale feasts, involving the consumption of vast quantities of meat and the drinking of wine, likely in communal celebrations dedicated to the gods.

Discussion:

Evaluate the significance of palatial religious centers in the context of Mycenaean sociopolitical structure. How did these centers contribute to the consolidation of power and authority?

Analyze the role of natural and rural sanctuaries in Mycenaean religion. How did these sites complement the religious functions of palatial centers?

Discuss the types of cultic activities prevalent in Mycenaean religious centers. How do these activities reflect the society's relationship with the divine?

Examine the evidence for religious feasting in Mycenaean centers. What are the implications of such feasts for our understanding of Mycenaean communal practices and social relations?

Exercises:

Compare the architectural and spatial organization of the religious centers at the Palace of Pylos and the Palace of Knossos. How do they reflect different aspects of Mycenaean religious practice?

Conduct a detailed study of a natural sanctuary, such as the Hagia Triada cave or the Mount Juktas peak sanctuary. Discuss the types of offerings found there and their potential significance in Mycenaean religion.

Analyze a Linear B tablet from Pylos that lists offerings to deities. Discuss the types of offerings and their potential meanings in the context of Mycenaean religious practice.

Mycenaean Deities and Religious Beliefs

The Mycenaean civilization, enveloped in the mysteries of its writing system and the passage of time, left a considerable legacy concerning its religious beliefs. Most insights into these beliefs stem from Linear B tablets, archaeological findings, and the analysis of sacred spaces. These sources combined paint a fascinating picture of the Mycenaean pantheon and their religious principles.

The Mycenaean Pantheon

The Mycenaean pantheon is largely recognizable to those familiar with later Greek religion. Several of the deities recorded in Linear B tablets correspond to gods and goddesses worshiped in the classical period. The tablets reveal that the Mycenaeans worshipped a broad range of deities, reflecting a complex and vibrant religious culture.

Poseidon, for example, is the most frequently mentioned deity in the Pylos tablets. Given his association with the sea, it is plausible to assume that he held a prominent role in a civilization so tightly linked to maritime activities. Other well-known deities include Zeus, Hera, and Dionysus. Their presence suggests that many beliefs of Mycenaean religion were incorporated into the subsequent classical Greek religious system.

However, a large number of deities that do not appear in later Greek religion are also mentioned, suggesting a rich local tradition. Some of these lesser-known deities might be associated with the natural world, healing, fertility, death, or other facets of life and the cosmos.

Deities such as Potnia (often translated as "Mistress"), a common epithet found on tablets, point to the reverence of female deities. Potnia might be seen as a precursor to goddesses like Athena or Artemis in later Greek religion, suggesting a continuity in the veneration of powerful female divinities.

Religious Beliefs and Practices

Mycenaean religious beliefs revolved around the appeasement and veneration of deities through ritualistic practices. Animal sacrifice, for instance, appears to have been a central part of religious ceremonies, serving as a form of communication with the gods. The remains of animals found at various religious centers substantiate this claim.

Offerings, as evidenced by the Linear B tablets, ranged from agricultural produce to crafted goods such as textiles, precious metals, and perfumed oil. Such offerings indicate that Mycenaean religion was an integral part of everyday life, connecting the mundane and the divine.

Another intriguing facet of Mycenaean religious practice is the prominence of females in the cultic activities. This can be inferred from the depiction of women in frescoes and the numerous figurines of women found at religious sites. The "phi" and "psi" figurines, typically associated with fertility, further hint at the possibility of a cult dedicated to a mother goddess.

Discussion:

Compare the Mycenaean pantheon with the later classical Greek pantheon. What continuities and changes can you identify?

Evaluate the role of offerings and sacrifices in Mycenaean religious practices. What do these practices reveal about the Mycenaeans' perception of the relationship between humans and gods?

Discuss the role of women in Mycenaean religious activities based on the archaeological evidence.

Exercises:

Analyze the religious significance of a deity mentioned in the Linear B tablets. How does this deity reflect Mycenaean society and culture?

Investigate the evidence for a particular type of religious practice in Mycenaean civilization, such as animal sacrifice or the making of offerings. Discuss its significance in the broader context of Mycenaean religious beliefs.

Based on the iconography of the "phi" and "psi" figurines, speculate on the possible characteristics and roles of a hypothetical Mycenaean mother goddess.

Mycenaean pantheon: Gods and goddesses

The Mycenaean civilization, with its rich tapestry of religious beliefs and practices, honored an extensive pantheon of gods and goddesses. These deities, each associated with specific domains or aspects of life, were venerated through various rituals and offerings. Some of these gods and goddesses would later find their places in the Greek pantheon, while others would vanish into the recesses of history.

Poseidon

The deity most frequently mentioned in the Linear B tablets found in Pylos is Poseidon, who later Greek tradition recognizes as the god of the sea and earthquakes. The Mycenaeans likely venerated Poseidon due to their maritime activities and his potential to either help or hinder their endeavors.

Poseidon, identified as "Po-se-da-o" in the Linear B script, holds an intriguing position in the Mycenaean pantheon. His ubiquity across the tablets found in Pylos, a significant Mycenaean center, indicates that he held an esteemed and influential place in their religious landscape.

From the standpoint of the Mycenaeans, a civilization deeply connected to the sea through commerce, maritime warfare, and exploration, Poseidon's position as the god of the sea would have been of critical import. The sea was a double-edged sword, bringing both prosperity through trade and potential danger from storms or rival civilizations. Thus, the veneration of Poseidon can be seen as a manifestation of their respect for, reliance on, and fear of the sea's unpredictable nature.

Poseidon's association with earthquakes, an element that appears in later Greek tradition, may also have originated from the Mycenaean period. Greece is a region prone to seismic activity, and the power to instigate or prevent such natural disasters would have made Poseidon a god of immense significance.

Archaeological evidence supports the high status of Poseidon in Mycenaean society. For instance, in Pylos, one encounters wall paintings depicting sea creatures, which may be associated with the cult of Poseidon.

Zeus

Zeus, one of the most prominent figures in later Greek mythology as the king of the gods, is also present in the Mycenaean pantheon. His presence in the Linear B tablets and the prominence of his cultic sites suggest that he was a significant figure in Mycenaean religious practices, perhaps occupying a similar position of supreme authority.

The presence of Zeus, or "Di-we" as inscribed on Linear B tablets, in the Mycenaean pantheon suggests an early inception of the deity who would later be considered the king of the gods in classical Greek mythology.

While it is unclear whether Zeus held a similar position of ultimate authority during the Mycenaean period, his presence in the religious records suggests a level of significance in the pantheon. His connection to the sky, as the later Greeks would understand him, may indicate that the Mycenaeans perceived him as a controller of weather and, by extension, agricultural success or failure, vital elements in any ancient civilization.

The Mycenaean cultic sites associated with Zeus point to his importance within their religious practices. For instance, archaeological evidence from Mount Lykaion, which later tradition identifies as the birthplace of Zeus, reveals a long history of ritual activity dating back to the Mycenaean period.

The depiction of Zeus in Mycenaean gem and seal iconography also attests to the significance of his cult. For example, a signet ring from Pylos shows a deity carrying a scepter, which scholars have speculated could represent Zeus. This indicates that his veneration was not limited to large-scale public rituals but was also a part of personal devotional practices.

In conclusion, both Poseidon and Zeus held significant positions in the Mycenaean pantheon, embodying the societal and environmental realities faced by the Mycenaeans. Their prominence in the Mycenaean period set the stage for their enduring roles in Greek religion and mythology.

Hera

Hera, later known as the wife of Zeus and the goddess of marriage, is another familiar name that appears in the Linear B texts. Her presence underscores the importance of familial and marital relationships within Mycenaean society.

In the Linear B tablets, Hera, known as "E-ra", emerges as a significant figure within the Mycenaean pantheon. Her presence attests to the fundamental role of marital and familial structures in Mycenaean society.

As in later Greek tradition, Hera's association with marriage in Mycenaean times suggests that she might have been perceived as a protector of marital bonds and familial harmony. These aspects were vital in the Mycenaean context, considering the pivotal role of family and kinship ties in maintaining social cohesion, ensuring property succession, and forming strategic alliances.

In addition to her connection to marriage, Hera might also have been venerated as a goddess associated with childbirth and child-rearing, another crucial aspect of maintaining and expanding familial and societal structures. Some scholars suggest that the worship of Hera might have involved rituals or offerings intended to secure her favor for a successful pregnancy and the healthy growth of children.

The exact nature of Hera's cult during the Mycenaean period is yet to be fully elucidated, and further research may throw light on this fascinating aspect of Mycenaean religion.

Dionysus

Interestingly, Dionysus, the god of wine, pleasure, and festivity in later Greek mythology, also features in the Mycenaean pantheon. His cult might be connected with ritual feasting and celebration, which appear to have been central aspects of Mycenaean religious and social life.

The presence of Dionysus, referred to as "Di-wo-nu-so" in the Linear B tablets, in the Mycenaean pantheon is indeed a fascinating aspect of their religious landscape. While later Greek tradition associated him primarily with wine, pleasure, and ecstatic frenzy, the precise role of Dionysus within the Mycenaean religious system remains a subject of scholarly debate.

The association of Dionysus with wine and ritual feasting could signify that his cult was linked to the practice of communal celebrations and the consumption of wine, which played a key role in Mycenaean society as a component of hospitality, status display, and religious rituals.

Dionysus might also have had connections to agrarian fertility and the vine's cultivation, considering the importance of viticulture in the Mycenaean economy. Some scholars have suggested that the worship of Dionysus could include rituals meant to ensure the vine's growth and the production of good quality wine.

Furthermore, the later Greek concept of Dionysus as a liminal deity, bridging the human and divine realms through ecstasy and mystic rites, might have early roots in the Mycenaean period, indicating intriguing possibilities regarding the nature of their religious experiences.

As with Hera, our understanding of Dionysus's role within Mycenaean religion is still evolving, offering fertile ground for further academic exploration.

Ares

Ares, who in later periods would be recognized as the god of war, appears in the Linear B tablets, underscoring the martial character of the Mycenaean civilization.

Ares, known as "A-re" in Linear B tablets, provides evidence of the significance of warfare and martial prowess in Mycenaean society. The Mycenaeans, as is well-documented, were a warrior culture, with military strength and heroism being paramount virtues.

The presence of Ares in the Mycenaean pantheon signifies the deep-rooted and institutionalized nature of warfare within their civilization. Ares was likely venerated as a divine protector of warriors, invoked for success in battle and, perhaps, to instill fear in their enemies. He may also have been associated with the martial virtues of courage, discipline, and strategic acumen.

Archaeological findings, including the presence of warrior grave goods in Mycenaean burial sites, align with the veneration of Ares, further illustrating the martial character of Mycenaean civilization.

Potnia

The term 'Potnia', often translated as 'Mistress' or 'Lady', appears frequently in the Linear B texts, usually followed by an epithet that designates a specific location or function. This title may represent a range of female deities venerated as divine mistresses of certain realms or activities. For example, Potnia Iqeja ("Mistress of Horses") and Potnia Wanon ("Mistress of Animals") reflect the importance of animals in Mycenaean society and its religion.

The term "Potnia," which translates as "Mistress" or "Lady," is a ubiquitous presence in the Linear B texts. However, this term does not refer to a single deity but appears to denote a category or type of goddesses, each associated with a specific realm or function as suggested by an appended epithet.

Potnia Iqeja ("Mistress of Horses") and Potnia Wanon ("Mistress of Animals") are two such examples that underline the pivotal role of animals within Mycenaean society and religion. These titles likely represented goddesses who oversaw the welfare, productivity, and protection of domestic and wild animals, respectively.

Other variations include Potnia Dabijo ("Mistress of the Land") and Potnia Periiwiyo ("Mistress of the House"). These titles potentially represented goddesses presiding over the fertility of the land and the domestic sphere, respectively, both of which were essential aspects of Mycenaean life.

The concept of "Potnia" offers an insightful glimpse into the nature of Mycenaean divine feminine, which encompassed a broad range of roles and functions. The veneration of these goddesses speaks volumes about the cultural, economic, and social priorities of the Mycenaean civilization.

The Mycenaean pantheon also includes a host of lesser-known deities who do not feature in later Greek religion, suggesting a religious system that was far more complex and multi-faceted than the one we encounter in classical Greek civilization.

Discussion:

Analyze the role of major deities such as Poseidon, Zeus, and Hera within the Mycenaean religious system. How might their prominence reflect the sociocultural values and concerns of Mycenaean society?

Discuss the possible identities and roles of the deities referred to as 'Potnia'. How might these goddesses reflect the gender dynamics within Mycenaean religion and society?

Compare the Mycenaean pantheon with the later Greek pantheon. What does this comparison reveal about the continuity and change in religious beliefs over time?

Exercises:

Choose one of the lesser-known deities in the Mycenaean pantheon. Based on the available archaeological and textual evidence, attempt to reconstruct the possible significance of this deity within Mycenaean religion.

Investigate the depictions of deities in Mycenaean art and iconography. How do these depictions contribute to our understanding of the characteristics and functions of the Mycenaean gods and goddesses?

Analyze the relationship between the Mycenaean deities and their later Greek counterparts. Discuss how the evolution of these deities might reflect broader changes in social and cultural values.

The importance of nature and fertility in Mycenaean religion

The Mycenaean civilization, flourishing from c. 1600 to c. 1100 BC on the Greek mainland, inherited and adapted various cultural aspects from their Minoan predecessors, including religious practices. This section will analyze the pivotal role of nature and fertility within Mycenaean religious belief systems, offering insights into the ways in which their spiritual life was entwined with the natural environment.

Nature in Mycenaean Religion

The Mycenaeans, like many ancient societies, placed significant emphasis on the natural world within their religious practices. This is evident in the archaeological record, particularly in Linear B tablets, which provide linguistic evidence of the Mycenaean pantheon and ritual practices. Deities representing natural elements were of utmost importance, underlining the culture's dependency on and respect for nature's forces.

Several Mycenaean deities were associated with natural phenomena. For instance, Poseidon, primarily known as the god of the sea in later classical Greek religion, was invoked as 'Earth-Shaker' in Linear B inscriptions, hinting at a more terrestrial, nature-centric role. Potnia, meaning 'Mistress' or 'Lady', was a title applied to several goddesses related to natural elements and animals.

Fertility in Mycenaean Religion

Fertility also figured prominently in the Mycenaean religious psyche. As an agrarian society reliant on crop cultivation and animal husbandry, the Mycenaeans venerated deities that represented or influenced fertility. In this context, the term fertility extends beyond human reproduction to include the fertility of the earth — the productivity of crops, livestock, and the successful change of seasons.

The Mycenaean pantheon comprised several deities related to fertility. Perhaps the most significant was the figure of Potnia, who appears frequently in Linear B texts and is often associated with fertility and agricultural abundance. The Linear B tablets from Pylos also mention a deity named 'Eleuthia', who is considered a goddess of childbirth, directly linking her to human fertility.

Challenges and Counterarguments

Interpretations of Mycenaean religion, including the prominence of nature and fertility, face several challenges. These primarily arise from our reliance on archaeological evidence and the limited number of decipherable Linear B tablets. Additionally, it is crucial to remember that the Mycenaean understanding of deities might have differed significantly from their classical Greek counterparts, despite sharing names and attributes.

Discussion Questions: How might reliance on nature influence the formation of a society's religious beliefs?

Exercise: Analyze a Mycenaean religious artifact, such as the gold rings from Pylos. Discuss how it may provide insights into their nature and fertility-centric beliefs.

Critical Thinking Challenge: Debate the assertion that the strong emphasis on nature and fertility in Mycenaean religion was primarily a result of their agrarian lifestyle. Could other factors have contributed to this emphasis?

Religious rituals and ceremonies in Mycenaean society

Mycenaean religion, flourishing during the Late Bronze Age (c. 1600-1100 BC), was an amalgamation of Indo-European elements, local Helladic features, and influences from Minoan Crete. However, our understanding of Mycenaean religious rituals and ceremonies is primarily extrapolated from archaeological findings and interpretations of Linear B tablets. In this section, we shall undertake a comprehensive exploration of religious practices in Mycenaean society.

Ritual Practice in Mycenaean Society

Religious rituals in Mycenaean society were likely performed in both public and domestic contexts, engaging various segments of the population in distinct manners. Sanctuaries, such as the one at Phylakopi on the island of Melos, were likely significant public spaces for the performance of communal rituals, underscoring the significance of shared spiritual experiences in strengthening societal bonds.

Animal sacrifice appears to have been a prominent part of Mycenaean ritual practice. Linear B tablets record offerings of cattle, sheep, and pigs, suggesting a form of communion with deities through these sacrifices. The offerings were likely a form of propitiation or gratitude, intended to curry divine favor and ensure the prosperity of the community.

Ceremonial Feasting and Libations

Ceremonial feasting and the offering of libations constituted significant components of Mycenaean religious ceremonies. Vast amounts of food and drink, such as wine and olive oil, were consumed and offered during these feasts. These practices can be interpreted as gestures of hospitality towards the gods, providing sustenance for them and reinforcing a sense of reciprocity between mortals and deities.

Burial Rituals

The Mycenaean society displayed a deep reverence for the dead, with elaborate burial rituals that suggest a belief in an afterlife. Tholos tombs and shaft graves, such as those at Mycenae, contained rich grave goods, signifying the societal status of the deceased and perhaps intended to equip them for the journey into the afterlife.

Challenges and Counterarguments

While our understanding of Mycenaean religious rituals and ceremonies is growing, it is vital to approach this knowledge with a degree of caution. Much of our information comes from archaeological evidence, which leaves ample room for interpretation and conjecture. Additionally, the absence of contemporary written narratives means that we must extrapolate ritual practices from administrative records, a methodology that has its limitations.

Discussion Questions: What can the nature of Mycenaean religious rituals tell us about the society's values and beliefs?

Exercise: Review Linear B tablets mentioning religious offerings and sacrifices. What do these records tell us about the nature and importance of animal sacrifice in Mycenaean religion?

Critical Thinking Challenge: Consider the role of feasting and libations in Mycenaean ceremonies. What might such practices suggest about the relationship between the Mycenaeans and their gods, and how might this compare to similar practices in other ancient societies?

The Collapse of the Mycenaean Civilization

The collapse of the Mycenaean civilization around 1200 BC represents a crucial turning point in the history of ancient Greece, marking the end of the Bronze Age and ushering in a period of transition and tumult, referred to as the Greek Dark Ages. The causes of this collapse have been the subject of rigorous scholarly debate. Various theories have been posited, which we shall explore here, bearing in mind that the collapse of a civilization is seldom attributable to a single cause, but rather, is usually the result of a confluence of factors.

Systemic Instabilities

The Mycenaean civilization, as with any complex society, was dependent on certain foundational elements for its stability. These elements included political stability, economic prosperity, and societal cohesion. The instability of any of these elements could lead to a cascade of consequences, jeopardizing the integrity of the civilization. Internal strife, including rebellion or political intrigue, could have eroded the authority of the ruling elite and destabilized the societal order.

Economic Disruptions

Economic disruption represents another potential cause of the Mycenaean collapse. Evidence suggests that the Mycenaeans had intricate trade networks spanning the Mediterranean. The interruption of these trade routes, potentially due to maritime piracy or the collapse of other regional civilizations, could have had a profound impact on the Mycenaean economy. It is also plausible that environmental changes or natural disasters led to agricultural failures, exacerbating economic distress.

Invasions and External Threats

The theory that external invasions precipitated the collapse of the Mycenaean civilization has been widely debated. The so-called "Dorian Invasion" is often cited as a potential cause, referring to the hypothesized invasion by Doric-speaking peoples from the north. However, the archaeological evidence to support a large-scale invasion is inconclusive, and this theory has been critiqued for its reliance on later historical sources.

Natural Disasters

A series of natural disasters, such as earthquakes or prolonged drought, could have also contributed to the Mycenaean downfall. The eastern Mediterranean is seismically active, and substantial earthquakes could have damaged infrastructure and disrupted societal functioning. Similarly, drought could have led to food shortages and societal instability.

Counterarguments and Concluding Thoughts

The collapse of the Mycenaean civilization remains a multifaceted and complex event. It is crucial to underscore that the above hypotheses are not mutually exclusive and may all have played a role to varying degrees. Further archaeological and historical research is needed to refine our understanding of this pivotal period in ancient history.

Discussion Questions: How does the collapse of the Mycenaean civilization compare to the fall of other ancient civilizations? What factors seem to be common across different societal collapses?

Exercise: Analyze various primary and secondary sources that discuss the Dorian Invasion theory. What are the strengths and weaknesses of this theory?

Critical Thinking Challenge: Consider the role of environmental changes in the collapse of the Mycenaean civilization. How might a changing climate or natural disasters impact a civilization, and can you find parallels in more recent historical or contemporary contexts?

Factors contributing to the decline of the Mycenaean civilization

The demise of the Mycenaean civilization is an intricate and multilayered phenomenon that has been analyzed from a plethora of perspectives over the years. As one delves into this topic, it becomes evident that it is not a straightforward, linear narrative, but rather an entangled web of causes and consequences, as complex as the society it pertains to.

Internal Factors

Social Instability: One of the internal factors that contributed to the decline of the Mycenaean civilization could have been social instability. This might have taken the form of civil unrest, dissatisfaction with the ruling elite, or social stratification leading to tensions between different segments of society. The archaeological record shows evidence of destruction and burning at several Mycenaean palace centers, which could indicate violent internal conflicts.

Economic Disruption: The Mycenaean economy, reliant on trade and agriculture, may have been disrupted by various factors, such as agricultural failures due to environmental changes or the collapse of trade networks. Evidence suggests that the late Mycenaean period saw a decline in the quality of craftsmanship and a reduction in the production of luxury goods, hinting at economic decline.

External Factors

Foreign Invasion: Theories of foreign invasion, particularly by the so-called "Sea Peoples" or Dorians, have been put forward as possible external factors contributing to the Mycenaean decline. However, the evidence supporting such large-scale invasions remains inconclusive.

Natural Disasters: The eastern Mediterranean region, where the Mycenaean civilization was located, is known for seismic activity. Earthquakes could have caused significant damage to infrastructure, leading to societal instability. Other natural disasters, such as drought or flooding, could have negatively impacted agriculture, leading to food shortages and further societal unrest.

Interplay of Factors

While each of these factors could have played a role in the decline of the Mycenaean civilization, it is more likely that a combination of them, acting together, led to its eventual collapse. An economic disruption could have exacerbated social tensions, while the damage caused by natural disasters could have made the society more vulnerable to foreign invasions. The interplay of these factors could have created a feedback loop of instability, contributing to the overall decline.

Considerations for Further Study

The downfall of the Mycenaean civilization underscores the complexity and interconnectedness of societal factors. It is an object lesson in the interplay of economic, social, and environmental elements, and how their instability can lead to societal collapse.

Exercise: Conduct a comparative analysis of the collapse of the Mycenaean civilization with that of other ancient civilizations. What similarities and differences do you observe?

Discussion Questions: What lessons can contemporary societies learn from the collapse of the Mycenaean civilization? How does the study of such ancient societies inform our understanding of societal resilience and vulnerability?

Critical Thinking Challenge: Think about the impact of climate change on modern societies. Drawing on the factors contributing to the decline of the Mycenaean civilization, predict potential outcomes if current environmental trends continue.

The impact of the collapse on religious practices and beliefs

The collapse of the Mycenaean civilization marks a significant turning point in the religious landscape of ancient Greece. The changes that ensued did not only constitute an end, but also a transformation and beginning of new religious practices and beliefs.

Religious Discontinuity

The first discernible effect of the collapse was a disruption in the previously held religious practices. The elaborate palatial religious ceremonies and rituals, evident from the Linear B tablets, seemed to have declined or even disappeared. The richly decorated palatial centers that served as central locations for these religious activities were destroyed and abandoned. Consequently, the priestly class that presided over these rituals also presumably diminished. The magnitude of the collapse, therefore, led to a dramatic religious discontinuity.

The Emergence of New Practices

Following the collapse, there was a profound shift in religious practices, moving away from palatial centers towards less formal and more personal modes of worship. The religion of the Dark Ages (as the period following the collapse is often referred to) is less well understood due to the scarcity of written records. However, archaeological evidence suggests the proliferation of open-air sanctuaries and an increased use of terracotta figurines, possibly indicating a more personal, household-based form of religious practice.

Moreover, it's during this time that the pantheon of gods started to take the shape more familiar to us from Classical Greek religion. While some of the gods worshipped in the Mycenaean period continued to be revered, others vanished, and new ones appeared. The goddesses seemed to have retained their preeminent status, possibly due to the importance of fertility in the subsistence-based economy of the time.

The Synthesis of Old and New

Even in this period of profound change, elements of continuity with the Mycenaean past can be discerned. Certain Mycenaean religious symbols and motifs continued to be used, suggesting a degree of cultural memory or resilience. It is plausible to posit that while the collapse led to the discontinuation of certain religious practices, it did not entirely erase the underlying beliefs.

Conclusion

The collapse of the Mycenaean civilization thus led to a period of religious transformation characterized by a blend of continuity and change. This transformation period laid the groundwork for the religious beliefs and practices of the Archaic and Classical Greece.

Exercise: Analyze the transformation of religious practices from Mycenaean civilization to the Dark Ages and beyond. What elements persisted and which ones were replaced?

Discussion Questions: How does societal collapse impact religious beliefs and practices? How do religion and society mutually influence each other during periods of significant change?

Critical Thinking Challenge: Drawing from the religious transformation following the Mycenaean collapse, consider the potential impact of a significant societal change (like a war or climate crisis) on contemporary religious practices and beliefs.

The transition period between the Mycenaean and Archaic Greek periods

The transition between the Late Bronze Age Mycenaean civilization and the ensuing Archaic period, which occurred roughly between the 11th and 8th centuries BCE, is also known as the Greek Dark Ages. This intermediary period was characterized by significant transformations across multiple domains, including socio-political organization, economic practices, and religious beliefs.

Socio-Political Changes

The Mycenaean period was marked by the existence of large, bureaucratic palace states. With the collapse of the Mycenaean civilization, these centralized structures of political power disintegrated. In their stead, smaller, more localized forms of governance emerged. This transition from palace states to smaller-scale polities resulted in a more decentralized power structure, setting the stage for the development of the polis or city-state structure that became characteristic of the Archaic period.

Economic Transformations

✧ The Disintegration of the Mycenaean Economic System

The economic system of the Mycenaean period was a complex structure, intricately linked to the political organization of the palatial centers. The economy was primarily redistributive in nature, with goods collected as taxes or tribute, stored in palaces, and then redistributed as per societal needs or for trade. However, with the collapse of these palatial centers around 1200 BCE, the economic system that sustained them also fell into disarray.

✧   Transition to a Subsistence Economy

The ensuing disruption led to the emergence of a more agrarian and self-sufficient economy. The production of surplus goods for trade was supplanted by the necessity of producing enough to survive. Hence, societies focused more on farming and animal husbandry, indicating a shift to subsistence agriculture.

This period witnessed a marked reduction in the variety and quality of pottery and other material goods, reflecting the decline in long-distance trade and the loss of specialized craftsmanship. Such changes suggest a relatively impoverished material culture compared to the preceding Mycenaean period.

✧   Decline and Resurgence of Trade

The collapse of the palatial centers and their economic systems brought about a significant decline in long-distance trade. This is evident in the reduced distribution of Mycenaean pottery in the broader Mediterranean area and the cessation of imported goods.

However, this situation gradually changed from the 9th century BCE onwards, signaling the end of the Greek Dark Ages. There was a resurgence of trade, both internal and external, accompanied by the reappearance of writing in the form of the Greek alphabet. These developments indicate the gradual integration of the Greek world into the wider economic networks of the eastern Mediterranean.

Conclusion

In conclusion, the collapse of the Mycenaean civilization prompted significant economic transformations. These included the disintegration of the redistributive economy, a shift towards subsistence farming, a decline in material culture, and a temporary cessation of long-distance trade. However, these changes were not permanent and the Greek economy began to revive by the 9th century BCE. These transformations illustrate the resilience and adaptability of these societies in the face of significant disruptions.

By considering these economic shifts, students can gain a deeper understanding of the complex interaction between economic systems, societal structures, and historical change. Furthermore, it encourages reflection on how societies respond to and recover from major disruptions, a theme of perennial relevance.

Religious Shifts

✧ The Decentralization of Religion

The Greek Dark Ages (c. 1200-800 BCE) saw a shift from the centralized, state-controlled religious practices of the Mycenaean period. With the collapse of the palatial centers, the uniformity of religious expression diminished. In its place, a more localized and diversified religious system emerged. Instead of grand palatial ceremonies, the focus shifted to local cults, family hearths, and open-air sanctuaries often located near significant natural landmarks, such as caves, springs, and groves.

This decentralization of religion facilitated a more intimate and personal form of worship. While the larger communal festivals and rituals still took place, the everyday religious experiences of most Greeks during this period would have been within their homes or local communities. The centrality of the household in religious observance is evidenced by the prevalence of domestic altars and small-scale household deities or 'daemons', who protected individual families and homes.

✧ Evolution and Syncretism in the Greek Pantheon

The Greek pantheon too underwent significant changes during the Dark Ages. Many of the deities central to the Mycenaean religious system, such as the goddess Potnia, disappeared or were absorbed into other deities. Meanwhile, gods and goddesses who had previously been minor or local figures began to rise in prominence. This reshaping of the pantheon can be seen as a form of syncretism, whereby previously distinct deities were merged, and their attributes reassigned to new or more regionally significant gods.

For instance, the Mycenaean deity Poseidon, who appears to have initially been associated with the earth and possibly horses, was transformed into the god of the sea. Similarly, Zeus, originally a sky deity, was over time imbued with attributes of justice, kingship, and order, becoming the supreme ruler of the gods. The fluid nature of these deities' identities reflects the adaptive nature of Greek polytheism, which allowed for the reconfiguration and reinterpretation of divine figures according to societal changes and needs.

✧ From the Dark Ages to the Archaic Period

By the end of the Dark Ages and the onset of the Archaic period (c. 800-500 BCE), there was a trend towards re-centralization and standardization in religious practices. This was likely influenced by the political changes occurring during this period, including the rise of the city-states (poleis) and the establishment of law codes. These changes led to the development of state-sponsored cults, the construction of monumental temples, and the organization of grand civic festivals.

In summary, the religious shifts from the end of the Mycenaean civilization through to the Archaic period were marked by decentralization, personalization, and syncretism, followed by a gradual return to more structured and communal practices. The transformation of the Greek pantheon mirrored these societal changes, as deities were reconfigured, replaced, or reshaped to meet the evolving needs and understandings of their worshippers.

Conclusion

The transition period between the Mycenaean and Archaic periods represents a pivotal phase in Greek history. It is a time of profound transformation, characterized by decentralization of political power, shifts in economic practices, and the reshaping of religious beliefs and practices. The changes that occurred during this period paved the way for the unique political, economic, and religious characteristics that would define the Archaic and Classical periods.

Exercises:

Compare the socio-political structures of the Mycenaean, Greek Dark Ages, and Archaic periods.

Discuss the economic changes that occurred during the transition period and their impact on societal structure.

Discussion Questions:

How did the transition period shape the religious beliefs and practices of the Archaic period?

How do societal transformations influence the development of economic and political structures?

Critical Thinking Challenge: Consider the impact of a major societal collapse on contemporary society. What kind of transformations might we expect in our political, economic, and religious structures?

The Greek Pantheon: Emergence and Development

The evolution of the Greek pantheon—its array of deities—offers fascinating insight into the development of Greek religious thought and societal values. Spanning from the prehistoric period through the Mycenaean civilization, the Greek Dark Ages, and into the Classical era, the pantheon's unfolding narrative is deeply interwoven with Greek history, politics, and culture.

Emergence of the Pantheon

✧   Prehistoric Roots: Minoan and Mycenaean Deities

The origin of the Greek pantheon reaches back into the prehistoric period. The Minoan civilization on Crete (2700–1450 BCE) offers some of the earliest evidence of religious belief in the region. While our understanding of Minoan religion is somewhat limited due to the undeciphered Linear A script, the archaeological evidence reveals a pantheon dominated by female deities, often depicted in association with natural elements and animals, particularly snakes. Notable among these is the iconic "Snake Goddess," depicted with serpents winding around her arms. This likely denotes a close relationship with the natural world, fertility, and possibly the underworld.

Subsequent to the Minoan civilization, the Mycenaean civilization (1600–1100 BCE) worshipped an array of deities, many of whom would later be incorporated into the Classical Greek pantheon. The decipherment of the Linear B script has yielded a wealth of information about Mycenaean deities. Tablets from Pylos, Knossos, and other Mycenaean centres list names like Zeus, Hera, Poseidon, Hermes, and others. However, it should be stressed that the nature of these deities might not correspond precisely to their Classical counterparts. For example, in the Mycenaean context, Poseidon appears to be primarily associated with the earth and earthquakes rather than the sea, as he would later be in the Classical era.

✧   From the Dark Ages to the Archaic Period: Localisation and Syncretism

The collapse of the Mycenaean palaces around 1200 BCE marked the onset of the Greek Dark Ages. This period was characterized by the decentralization of power and the loss of literacy, resulting in a greater regional diversity of religious practices. Localised cults emerged, often worshipping deities tied to specific geographical features or communities.

By the end of the Dark Ages and into the Archaic period (800–500 BCE), a process of religious syncretism began to take shape. As various poleis came into contact through trade, warfare, and colonisation, their individual deities were often identified with one another. This resulted in the assimilation of gods and goddesses of different regions into singular divine figures.

✧   The Classical Pantheon: Hierarchization and Standardization

By the Classical period (500–323 BCE), the Greek pantheon had taken on a more structured and hierarchical form. The gods were typically depicted as a family, with Zeus as the patriarch. Other gods and goddesses had their own distinct domains and attributes, and their relationships with each other and with humanity were codified in myth and ritual. This period also saw the production of monumental temples dedicated to individual deities, reflecting their accepted positions within the pantheon.

In conclusion, the emergence of the Greek pantheon was a process that spanned centuries and was influenced by a multitude of social, political, and cultural factors. From the female-centric pantheon of the Minoans to the complex, hierarchical family of gods in the Classical period, the evolution of the Greek pantheon reflects the changing dynamics of the societies that worshipped them.

Evolution During the Greek Dark Ages and Archaic Period

The Greek Dark Ages: Transition from Mycenaean Religion
The Greek Dark Ages (c. 1100–800 BCE) represents a time of profound change. With the disintegration of the Mycenaean civilization came a breakdown of the established religious order. The grand palatial centres with their formalized religious practices gave way to small, dispersed communities, each evolving and developing its own distinct religious traditions.

In the absence of a centralized religious authority, localized cults flourished, some of which may have had roots in the Mycenaean era, while others could have developed anew. The loss of literacy during this period further fostered the diversification of religious beliefs and practices. Religious narratives and mythologies were preserved and disseminated through oral traditions, which by their nature allowed for variations and regional adaptations.

Hesiod's "Theogony," composed in the late 8th century BCE, provides a unique insight into the religious landscape of the time. This epic poem introduced a new cosmology, genealogies of the gods, and narratives that would profoundly influence later conceptualizations of the pantheon.

✦ The Archaic Period: Emergence of a Unified Pantheon

With the advent of the Archaic period (800-500 BCE), there was a trend towards greater cohesion in the pantheon. As communities began to establish themselves as city-states (poleis), each polis typically chose a patron deity, who was worshipped with special fervour. The process of synoecism—the unification of nearby settlements into a single political entity—may have also encouraged the merging of local deities and religious practices.

During this period, the gods of the Greek pantheon began to acquire the attributes and domains of influence for which they are best known today. Zeus emerged as the father of gods and men, the enforcer of justice and fate, and the lord of the sky and thunder. Athena solidified her role as the goddess of wisdom, strategic warfare, and crafts. Meanwhile, Apollo's association with music, prophecy, healing, and the sun became more pronounced.

The Homeric Hymns, a collection of ancient Greek hymns dedicated to the gods, illustrate these shifts in divine roles and functions. Composed during the Archaic period, they offer a vivid portrayal of the gods in their various aspects. They also reflect the increasing importance of certain deities, such as Zeus, Hera, Athena, and Apollo, marking a significant step towards the hierarchical structure of the Classical pantheon.

In summary, the Greek Dark Ages and the Archaic period witnessed a remarkable transformation in the Greek religious landscape. From the ruins of the Mycenaean palatial systems, a new pantheon emerged, shaped by local traditions, socio-political changes, and the creative force of poetic imagination. This evolution set the stage for the further development of Greek religion in the Classical period and beyond.

The Classical Period and Beyond

✦ The Classical Period: Standardization and Structuring of the Pantheon

The Classical period in Greece (5th-4th centuries BCE) was marked by a significant consolidation and refinement of the pantheon. By this time, the pantheon had evolved into a structured assembly of gods and goddesses, each possessing distinct roles, areas of influence, and characteristics. Some of these divine figures, such as Athena and Poseidon, were intimately linked to the city-states that worshipped them. Others, like Apollo and Artemis, were associated with more universal concepts, such as light, prophecy, and wilderness.

The gods and goddesses of this period were not only characters in a vast array of myths and stories but also the objects of a diverse array of ritual practices. The construction of monumental temples, the dedication of statues, and the observance of regular festivals and rites were all means by which the Greeks manifested their devotion to the divine. Indeed, religion was not a separate domain of life in the Classical Greek world but deeply woven into the fabric of society, politics, and culture.

✧   Hellenistic Religion: Greek Pantheon Beyond Greece

The conquests of Alexander the Great in the 4th century BCE spread Greek culture, including its religious beliefs, across a vast geographic area, from Egypt to India. In these new lands, Greek gods and goddesses were often syncretized with local deities, resulting in hybrid forms of worship. For example, in Egypt, the Greek god Zeus was equated with the native Egyptian god Amun, resulting in a combined deity known as Zeus-Ammon.

✧   The Roman Era and the Christianization of the Empire: The Decline of the Greek Pantheon

With the rise of Rome, Greek religion was again disseminated widely, as the Romans assimilated Greek deities into their own pantheon, often equating Greek gods with their own. For example, the Greek god Hermes was identified with the Roman Mercury, while the Greek Aphrodite was seen as equivalent to the Roman Venus. This process of syncretization often preserved and even expanded the worship of Greek deities.

However, with the official endorsement of Christianity by Emperor Constantine in the 4th century CE and the subsequent Christianization of the Roman Empire, the Greek pantheon's influence began to wane. The traditional forms of Greek religion, along with its pantheon, gradually faded into the background, replaced by the monotheistic faith of Christianity.

In conclusion, the history of the Greek pantheon from the Classical period and beyond is one of continuity and change, preservation and transformation. Even as the pantheon evolved, adapted, and eventually declined, it left a lasting imprint on the cultural, religious, and philosophical landscape of the ancient world, an influence that continues to reverberate in our contemporary world.

Conclusion

The Greek pantheon's emergence and development reflect a dynamic interplay between societal transformation, political shifts, and evolving religious ideas. From its early genesis in the Bronze Age to its final iterations in the Classical period, the pantheon functioned as a spiritual mirror to Greek society, encapsulating its values, fears, hopes, and aspirations.

Exercises:

Examine how the functions and roles of a deity, such as Athena or Zeus, evolved over time.

Discuss the societal and cultural factors that influenced the development of the Greek pantheon.

Discussion Questions:

How did societal changes during the Greek Dark Ages impact the evolution of the Greek pantheon?

How did the religious narratives, such as those presented in Hesiod's "Theogony," shape the Greek understanding of their pantheon?

Critical Thinking Challenge: Contemplate the influence of political power dynamics, such as the rise of city-states, on the formation and development of the Greek pantheon.

The merging of Mycenaean deities with other Greek divinities

The blending and evolution of religious concepts—known as syncretism—is a common phenomenon in human history. Among the most salient examples of syncretism in ancient times is the merging of Mycenaean deities with the pantheon of other Greek divinities, a process that played out over centuries and was intricately tied to social, cultural, and political changes.

The Mycenaean Deities

The Mycenaean civilization, which flourished in Greece during the Late Bronze Age (c. 1600–1100 BCE), provides us with the earliest written evidence of Greek religious practices. This evidence is primarily in the form of Linear B tablets, an early form of Greek script. While the tablets are primarily administrative records, they also mention a number of deities, allowing us to piece together the religious landscape of Mycenaean Greece.

Linear B and the Documentation of Mycenaean Deities: The Linear B script, deciphered by Michael Ventris and John Chadwick in the mid-20th century, is predominantly utilitarian in nature, detailing matters such as taxation, inventory, and personnel records. However, within these dry administrative documents, references to various deities appear. These deities were often linked with specific places or functions, offering us insights into their roles within the Mycenaean religious system.

The Pantheon of Mycenaean Deities: Many of the deities mentioned in the Linear B tablets correspond to gods and goddesses who would later be central to the Classical Greek pantheon. For instance, Zeus (Di-we), Hera (E-ra), Poseidon (Po-se-da-o), Artemis (A-te-mi-to), Hermes (E-ma-a), and Dionysus (Di-wo-nu-so) all appear in the Mycenaean texts. However, the roles and characteristics attributed to these deities within the Mycenaean religious framework might have differed significantly from their later Classical conceptions.

The Nature and Roles of the Mycenaean Deities: A crucial factor to bear in mind is that the attributes of these gods during the Mycenaean period might not align neatly with their Classical counterparts. For example, Poseidon, who was known as the god of the sea in Classical mythology, seems to have been primarily associated with the earth and earthquakes in the Mycenaean context. Similarly, Zeus appears to have been a more specialized deity, associated with the sky and possibly fertility, a far cry from the universal sovereign he would become in later Greek mythology. Moreover, there were deities, such as the "wanax" (wa-na-ka), the king or the lord, who do not appear in the later pantheon, suggesting that the Mycenaean pantheon underwent significant changes over time.

The Cult of the Deities: The cult practices of the Mycenaean period also differ from later times. Archaeological evidence, such as the remains of sacrificial animals found in palatial centers, suggests that animal sacrifice played a key role in Mycenaean religious rituals. The tablets also provide information about offerings made to the deities, often in the form of agricultural products, attesting to a deeply reciprocal relationship between the worshippers and their gods.

In conclusion, the Mycenaean civilization, as represented through the Linear B tablets, offers a fascinating window into the early stages of Greek religious thought. It demonstrates that the gods of the Classical Greek pantheon had their roots in the Mycenaean age, albeit in forms and roles that were significantly different. This diversity underscores the fluidity of divine identities, as gods were reimagined and reinterpreted in response to changing social, political, and cultural contexts.

The Greek Dark Ages and the Archaic Period

The Greek Dark Ages (c. 1100–800 BCE), also known as the Homeric Age due to its association with the works of Homer, marked a significant transition in Greek history. It followed the collapse of the Mycenaean civilization, a tumultuous event that precipitated profound societal changes. Centralized palatial systems disintegrated, making way for smaller, more dispersed communities. Such drastic shifts in societal structure engendered critical implications for religious beliefs and practices.

Decentralization and Localization of Cults: The fall of palatial systems and the move toward localized communities naturally affected religious practices. With the disintegration of centralized structures, cults became localized, resulting in the diversification of religious traditions. This localization can be observed in the increased prominence of local heroes and deities, who often bore a direct relationship to the landscape and history of specific communities.

Syncretism and the Archaic Era: The subsequent Archaic era (c. 800–480 BCE) was a period of cultural and political renaissance that saw the rise of city-states (poleis) and the establishment of democratic governance in Athens. As Greece emerged from its 'dark age', the landscape of the divine realm was also transformed. Syncretism, the merging of different religious traditions, became a crucial process in shaping the Greek pantheon. Mycenaean deities, influenced by local and imported divinities, gradually coalesced into new godly figures.

Influence of External Factors: The reshaping of the Greek pantheon was not an isolated process but was influenced by a myriad of external factors. These included local traditions, the emergence of city-states, inter-regional contact and trade, and societal needs and anxieties. For instance, interaction with Eastern cultures, especially through colonization and trade, brought new religious ideas and practices to Greece, which then left an indelible mark on the Greek pantheon.

Homeric and Hesiodic Contributions: Literary works played a pivotal role in this transformation. Homer's Iliad and Odyssey, and Hesiod's Theogony and Works and Days, codified the narratives of the gods, offering structure and coherence to disparate myths. They did not merely record existing religious beliefs but actively contributed to the standardization and interpretation of these beliefs. The synthesis of previously distinct deities into unified figures was one significant outcome of this process.

For example, Zeus, initially a Mycenaean sky deity, underwent a profound transformation during this period. Influenced by the attributes of other divinities and reflecting the changing societal needs, Zeus evolved into the patriarchal figure and supreme ruler of the pantheon. His transformation from a relatively specialized deity to a universal sovereign is emblematic of the broader process of syncretism and consolidation that characterized this period.

In sum, the Greek Dark Ages and the Archaic period, while fraught with societal upheaval, marked a fertile phase in the evolution of Greek religious thought. It was during this period that the foundations of the classical Greek pantheon were laid, through a process marked by localization, syncretism, and literary standardization. The result was a richly textured religious system that would come to dominate the Hellenic world and leave a lasting legacy on Western civilization.

Conclusion

The merging of Mycenaean deities with other Greek divinities was not a uniform or unilateral process. Instead, it was a complex and organic development, reflecting the ongoing dialectic between tradition and change, local and panhellenic identities, and political realities and ideological needs.

Exercises:

Analyze how the Homeric Epics and Hesiod's "Theogony" contributed to the merging of Mycenaean deities with other Greek divinities.

Explore the case of a specific deity, such as Athena or Demeter, tracing their evolution from the Mycenaean period to the Classical era.

Discussion Questions:

How did changes in social and political structures during the Greek Dark Ages influence the merging of Mycenaean deities with other Greek divinities?

In what ways do the merged deities reflect the cultural, societal, and political realities of their era?

Critical Thinking Challenge: Evaluate the role of syncretism in the development of religious systems. Consider how the case of the Mycenaean deities fits into broader patterns of religious change and evolution.

The influence of Minoan religious elements on the Greek pantheon

The Minoan civilization, which flourished on Crete from approximately 2700 to 1450 BCE, was among the most advanced in the ancient world and exerted considerable influence over the subsequent cultures, including Mycenaean and Classical Greek civilizations. One of the most significant aspects of this influence was in the realm of religion, where a number of Minoan elements found their way into the Greek pantheon.

Minoan Religion and Its Characteristics

Minoan religion was characterized by a pantheon of female deities, associated with nature, fertility, and animals, particularly snakes. The depictions of these deities, often seen in frescoes, terracotta figurines, and seals, suggest a vibrant cult with elaborate rituals and ceremonies.

One of the most iconic images is the "snake goddess," frequently depicted with snakes entwined in her hands. Additionally, the Minoans held rituals in natural settings such as caves, mountaintops, and forests, as well as in complex palatial and non-palatial architectural sites, including the famous "palace" of Knossos.

The religious system of the Minoan civilization, flourishing in Crete during the Bronze Age (3000–1450 BCE), was characterized by an array of distinctive attributes, reflecting the unique socio-cultural and environmental contexts of the Minoans.

Female Deities and Fertility Cult: A central aspect of Minoan religion was its focus on female deities, which stood in stark contrast to the predominantly male-oriented pantheons of many contemporary civilizations. These deities were often associated with nature and fertility, underscoring the Minoans' profound reverence for the natural world and its generative powers. Many scholars argue that this emphasis on fertility deities suggests a religion that was deeply entwined with agricultural cycles and practices. It is thus surmised that the Minoans perceived a divine presence in the natural forces that governed their subsistence and survival, venerating them in the form of female deities.

Symbolism and Iconography: Minoan religious iconography, as discerned from frescoes, terracotta figurines, seals, and other archaeological artifacts, is replete with vibrant symbols and motifs. Among the most iconic is the depiction of a "snake goddess," a female figure shown holding snakes in her hands. The snake, an animal frequently associated with regeneration and the earth's fertility in many cultures, was thus a potent religious symbol in Minoan Crete. It is also noteworthy that the iconography frequently depicted animals, such as bulls, birds, and bees, suggesting a religion deeply interconnected with the surrounding natural and animal world.

Sacred Spaces and Ritual Practices: The Minoans conducted their religious rituals in a variety of settings. Natural landscapes, including caves, mountaintops, and forests, were imbued with sacredness and served as places of worship. Such a pattern indicates a belief system where the divine was not confined to man-made temples but was perceived to reside in and emanate from nature itself.

Simultaneously, the Minoans also erected complex architectural structures for religious practices. The famous "palace" of Knossos, with its labyrinthine design and elaborate frescoes, is one such example. There were also several "peak sanctuaries" located atop mountains, where votive offerings were made.

Ceremonial Practices: Minoan religion appears to have involved a variety of rituals and ceremonies, some of which are tantalizingly depicted in their frescoes. For instance, the 'Bull-Leaping' fresco from Knossos depicts an acrobatic ritual involving bulls, possibly indicating a ceremonial tradition associated with these animals. Other rituals may have involved processions, music, dance, and feasting, as indicated by various artifacts.

The absence of a defined clergy: Unlike some contemporaneous religions, there is little evidence in Minoan religion of a distinct priestly class. The rituals and ceremonies seem to have been communal activities, with participation from various segments of society. Some scholars suggest that this characteristic might reflect a relatively egalitarian social structure.

In conclusion, Minoan religion, characterized by its emphasis on female deities, a strong connection to nature and fertility, vibrant iconography, diverse sacred spaces, and seemingly egalitarian ceremonial practices, offers a fascinating study of a Bronze Age religious system. It stands as a testament to the Minoans' unique understanding of the divine and their place within the natural world. The understanding and interpretation of Minoan religion, however, remain a challenging task due to the lack of decipherable written records, encouraging researchers to continually piece together information through ongoing archaeological and iconographic studies.

The Influence on the Greek Pantheon

With the advent of the Mycenaean civilization, which came into close contact with the Minoans through trade and later conquest, Minoan religious elements started to blend with the Mycenaean and, eventually, the Greek pantheon.

A prominent instance of this influence can be found in the figure of the Greek goddess Artemis, who inherited traits from the Minoan "mistress of animals." Artemis' association with the wilderness, hunting, and animals echoes the nature-centric beliefs of the Minoans.

Similarly, the Minoan "snake goddess" appears to have contributed to the formation of several Greek deities, including Athena, who is occasionally depicted with a snake, and Hera, whose temple in Argos featured snake-themed decorations.

The influence also extended to religious architecture and practices. For example, the Minoan tradition of peak sanctuaries, where offerings were made at mountaintops, is mirrored in the later Greek practice of erecting temples in high places, such as the Acropolis in Athens.

Conclusion

The influence of Minoan religious elements on the Greek pantheon underscores the dynamic and syncretic nature of religious systems. The adoption and adaptation of Minoan deities and rituals reflect the Greeks' cultural interactions and their flexible approach to religious syncretism.

Exercises:

Identify and analyze instances of Minoan influence in the representations of Greek goddesses such as Artemis, Athena, and Hera.

Discuss the impact of Minoan architecture and ritual practices on Greek religious customs.

Discussion Questions:

How did the Minoan focus on female deities and nature-centric worship influence the religious beliefs of the Mycenaean and later Greek civilizations?

How do the adoptions and adaptations of Minoan elements reflect the Greek approach to syncretism and cultural interaction?

Critical Thinking Challenge:

Evaluate the Minoan influence on the Greek pantheon in the context of broader cross-cultural exchanges in the ancient Mediterranean world. Consider how this influence reflects the interplay of cultural continuity and change in the evolution of religious systems.

The formation of major Greek gods and goddesses during the Archaic period

The Archaic period in Greece (800–480 BCE) was a time of profound cultural evolution and was pivotal in the formation of the Greek pantheon. Drawing from the influences of the preceding Mycenaean civilization and its interaction with other cultures, such as the Minoan civilization, the Greeks during this period developed a distinct religious system that still captures the world's imagination.

The Greek Pantheon: An Overview

The Greek pantheon was a complex system of deities and semi-divine beings, each having a specific sphere of influence and associated symbols. There were twelve principal Olympian gods, who were believed to reside on Mount Olympus, the highest peak in Greece.

Zeus, the king of the gods, presided over the sky and was associated with thunderbolts. Hera, his wife, was the goddess of marriage, while their daughter Athena was the goddess of wisdom and warfare. Poseidon, brother of Zeus, ruled over the sea, and Demeter, their sister, was the goddess of agriculture. These are examples of the intricate web of divine entities that the Greeks believed influenced their daily lives and the natural world.

Formation of Major Greek Gods and Goddesses

During the Archaic period (800-480 BCE), the intricate narratives and characteristics associated with the major Greek gods and goddesses were progressively formulated and codified. This formation process, far from being a sudden or isolated development, was a nuanced and dynamic one, drawing significantly from a variety of influences, including the religious frameworks of the preceding Mycenaean and Minoan civilizations.

Consider the case of Zeus. In the Mycenaean period, Zeus was predominantly associated with meteorological phenomena, effectively functioning as a weather deity. Yet, during the Archaic period, the figure of Zeus underwent substantial evolution. He was progressively recast into a universal sovereign, embodying not just the power of the skies but also the concepts of law, order, and justice. This transformation from a somewhat limited weather deity into the supreme arbiter of justice and social order signifies the conceptual expansion in the Greek perception of divinity. It also underscores how deities could evolve over time, adapting to the shifting religious, social, and philosophical landscapes.

Athena offers another revealing example of this transformative process. Traces of Athena, as a deity associated with the city and warfare, can be traced back to the Mycenaean period, substantiated by the 'Linear B' tablets found at Pylos. Nevertheless, her evolution did not halt with the end of the Mycenaean civilization. During the Archaic and Classical periods, Athena transformed into a multifaceted goddess, patronizing not just warfare, but also wisdom, crafts, and strategic planning. This embellishment of Athena's portfolio, adding layers to her divine persona, exemplifies the dynamism inherent in the Greek religious imagination.

It would be remiss to confine the exploration of the formation of Greek deities solely within the geographical or cultural bounds of Greece. Indeed, the Greek pantheon and mythology were also shaped profoundly by their interaction with other cultures, especially those of the East. Through the processes of colonization, trade, and cultural exchange, the Greeks were exposed to an array of religious practices and ideas.

The impact of these Eastern influences is discernible in the transformation of Greek gods during the Archaic period. One such deity is Apollo, who seems to have had no clear Mycenaean precursor. Apollo, in the Greek pantheon, is associated with an array of spheres such as music, prophecy, healing, and light, which includes the sun. Notably, the sun and prophecy were significant elements in several Eastern religions. The association of Apollo with these aspects is indicative of the syncretic adoption of foreign elements, amalgamating them seamlessly into the indigenous religious fabric.

In conclusion, the formation of the major Greek gods and goddesses was a dynamic, multifaceted process, involving the continuous evolution of deity characteristics and narratives over time, drawing from the Mycenaean and Minoan past, and assimilating influences from encounters with foreign cultures. The end product was a richly diverse and complex pantheon, reflecting the unique cultural trajectory of the Greek civilization and its constant interaction with a broader Mediterranean world. The study of this formation process offers fascinating insights into the fluidity of ancient religions and the complex cultural interactions that shaped them.

Conclusion

The Greek pantheon that emerged during the Archaic period reflects a synthesis of domestic and foreign influences, a testament to the cultural dynamism of this era. The deities, each with their unique narratives and attributes, offer us a complex mirror into how the ancient Greeks perceived their world and their place in it.

Exercises:

Analyze the evolution of Zeus from the Mycenaean period through the Archaic period. What changes in his attributes and worship can you identify?

Compare the characteristics of the Greek goddess Athena in the Archaic period with those of a female deity from the Minoan period. Can you trace any influences?

Discussion Questions:

How did the Greek deities evolve during the Archaic period to reflect changes in society and culture?

In what ways did interaction with Eastern cultures influence the formation of the Greek pantheon during the Archaic period?

Critical Thinking Challenge:

Consider the formation of major Greek gods and goddesses in the context of Greece's geographical location and historical interactions. How did these factors influence the development of the Greek pantheon? Can you identify similar processes of religious evolution in other historical or contemporary contexts?

The Role of Homer and Hesiod in Shaping Greek Mythology

In understanding the evolution of Greek mythology, one must delve into the profound influences of Homer and Hesiod, two preeminent figures of ancient Greek literature. Their works, notably the Homeric epics and Hesiod's 'Theogony' and 'Works and Days', played a crucial role in shaping and disseminating Greek mythology, thereby serving as vital links between the archaic oral traditions and the later literary canon.

Homer's Influence

Homer, the reputed author of the "Iliad" and the "Odyssey," had an indisputable influence on Greek mythology. His epic poems, centered around the Trojan War and its aftermath, formed an expansive corpus of mythological narratives, characters, and tales. These narratives provided not merely shape and form to diverse mythological accounts, but they also endowed the gods and heroes with distinct personas, moral orientations, and ethical quandaries.

One significant element of Homeric epics is the anthropomorphization of the deities. Gods and goddesses in Homer's work display a range of human emotions and motivations. They meddle in human affairs, often taking sides with different heroes and, thus, underscoring the juncture between the divine and human spheres. This representation was a notable shift from the Mycenaean religious practices, where deities were envisioned more as distant and awe-inspiring entities.

By providing personalities to gods and heroes, Homer contributed to the vividness and relatability of Greek mythology. For instance, in the "Iliad," Achilles' wrath and heroic valor, Agamemnon's pride, and Hector's nobility were conveyed not just through their actions but also through their interactions with gods. These interactions presented an image of gods who could be reasoned with, petitioned, and even manipulated. Thus, Homer's depiction of gods resonated with the common populace, making them accessible and allowing for a more intimate connection between humanity and the divine.

Moreover, Homer's epics were not merely tales of heroic deeds; they explored intricate issues of morality, honor, wrath, revenge, and love. These tales served as an essential source for moral education, presenting ethical quandaries and their resolutions through the actions of gods and heroes.

Another noteworthy aspect of Homer's influence is the incorporation of ritualistic practices within his epics. In both the "Iliad" and "Odyssey," the depiction of rituals, prayers, and sacrifices reflected contemporary religious practices, thereby offering us glimpses into the religious life of ancient Greeks. Furthermore, the repetition of these rituals in the epics could have served to reinforce these practices among the listeners and readers, thereby shaping Greek religious behavior.

Despite the significant influence of Homer on Greek mythology, it is crucial to remember that his works were part of a broader tradition. Greek mythology, like its religion, was not a static or uniform entity but was a dynamic system subject to variations, adaptations, and regional differences. Homer's epics, therefore, should not be seen as definitive texts but rather as one among many sources that shaped Greek religious and mythological landscapes.

In conclusion, through his epics, Homer indelibly impacted Greek mythology, shaping the character of gods and heroes, infusing myths with moral dimensions, and reflecting ritualistic practices. His contribution, however, should be understood within the larger, fluid tradition of Greek mythology and religion. By studying Homer's influence, we can appreciate the complexity and richness of Greek mythology, and its deep entwinement with the cultural, moral, and religious fabric of ancient Greek society.

Hesiod's Contribution

Hesiod, another monumental figure in ancient Greek literature, is particularly recognized for his works "Theogony" and "Works and Days". "Theogony" introduces an account of the world's origin and the genealogy of the gods, thereby acting as a cosmogonic and theogonic narrative. This work methodically organizes the Greek pantheon, detailing the lineage of gods, their responsibilities, and interconnections. The story of chaos transforming into an ordered universe under the governance of Zeus provided a coherent structure to disparate myths, significantly influencing subsequent cosmological narratives.

In "Theogony", Hesiod outlines the primordial beginnings from Chaos to the reign of Zeus, the Sky God. In doing so, Hesiod provides a systematized account of divine genealogy and the complex relationships among the gods. For instance, the Titanomachy, a mythical ten-year war between the Titans and the Olympians, depicts the struggle and subsequent succession of power from one generation of gods (Titans) to the next (Olympians). Such narratives not only rationalize the power structures within the pantheon but also mirror societal transitions and the legitimization of power structures within human societies.

Contrarily, "Works and Days" presents moral and practical instructions for men, embodying a wisdom tradition. The work offers a glimpse into the socio-economic conditions of the time. Moreover, it incorporates the myth of Prometheus and Pandora, pivotal figures in Greek mythology. The narrative of Prometheus, the Titan who defied Zeus by stealing fire for humans, and Pandora, the first woman whose curiosity led to the release of all evils into the world, underscores the complexities of human life and the divine-human relationship.

Hesiod's works also feature the theme of divine justice and retribution. The tale of Prometheus's punishment and the ensuing suffering of humans through Pandora's actions underscores the concept of divine retribution. Similarly, in "Works and Days",

Hesiod emphasizes the importance of hard work, justice, and righteous living, cautioning against deceit and laziness. Thus, Hesiod's works served as both a source of moral and ethical guidance and a reflection of societal norms and values.

Moreover, through the structured pantheon and systematic genealogy of gods presented in "Theogony", Hesiod contributed to the development of Greek mythology by introducing consistency and order. His works had a profound influence on Greek religious thought by providing a theological basis for religious practices, shaping the perception of the divine, and reinforcing societal values.

However, like Homer's works, Hesiod's narratives should not be viewed as definitive accounts. Greek mythology was a complex, multifaceted tradition with diverse regional variations and interpretive possibilities. Therefore, the influences of Hesiod should be understood as one of the many layers shaping the intricate tapestry of Greek mythology.

In conclusion, through his works, Hesiod had an indelible impact on Greek mythology and religion, structuring the pantheon, defining divine-human relationships, and outlining ethical and moral principles. By examining Hesiod's influence, we can further appreciate the complexities of Greek mythology and its deep intertwining with the social, moral, and religious fabric of ancient Greek society.

Impact on Greek Mythology

The contributions of Homer and Hesiod have served as a cornerstone in the formation of Greek mythology, granting structure, coherence, and depth to an extensive array of myths. Their narratives did not solely mould the religious beliefs and practices of the ancient Greeks; they also offered a moral and ethical compass that permeated into various aspects of their socio-cultural life.

The Homeric and Hesiodic cosmogonies granted Greek mythology its systemic structure, organizing the divine world and laying down the genealogical hierarchy of gods. They also provided identities to the gods, infusing them with human-like qualities and emotions, an aspect that allowed the ancient Greeks to perceive their deities as entities with whom they could relate. This anthropomorphization of gods, as well as the depiction of the divine-human interaction, were integral to the formation of a personalized religious experience in ancient Greece.

In the narratives of Homer and Hesiod, one discerns a palpable transition from the somewhat remote and elemental deities of the Minoan and Mycenaean cultures towards more complex, anthropomorphized gods and goddesses. This evolution showcases not only a progression in the theological constructs but also underscores the dynamic nature of religious transformation, an area of study that is essential for understanding the evolution of societies and cultures at large.

The influence of Homer and Hesiod extended beyond the realm of literature and religion, penetrating deeply into the educational system of ancient Greece. The narratives they provided, teeming with tales of heroes, gods, and moral lessons, were integral to the 'paideia' – the Greek system of education. They not only acted as literary textbooks but also served as ethical guides, setting standards for heroism, honour, and moral conduct. Consequently, the influence of these works was far-reaching, shaping the moral and cultural ethos of ancient Greek society.

Further, their impact was observable in the visual arts of the period. Scenes from the epics and theogonic narratives often found expression in sculpture, pottery, and other forms of art. This wide-ranging depiction reflects the extent to which these works were embedded in the societal consciousness of the Greeks.

Moreover, the depiction of a wide range of characters - gods, demigods, and mortals - and their complex interrelationships in the Homeric and Hesiodic narratives also offered an important platform for the exploration of a myriad of themes such as power, justice, love, vengeance, honour, and the human condition. Thus, these narratives not only enriched the mythic imagination but also provided a deep and profound reflection on life's existential dilemmas.

In conclusion, the works of Homer and Hesiod significantly influenced Greek mythology and beyond. Their narratives lent coherence and depth to the diverse myths, infused the gods with distinct personalities, provided a moral and ethical framework, and significantly influenced the socio-cultural and artistic expressions of ancient Greece. By understanding their influence, we gain not only a deeper insight into Greek mythology but also a nuanced appreciation of the dynamic interplay between mythology, culture, religion, and society in ancient civilizations.

Exercises:

Examine how Homer's depiction of gods in the 'Iliad' and the 'Odyssey' differ from the representation of gods in Mycenaean religious practices.

Analyze Hesiod's 'Theogony' and its influence on the structuring of the Greek pantheon.

Discussion Questions:

What roles do Homer and Hesiod's works play in shaping Greek mythology and the perception of deities?

How did the narratives of Homer and Hesiod influence the socio-cultural life of the Greeks?

Critical Thinking Challenge:

Consider the cultural and historical context in which Homer and Hesiod composed their works. How did these contexts shape their narratives? Furthermore, how did their works, in turn, influence the socio-cultural and religious milieu of their time? Can you identify similar dynamics in the context of other mythologies or religious systems?

The significance of Homer's epics in preserving Mycenaean and Greek religious narratives

The Homeric epics, namely the 'Iliad' and the 'Odyssey', are cornerstones of Western literature, providing a comprehensive panorama of Greek society, culture, and religion. Their importance in preserving Mycenaean and Greek religious narratives cannot be overstated. They serve as profound reservoirs of ancient Greek religiosity and offer a rare glimpse into the transition from the Mycenaean era to the Archaic period, framing an intricate tapestry of mythical narratives, moral values, and socio-cultural norms.

Homeric Epics as Cultural Memories

Homer's epics, composed during the 8th century BCE, represent a pivotal point in Greek literature where oral tradition coalesced into a monumental written narrative. They preserve a palimpsest of memories from the Bronze Age Mycenaean civilization, which collapsed around 1100 BCE, and the evolving religious consciousness of Archaic Greece.

The Trojan War, around which the 'Iliad' revolves, reflects echoes of Mycenaean military expeditions and their associated narratives. The 'Iliad' and 'Odyssey' are replete with descriptions of religious rituals, prayers, sacrifices, and the intervening role of gods in human affairs – elements traceable back to the Mycenaean era but also illustrative of the evolving religious practices of the Archaic period.

Homeric Epics as Religious Texts

The Homeric epics serve as quasi-religious texts that elucidate the Greek pantheon, divine-human interactions, and the ethical framework underpinning Greek society. The gods in Homer's epics are anthropomorphic, possessing human-like characteristics and emotions, reflecting a shift from the more remote deities of the Mycenaean period.

The epics illustrate the practice of hero worship, a prominent feature of Greek religion. Heroes like Achilles and Odysseus embody exceptional human qualities and are accorded semi-divine status. They provide a moral and ethical compass for the society, and their tales of bravery, cunning, and perseverance continue to shape societal norms and values.

Homer's Epics as Sources of Myth

Homer's epics also serve as a crucial source of Greek myth. They provide narratives for a multitude of gods, demigods, heroes, and other mythological creatures, preserving and disseminating their stories for future generations. The narratives of the epics are deeply intertwined with the religious life of the Greeks, guiding their understanding of the cosmos, the divine, and their place within it.

Conclusion

In summary, Homer's epics play a significant role in preserving Mycenaean and Greek religious narratives. They offer a bridge between the Mycenaean past and the evolving religious consciousness of the Archaic period, encapsulating the transition within their epic narratives. Through their portrayal of gods, heroes, and religious rituals, they provide an invaluable insight into the religious life of ancient Greeks.

Exercises:

Examine specific rituals or religious practices described in the 'Iliad' or the 'Odyssey'. How do these reflect the Mycenaean influence and the evolving religious consciousness of the Archaic Greeks?

Discussion Questions:

How does the anthropomorphic portrayal of gods in Homer's epics differ from the earlier representations of deities in the Mycenaean period?

Critical Thinking Challenge:

Consider the narratives of Achilles and Odysseus in the Homeric epics. How do these heroes embody the ethical and moral values of their time? How do their stories reflect the religious beliefs and practices of the ancient Greeks?

Hesiod's Theogony and its role in defining the genealogy of the gods

"Theogony," a poem attributed to Hesiod, a contemporary of Homer, is a seminal work that systematically presents the genealogy of Greek deities. Hesiod's composition is invaluable in understanding the conception of the cosmos, the hierarchy of gods, and the creation myths of ancient Greece. Composed in the late 8th or early 7th century BCE, "Theogony" is a narrative that combines cosmogony (creation of the world) with theogony (birth of the gods), offering an intricate map of divine familial relations and power struggles.

Hesiod's Theogony: A Cosmic Family Tree

In the epic poem, Hesiod delineates the origins and lineage of the Greek deities, establishing a complex familial network of gods, titans, and primordial entities. The narrative begins with Chaos, the primordial void, followed by the advent of Earth (Gaia), Tartarus (the underworld), Eros (Love), Erebus (Darkness), and Night (Nyx). From these primeval beings sprang the next generation of gods, notably the Titans, who were subsequently overthrown by their offspring, the Olympian gods, led by Zeus.

A striking feature of the "Theogony" is the depiction of gods not as abstract divine entities, but as characters with human-like characteristics and family relationships. The poem showcases generational conflicts, matrimonial alliances, rebellions, and successions, mirroring the dynamics of a human aristocratic society.

Hesiod and the Structuring of the Divine Order

Hesiod's "Theogony" played a cardinal role in defining the divine order of the Greek pantheon. The structured genealogy brought coherence and order to what was previously an array of scattered divine entities. It helped establish the supremacy of the Olympian gods, notably Zeus, over the Titans and primordial deities.

By narrating the sequence of cosmic succession, from Chaos to the Titans and then the Olympian gods, Hesiod proposed a sense of progression and cosmic justice.

The omnipotence of Zeus, established by his victory over the Titans, signified the triumph of order over chaos and the imposition of moral righteousness over the universe.

Hesiod's Contribution to Greek Cosmology

The cosmological narrative of the "Theogony" offers insights into the ancient Greeks' understanding of the universe's structure. Hesiod depicted an anthropocentric cosmos, with the Earth at its center, surrounded by the river Oceanus, and capped by the heavens, home to the gods. This cosmology would shape Greek philosophical thought and literature for centuries.

Conclusion

Hesiod's "Theogony" represents a foundational text for understanding Greek mythology and religion. The intricate genealogical web woven by Hesiod offers a comprehensive framework to understand the relationships among the Greek gods and their roles in the cosmos. It set the stage for the articulation of Greek religious thought and offered a cosmological narrative that resonated with the intellectual spirit of the Archaic age.

Exercises:

Analyze the narrative of the 'Titanomachy' in the "Theogony". How does this conflict reflect the societal changes and power dynamics in ancient Greece?

Discussion Questions:

How did Hesiod's "Theogony" contribute to the formation of the Greek pantheon and the establishment of a divine hierarchy?

Critical Thinking Challenge:

Consider Hesiod's anthropomorphic depiction of gods. What does this human-like portrayal tell us about the worldview and beliefs of ancient Greeks? How does it differ from or align with other ancient or modern religious conceptions of divinity?

How epic poetry influenced Greek religious beliefs and practices

Epic poetry, with its grand narratives and heroic exploits, played a vital role in shaping ancient Greek religion. These epics, notably the Homeric poems, "The Iliad" and "The Odyssey," and Hesiod's "Theogony" and "Works and Days," exerted profound influence on the formation and evolution of Greek religious beliefs and practices. The influence is evident in the mythology, the depiction of deities, and the embodiment of ethics and values that pervaded Greek society.

Epic Poetry as a Source of Mythology

One of the primary contributions of epic poetry to Greek religion is its rich repertoire of myths, offering detailed narratives about gods, heroes, and the world's creation. Hesiod's "Theogony" traces the lineage of the gods, laying the foundation for the Greek pantheon and cosmology. Homer's epics offer a vibrant portrayal of the gods and their interactions with humans, with the Homeric gods often displaying human-like characteristics. These narratives brought the divine world closer to the human world, giving tangible form to abstract religious concepts.

Epic Poetry and the Anthropomorphic Pantheon

The influence of epic poetry is perhaps most apparent in the anthropomorphism of Greek deities. Epic poets portrayed gods in human form, ascribing to them human emotions and motivations. This anthropomorphic representation not only made the gods more relatable but also reflected the human-centered worldview of the Greeks. The gods of Homer and Hesiod are not distant divine beings but active participants in human affairs, showcasing the intimate connection between the divine and human realms.

Epic Poetry and Ethical Norms

Epic poetry also contributed to the ethical framework of Greek religion. Homeric and Hesiodic poetry are replete with moral lessons, often delivered through divine interventions and the fates of heroes. Respect for the gods, adherence to oaths, hospitality, and the concept of 'hubris' (excessive pride or self-confidence) followed by 'nemesis' (retribution), are recurring themes in these epics. The ethical principles conveyed through epic poetry provided moral guidance and shaped religious conduct in Greek society.

Epic Poetry and Ritual Practices

Epic poetry also had implications for Greek religious rituals. Homeric descriptions of sacrificial practices, funeral rites, and supplications influenced real-life ceremonies. They provided a blueprint for ritual actions, thus integrating the narratives of epic poetry into everyday religious life.

Conclusion

The impact of epic poetry on Greek religion was profound and multifaceted. It offered a rich tapestry of myths, shaped the character of the Greek pantheon, infused religious conduct with ethical norms, and informed ritual practices. As such, epic poetry was not just a form of entertainment; it was a medium through which the ancient Greeks explored, understood, and articulated their religious beliefs and practices.

Exercises:

Analyze the depiction of the gods in the Homeric poems. How does this portrayal influence the understanding of the divine in ancient Greek religion?

Discussion Questions:

How did the ethical norms presented in epic poetry shape Greek religious practices and societal values?

Critical Thinking Challenge:

Consider the anthropomorphic portrayal of gods in Greek epic poetry. How does this human-centered depiction compare with divine representations in other ancient religions?

Conclusion

Summary of Mycenaean Religious Beliefs and Their Impact on the Development of Greek Mythology

Mycenaean civilization, at its zenith from 1600 to 1100 BCE, substantially influenced the development of Greek mythology. The Mycenaeans inherited and integrated a wealth of religious beliefs from the Minoans, including a pantheon of deities that bore striking resemblances to the later Greek gods and goddesses. The gods of the Mycenaeans, including Poseidon, Zeus, Hermes, and Hera, were absorbed into the religious landscape of the Greeks, shaping the foundational structure of the Greek pantheon.

Linear B tablets reveal traces of Mycenaean religious rituals, including sacrifices and offerings, which would echo in later Greek cult practices. These religious beliefs and practices, deeply ingrained in Mycenaean society, formed a significant part of the religious legacy that the Mycenaeans bequeathed to the Greek civilization.

Reflection on the Significance of the Transition Period for the Evolution of the Greek Pantheon

The period following the decline of the Mycenaean civilization, often referred to as the Dark Ages (c. 1100-800 BCE), played a pivotal role in the evolution of the Greek pantheon. Despite the societal disintegration that characterized this era, the Mycenaean religious beliefs persisted and intermingled with new ideas, leading to a pantheon that was a blend of old and new elements.

The deities underwent a transformation during this period. Some Mycenaean deities faded into obscurity, while others were syncretized with similar divinities from other cultures. The anthropomorphic traits of the gods, their roles, and hierarchies became more defined during this transitional period. By the time of the Archaic Period (c. 800-500 BCE), the Greek pantheon, as we understand it today, was largely in place.

The Lasting Legacy of Mycenaean Religion in Greek Culture and Its Influence on Western Civilization

Mycenaean religion, despite its prehistoric origins, left an enduring legacy in Greek culture. The religious beliefs, myths, and ritual practices of the Mycenaeans became the cornerstones of Greek religion, which in turn significantly influenced Western civilization.

The impact of Mycenaean religion is discernible in the Greek pantheon, the epic poetry of Homer and Hesiod, and the ethical and philosophical discourses that informed Greek society. The Greek gods, with their human-like attributes and complex personalities, not only played a crucial role in Greek literature and art but also shaped the Greek understanding of the cosmos and human nature.

The influence of Mycenaean and, by extension, Greek religious beliefs extended beyond the confines of Greece. As Greek culture spread across the Mediterranean through conquest and trade, so did its religious ideas. The Romans, most notably, absorbed the Greek gods into their pantheon, leading to a remarkable cultural synthesis. The myths, religious practices, and philosophical ideas rooted in Mycenaean and Greek religion left a profound imprint on Western literature, art, philosophy, and theology, making it a pivotal aspect of our cultural heritage.

Chapter 7: The Influence of Minoan and Mycenaean Cultures on Greek Religion

The labyrinthine corridors of Greek religion and mythology, replete with a pantheon of anthropomorphic gods, goddesses, heroes, and myriad supernatural beings, stand as one of the most vivid and intriguing facets of the cultural heritage of Greece. The inception of this pantheon, far from being a singular or isolated event, is embedded in a matrix of cultural interactions and historical evolutions spanning millennia. The cultures that significantly contributed to this intricate weave were those of the Minoans and the Mycenaeans, the advanced civilizations that predate Classical Greece. Both cultures, in their distinct ways, bequeathed a rich corpus of religious ideas, practices, and iconographies that would shape the Greek pantheon and its attendant myths.

In this chapter, we shall delve into the profound influence of the Minoan and Mycenaean cultures on Greek religion. We shall explore the religious ideas of these early cultures, how these ideas were transmitted to the Greeks, and the ways in which they were absorbed, adapted, and transformed in the Greek religious milieu.

The Minoan civilization, thriving on the island of Crete from approximately 3000 to 1450 BCE, was characterized by its advanced urban planning, sophisticated art, and a religious tradition that seems to have been dominated by female deities and nature worship. The subsequent Mycenaean civilization, centered in mainland Greece from around 1600 to 1100 BCE, appears to have incorporated and modified Minoan religious practices, while also introducing its unique contributions.

This chapter provides an overview of the impact of these civilizations, drawing on archaeological discoveries, the decipherment of Linear B script, and subsequent interpretations by historians and archaeologists. Through a comparative study of Minoan and Mycenaean religions, we aim to illuminate the threads of continuity and transformation that culminated in the rich tapestry of Greek religion.

As we traverse through the layers of time, we will also explore contentious debates among scholars regarding the interpretation of the archaeological and textual evidence. We encourage students to critically analyze the available evidence, engage with varying interpretations, and formulate their nuanced understanding of this complex subject. The journey promises to be one of exploration and discovery, offering invaluable insights into the birth and development of one of the world's most influential religious systems.

Overview of Minoan and Mycenaean civilizations

The ancient Minoan and Mycenaean civilizations, residing on the cusp of the Bronze Age and the nascent stirrings of classical antiquity, cast a profound influence upon subsequent Greek culture and religion. Both civilizations emerged in a region characterized by its vibrant cultural interactions, territorial rivalries, and trade networks, which fostered an environment ripe for the exchange and modification of religious ideas.

The Minoan civilization, named after the legendary King Minos, blossomed on the island of Crete, with its duration traditionally segmented into three periods: the Early Minoan (EM, circa 3000–2100 BCE), Middle Minoan (MM, circa 2100–1600 BCE), and Late Minoan (LM, circa 1600–1100 BCE) periods. Notable for their remarkable frescoes, pottery, and labyrinthine palace complexes such as Knossos and Phaistos, the Minoans demonstrated an advanced understanding of architecture and aesthetic expression. The complexity of Minoan art, with its recurring motifs of nature, animals, and seemingly divine figures, suggests a rich spiritual life.

Interestingly, Minoan religion appears to have emphasized female deities, often portrayed amidst nature or animals, hinting at a potential matriarchal socio-religious structure. However, the absence of deciphered written records from this civilization leaves much to conjecture and interpretation based on archaeological findings, leading to divergent scholarly theories.

The Mycenaean civilization, contemporaneous with the Late Minoan period and extending to around 1100 BCE, originated on the Greek mainland with prominent centers at Mycenae, Tiryns, and Pylos. The Mycenaeans are often credited with the introduction of the Greek language and Linear B script, providing invaluable written records that shed light on their socio-political structure and religious beliefs. The decipherment of Linear B tablets has revealed references to various deities, some of whom show continuity with the later Greek pantheon.

Mycenaean religion, in comparison to the Minoan, appears to have been more oriented towards male deities and hierarchical in its divine and socio-religious structure, perhaps reflecting the warrior-centric nature of Mycenaean society. The Mycenaeans seemingly integrated Minoan religious elements with their indigenous beliefs, evidenced by the presence of Minoan symbols and deities in Mycenaean contexts and the modification of Minoan religious sites.

It is important to note that the distinctions and characterizations of these civilizations are not devoid of challenges and ambiguities. Our knowledge of these cultures is constrained by the incomplete and often enigmatic archaeological and textual evidence, inviting continuous scholarly dialogue and reinterpretation. In the following sections, we shall explore these civilizations' specific contributions to Greek religion, emphasizing the process of cultural adaptation and transformation that led to the rich and multifaceted Greek religious tradition.

Significance of studying their influence on Greek religion

It is indeed an intriguing endeavor to trace the origins and evolution of religious beliefs, rituals, and myths, all of which constitute an integral part of a society's cultural fabric and worldview. The study of Minoan and Mycenaean influences on Greek religion holds a unique place in such an exploration. Understanding the complex interplay between these early civilizations and their successive influence on Greek religion offers valuable insights into cultural transmission, adaptation, and transformation processes.

Firstly, the investigation of Minoan and Mycenaean religions can contribute significantly to the identification of continuity and change in religious phenomena. By comparing Minoan, Mycenaean, and subsequent Greek religious elements, scholars may trace the persistence of specific symbols, rituals, and deities, as well as the emergence of novel religious practices and concepts. Such an examination can reveal the dynamic nature of religious traditions and the ways they respond to socio-cultural shifts, such as changes in political power, technological advancements, and intercultural interactions.

Moreover, the analysis of these ancient religions helps in dissecting the diverse influences shaping Greek mythology, a central aspect of Greek religion. Myths are not merely fantastical narratives; they are imbued with deep cultural, moral, and metaphysical significances, reflecting the human endeavor to comprehend the world and the human condition. The Minoan and Mycenaean contributions to the Greek mythological corpus, such as elements related to the myths of Minos, Daedalus, and the Labyrinth in Crete or the heroic tales connected to Mycenae, can be better understood within the broader framework of these civilizations' cultures and worldviews.

Additionally, studying the Minoan and Mycenaean influence offers an opportunity to critically engage with the complexities and limitations of archaeological and literary evidence. The decipherment and interpretation of archaeological artifacts and inscriptions is a challenging task that involves a sophisticated understanding of material culture, ancient scripts, and linguistics. This process can foster critical thinking skills, cautioning students against overgeneralization and encouraging a balanced evaluation of multiple interpretations.

Lastly, the investigation of Minoan and Mycenaean influences on Greek religion can illuminate the interconnectedness of ancient Mediterranean cultures and their enduring legacies. The study promotes a holistic understanding of the ancient world, where cultures were not isolated entities but participated in intricate networks of exchange and interaction. This recognition fosters an appreciation of cultural diversity and the transformative power of intercultural engagements, insights that remain pertinent to our increasingly globalized world.

Thus, the exploration of Minoan and Mycenaean influences is not a mere antiquarian pursuit. It is a vibrant field of study that offers profound insights into human culture, imagination, and the quest for meaning, bridging the temporal gap and connecting us with our ancient past in enlightening ways.

The interconnectedness of ancient Mediterranean cultures

A fundamental tenet of historical and cultural analysis acknowledges that no civilization exists in a vacuum. The sphere of the ancient Mediterranean is a compelling exemplar of this principle, demonstrating a vibrant matrix of interconnection, interaction, and influence among various cultures. This interplay significantly shaped societal, artistic, technological, and importantly for our context, religious landscapes, generating a dynamic and complex cultural tapestry that extends beyond geographical and temporal boundaries.

A grand narrative of interconnectivity begins with the emergence of the Minoan civilization on Crete and the Cycladic culture in the Aegean Sea. The Minoans, in particular, built a formidable maritime empire, establishing extensive trade networks that enabled cultural and religious interaction with multiple regions, including Egypt, the Near East, and the Cyclades. Evidence from archaeological excavations, such as Minoan-style frescoes in Egyptian Thebes and Egyptian artifacts in Minoan Crete, underline the existence of such intercultural exchanges.

With the ascendancy of the Mycenaean civilization in mainland Greece, which likely incorporated elements of Minoan culture through a process of cultural assimilation or syncretism, the scope of Mediterranean interconnectivity expanded further. Mycenaean artifacts discovered in places as distant as Italy, Anatolia, and even the Levant bear testimony to this wide-ranging cultural interaction. Consequently, the Mycenaean religious and mythological components would have permeated these regions, enhancing the dissemination of particular deities, rituals, and mythic narratives.

Following the collapse of the Mycenaean civilization, a period known as the "Dark Ages" ensued, leading to a temporary hiatus in these extensive intercultural connections. However, with the advent of the Archaic period, the Greek city-states embarked upon a new era of expansion and exploration, forging alliances, initiating conflicts, establishing colonies, and revitalizing trade routes across the Mediterranean. These activities, in turn, influenced and were influenced by the religious beliefs and practices of the interacting cultures, contributing to the Greek pantheon's evolving character.

This intricate web of interconnections was not a one-way avenue of influence. The cultures that interacted with the Greeks, such as the Egyptians, Phoenicians, and Etruscans, also left indelible imprints on their religion and mythology. For example, the Greek god Hermes may have been influenced by the Egyptian Thoth, and the Phoenician Melqart may have contributed to the Greek conception of Heracles.

In essence, the religious and cultural milieu of the ancient Mediterranean was a dynamic, interactive sphere, where elements were adopted, adapted, and transformed in response to a multitude of factors, including trade, politics, migration, and warfare. This understanding calls for a nuanced interpretation of ancient cultures that recognizes the intricate tapestry of interconnections that underlie the development of cultural phenomena, including religion. It is a reminder of the shared human history and the rich cultural symbiosis that has shaped our collective past. In essence, to comprehend Greek religion is to embark upon a journey that traverses the ancient Mediterranean's cultural horizons, reflecting an interconnected world that still resonates with our contemporary reality.

The Minoan Civilization: Religion and Iconography

The Minoan civilization, flourishing on the island of Crete from around 2000 to 1450 BC, left behind a rich repository of archaeological evidence, providing us with insights into their religious beliefs, practices, and iconography. However, due to the lack of deciphered textual evidence, much of our understanding depends upon material culture, including frescoes, statuettes, pottery, and the architecture of the palace-temples.

A central characteristic of Minoan religion seems to be its theogonic orientation. The figure of the goddess, portrayed in various roles and often accompanied by nature motifs, is a recurrent feature, suggesting a possible matriarchal or matrifocal religious system. The "snake goddess" figurines found at the palace of Knossos offer fascinating insight. Depicting women with exposed breasts, holding or surrounded by serpents, these figurines might point towards a fertility cult, a common theme in ancient Near Eastern and Mediterranean religions. However, this interpretation remains speculative due to our limited knowledge of Minoan language and culture.

Other prominent symbols in Minoan religious iconography include the bull and the double axe. The bull is a recurring motif in Minoan frescoes and ceramics, with depictions of bull-leaping rituals perhaps suggesting a form of bull worship or a ritual of passage. The double axe, or 'labrys,' is another significant religious symbol, often found in archaeological sites associated with Minoan religion. It has been suggested that the term 'labyrinth,' referring to the palace complex at Knossos, is derived from 'labrys,' possibly indicating the presence of a religious function or ritual involving the double axe.

Minoan religious practice also appears to have encompassed natural elements, with evidence of worship in open-air sanctuaries, peak sanctuaries, and cave sites, suggesting a veneration of natural landscapes and possibly an animistic belief system. Items such as stone libation tables and clay figurines, often found in these sites, further support the notion of outdoor rituals.

Palatial complexes, such as Knossos, Phaistos, and Malia, present a distinctive architectural feature: the 'lustral basin'—a small, sunken room accessed by a set of steps, typically lined with gypsum. While initially believed to be used for ritual purification, recent interpretations propose they may have served as repositories for sacred objects or spaces for initiation rituals.

The legacy of Minoan religion and its influence on subsequent Greek religion is a subject of ongoing scholarly debate. The ubiquity of the goddess figure and the symbols of the bull and double axe persist into Mycenaean and later Greek iconography. However, discerning direct lines of transmission is challenging due to the complexities of cultural interaction, evolution, and syncretism. Furthermore, the decipherment of Linear A, the script used for Minoan administrative purposes, remains a challenge that, once accomplished, will undoubtedly provide a more comprehensive understanding of Minoan religious beliefs and practices.

To encapsulate, the study of Minoan religion, though fraught with interpretive challenges, contributes valuable dimensions to our understanding of ancient Mediterranean religions. Its distinctive iconography, emphasis on natural and palatial spaces for worship, and possible focus on goddess worship present a compelling religious panorama that reverberates through later Greek religious thought, offering us a lens into the rich tapestry of interconnected ancient Mediterranean religious landscapes.

Overview of Minoan religious practices and beliefs

While the decipherment of Minoan script, known as Linear A, remains an unfinished task, we are not left bereft of information regarding Minoan religious practices and beliefs. Evidence gleaned from archaeological discoveries—art, artifacts, and architecture—offers valuable insights into the Minoan spiritual world.

An apparent pantheistic feature of Minoan religion can be discerned from the archaeological record. Deities associated with natural phenomena—mountains, caves, trees, animals, and the underworld—figure prominently in Minoan iconography. This strong nature-oriented focus suggests a religion deeply embedded in the rhythms of the natural world and reflective of the agrarian structure of Minoan society.

Fertility cults also appear to have been of significant import, as suggested by a prevalence of female figurines, often depicted with snakes or doves, symbols that may denote regenerative aspects of nature and are linked to fertility in many ancient cultures. The recurring theme of a dominant female deity, arguably a goddess, could also point to a form of goddess worship.

Rituals seem to have played a central role in Minoan religious life. 'Ritual' here is understood as a structured set of actions performed in a sacred context, aimed at communicating with the divine. Bull-leaping frescoes and figurines discovered at Knossos suggest the possibility of ritualistic bull-leaping, possibly a rite of passage, a fertility ritual, or a form of bull worship. Moreover, the presence of sacrificial altars, libation tables, and 'lustral basins' at palace sites indicate elaborate rituals involving offerings or purification.

Moreover, the locations of Minoan religious activities varied. The grand palatial complexes served as central religious sites, often housing shrines and lustral basins. However, numerous peak sanctuaries, cave sanctuaries, and villas scattered across Crete and the Aegean islands suggest that Minoan religious practice was not confined to palaces alone. These outdoor sanctuaries, often located in geographically significant places—mountain peaks or caves—support the theory of an animistic Minoan belief system that venerated natural elements and landscapes.

Ancestor worship may have been another component of Minoan religion. The presence of burial goods, such as precious jewelry and pottery in Minoan tombs, indicates a belief in an afterlife, a common theme in many ancient religions. However, without written records, it is challenging to ascertain the specific nature of these beliefs and the extent to which they influenced Minoan society.

In sum, while the full spectrum of Minoan religious beliefs and practices remains an enigma due to the undeciphered Linear A, the material evidence points towards a complex and multifaceted religious system. It likely involved goddess worship, fertility rites, bull rituals, nature veneration, possibly ancestor worship, and encompassed both grand palaces and the natural landscapes of Crete as spaces of worship. It is important, however, to interpret these findings with caution, recognizing the potential for varied local religious practices within the Minoan civilization and the limitations imposed by our reliance on material culture in the absence of comprehensible written sources.

Minoan religious centers and their architectural features

The architecture of Minoan religious centers presents a fascinating kaleidoscope of features that not only reflect the socio-cultural milieu of Minoan civilization but also underscore the integral role of religious activities within this society. It must be noted, however, that our understanding of Minoan religious architecture is primarily based on archaeology, and this interpretive lens may come with certain limitations and predispositions.

Palaces, such as those found at Knossos, Phaistos, and Malia, served as prominent religious centers in Minoan Crete. These complexes, equipped with significant architectural features such as courts, storage rooms, shrines, and residential quarters, likely functioned as ceremonial, economic, and administrative hubs. Within these palaces, distinct areas designated for religious activity can be discerned.

One key feature of Minoan palace architecture is the 'lustral basin,' a type of sunken room often associated with purification rituals. Although the term 'lustral' (derived from 'lustratio,' a Roman purification rite) might be a misnomer, it has nonetheless been widely accepted in the archaeological discourse. These basins, often lined with gypsum and accessed via steps, are frequently located near light wells, suggestive of an interplay between architecture and natural elements for ceremonial purposes.

Another noteworthy feature is the 'pillar crypt,' a small, pillar-supported room often found adjacent to a lustral basin. While the exact function of pillar crypts is disputed, the recurring association with lustral basins may suggest a ritualistic purpose.

Minoan palaces often housed 'shrines,' spaces designated for religious worship. These areas are characterized by the presence of 'cult objects,' such as stone or terracotta figurines, double axes, and ritual tables. Shrine rooms often feature 'horns of consecration,' a symbol that possibly represented the sacred bull or mountains, underscoring the nature-oriented elements of Minoan religious belief.

Outside the palatial complexes, 'peak sanctuaries,' positioned on mountain summits, and 'cave sanctuaries,' nestled within naturally occurring caves, offered alternative spaces for religious activities. These sanctuaries, devoid of monumental architecture, relied on their natural surroundings for their sacredness. Archaeological findings, including pottery, figurines, and stone altars, suggest that these were active sites of worship, perhaps serving the broader populace as opposed to the more restricted access of palace-based religious activities.

In conclusion, the architectural features of Minoan religious centers—whether in palatial complexes or natural sanctuaries—offer a window into the spiritual world of Minoan civilization. Their sophistication and diversity reflect a complex society deeply engaged with its natural surroundings and the unseen world of the divine. However, without written records, the specifics of their function and symbolism remain subjects of conjecture and debate, reminding us of the interpretive nature of archaeology.

Iconography in Minoan religious art and its symbolism

The Minoan civilization is renowned for its exquisite art, which is imbued with a rich panoply of iconography reflecting religious beliefs and ritual practices. While we must exercise caution in interpreting these images due to the absence of comprehensive written records, the thematic consistency across various mediums of Minoan artistry affords us some insight into their religious symbolism.

One of the most pervasive motifs in Minoan religious iconography is the figure of the bull. Bull's heads, horns, and scenes of bull-leaping, or "taurokathapsia," frequently appear in Minoan frescoes, seal stones, and ceremonial vessels. The emphasis on the bull may represent a form of animal worship, with the bull symbolizing strength, fertility, and possibly the sun, given its association with light and heat. However, the precise meaning of the bull-leaping ritual remains a matter of scholarly debate. It might symbolize a rite of passage, a form of religious worship, or perhaps a cosmological myth.

The "horns of consecration" are another common symbol found in Minoan religious architecture and art. They are thought to represent the horns of a sacred bull, or possibly an abstract depiction of mountain peaks. They are often associated with sacred spaces, perhaps signifying a boundary between the mortal world and the divine.

In terms of human figures, the most prominent is arguably the "snake goddess" or "faience goddess" figurines. These female figures, often depicted with exposed breasts, holding or surrounded by snakes, are interpreted as deities or priestesses. Their elaborate attire and commanding pose suggest high social or religious status. The snakes, associated with the earth, regeneration, and the cycle of life and death, may indicate these figures' role in fertility or chthonic (underworld) cults.

Another recurring theme in Minoan iconography is the depiction of nature, with marine life, birds, and flowers featuring prominently in frescoes, pottery, and jewelry. These natural motifs might reflect the Minoans' deep appreciation of the natural world, reinforcing the conjecture that Minoan religion was nature-oriented.

In conclusion, the iconography in Minoan religious art reveals a complex spiritual worldview wherein animals, humans, and natural elements are closely interlinked. However, interpretations of this symbolism remain speculative due to our limited understanding of Minoan language and culture. As scholars, we are reminded of the complexities and uncertainties involved in interpreting the visual culture of a civilization primarily through archaeological evidence. Each piece of art serves not only as an artifact but also as a conduit for engaging with the complexities of Minoan belief systems, encouraging ongoing dialogue and inquiry.

Minoan Goddesses and Their Impact on Greek Religion

One of the defining characteristics of the Minoan religious sphere was the prominence of female deities, as evidenced by the plethora of feminine iconography in their art and architecture. This focus on the divine feminine had a substantial influence on the evolution of Greek religion and shaped its pantheon in profound ways.

While our understanding of Minoan goddesses remains imperfect due to the absence of decipherable written records, the existing archaeological and iconographic evidence allows us to hypothesize about their nature and roles. Several recurring motifs and symbols in Minoan religious art suggest the existence of a mother goddess or a group of goddesses associated with fertility, nature, animals, and possibly the underworld. These divine feminine entities were the central figures of Minoan worship, as opposed to the patriarchal orientation of many later religions.

The influence of these Minoan goddesses on Greek religion can be seen in several ways. Firstly, many characteristics of the Minoan goddesses seem to have been incorporated into the personas of Greek goddesses. For example, the Minoan "snake goddess" or "faience goddess" may have influenced the Greek goddesses Athena, who is sometimes depicted with a snake, and Demeter, associated with fertility and the cycle of life and death. Additionally, the nature-oriented aspect of Minoan religion may have influenced the conceptualization of Artemis, the Greek goddess of wildlife and hunting.

Secondly, the Minoan focus on female deities may have contributed to the relatively balanced gender representation in the Greek pantheon. Unlike many ancient religions, which were heavily dominated by male deities, the Greek pantheon included numerous powerful and complex goddesses who played crucial roles in mythology and religious practices.

Lastly, the likely existence of priestesses in Minoan religion, suggested by various depictions of women in religious contexts, might have influenced the institution of priestesses in Greek religion. Although the status and roles of priestesses varied among different city-states and periods in ancient Greece, they were integral to many religious rituals and held significant societal prestige.

In conclusion, while the precise nature of Minoan goddesses and their worship remains somewhat enigmatic, their influence on the evolution of Greek religion is indisputable. The Minoan emphasis on female divinities contributed to the gender diversity of the Greek pantheon and the presence of powerful goddesses with complex personalities and domains. These Minoan roots underscore the dynamic and multifaceted nature of Greek religion, reminding us of the deep historical and cultural layers beneath the myths and gods that are familiar today.

The prominent role of goddesses in Minoan religion

In Minoan society, religion served as a central fulcrum of culture and community, and within its religious framework, the preponderance of feminine deities was a striking feature. In contrast to the predominantly male-oriented pantheons of many ancient civilizations, Minoan religion assigned a prominent place to goddesses, which sheds light on the unique societal structure and gender dynamics of Minoan civilization.

The prevalence of goddesses in Minoan religion is primarily inferred from the extensive array of female figurines and frescoes discovered in palaces, sanctuaries, and peak sanctuaries across Crete. These images often portray women in dynamic and assertive poses, engaging in rituals or surrounded by symbols of nature and fertility. Such depictions signal a high degree of reverence towards female deities and suggest their central role in Minoan religious practices and societal life.

The famed "Snake Goddess" figurines represent one of the most explicit examples of the significance of goddesses in Minoan religion. These statuettes typically feature a woman, or perhaps a goddess, holding one or more snakes in her outstretched hands, a powerful symbol that has been interpreted as a representation of authority and control over natural forces. Similarly, the "Poppy Goddess" figurine, adorned with a crown of poppy capsules, a symbol associated with sleep and death, signifies the possible existence of a goddess with dominion over the transition between life and death.

In addition, there is the figure often referred to as the "Mistress of Animals" found in various Minoan sealstones and ring-seals. This female figure, often depicted in a flanked position by wild animals, strongly suggests the existence of a potent nature goddess. By extension, this suggests an inherent respect for the natural world and its processes within the Minoan spiritual paradigm.

The emphasis on goddesses in Minoan religion may also point towards a matrifocal social structure, although this notion remains subject to scholarly debate. However, it is plausible that the preeminence of goddesses in religious contexts could reflect the significant roles of women in Minoan society. The depictions of women participating in religious ceremonies and rituals, as well as the possible existence of priestesses, offer a glimpse into the active involvement of women in Minoan religious life.

To summarize, the prominence of goddesses in Minoan religion reveals a rich spiritual landscape that valued the feminine divine. The diverse portrayals of goddesses and their associations with nature, fertility, and the cycle of life and death exhibit a profound veneration for natural processes and the feminine principle. This unique religious aspect of Minoan civilization elucidates its distinct cultural identity and provides invaluable insight into the societal roles and perceptions of women in this ancient society.

The assimilation of Minoan goddesses into the Greek pantheon

The profound influence of Minoan religion on subsequent Greek religion is most discernible in the assimilation and adaptation of Minoan goddesses into the Greek pantheon. This intriguing process of cultural syncretism not only underscores the interconnectedness of ancient Mediterranean cultures, but also provides valuable insights into the evolution of religious beliefs and practices.

The prominence of the Great Goddess, who appears to have held dominion over nature, fertility, and possibly the underworld in Minoan religion, has led scholars to draw correlations between this figure and several goddesses of the Greek pantheon. The most salient example is the connection posited between the Minoan Great Goddess and the Greek goddesses Demeter, Persephone, and Artemis.

The Minoan Great Goddess, often represented amidst nature or animals, exhibits strong similarities with the Greek goddess Artemis, who is associated with wild animals and the wilderness. The possible connection between the Minoan Snake Goddess and Artemis is particularly intriguing, considering the latter's association with childbirth and the life-giving aspect of snakes in ancient symbolism.

The Greek goddess Demeter, a central figure in the Eleusinian Mysteries and known for her role as a fertility goddess overseeing the agricultural cycle, may also have evolved from the Minoan Great Goddess. The emphasis on fertility, agricultural abundance, and the cycle of life and death in the cult of Demeter parallels the themes associated with the Minoan Great Goddess.

Persephone, the Greek goddess of the underworld and the springtime growth of vegetation, provides yet another example of the assimilation of Minoan religious aspects. Given the Minoan Great Goddess's hypothesized dominion over the underworld and fertility, the parallels with Persephone are noteworthy. This correlation might also shed light on the origins of the Eleusinian Mysteries, an initiation ceremony in Greek religion that centered around the myth of Demeter and Persephone.

It is essential to note that the process of assimilation was not a matter of direct adoption. The Greek goddesses are not mere reproductions of the Minoan deities. Instead, they represent a fusion of Minoan elements with local religious traditions, resulting in a unique synthesis that formed an integral part of the distinctive Greek religious landscape.

Moreover, the assimilation process speaks volumes about the nature of ancient religions, highlighting their fluidity and adaptability. The assimilation of Minoan goddesses into the Greek pantheon underscores how ancient societies would adopt, adapt, and transform foreign religious elements, weaving them into their own spiritual fabric to meet their specific cultural and societal needs.

In conclusion, the study of the assimilation of Minoan goddesses into the Greek pantheon offers an enlightening perspective on the continuity and evolution of ancient Mediterranean religions. This phenomenon testifies to the permeability of religious boundaries and the shared spiritual heritage that bound these ancient societies together.

The influence of Minoan religious concepts on Greek goddess worship

The fertile ground of religious syncretism in the ancient Mediterranean world allowed for the transference and adaptation of diverse spiritual concepts. In this context, the influence of Minoan religious beliefs and practices on the worship of goddesses in the Greek pantheon is of considerable scholarly interest. This influence provides a window into understanding the dynamic interaction between different religious traditions and their mutual shaping.

The pre-eminence of goddesses in Minoan religion appears to have substantially influenced the development of Greek goddess worship. The Minoans' matrifocal religious system, wherein the female deities held significant authority and influence, seemingly served as a precedent for the considerable role played by goddesses such as Hera, Athena, and Aphrodite in Greek mythology. The power, complexity, and central positions these figures assumed within the Greek pantheon might be viewed as an extension of the Minoan religious tradition, indicating a continued reverence for the divine feminine.

One of the most potent symbols of the intercultural religious interaction between the Minoans and the Greeks is found in the labyrinth motif. The labyrinth is heavily associated with the Minoan myth of the Minotaur, contained within the elaborate palace complex of Knossos, which was presumably used for religious ceremonies. In Greek mythology, the labyrinth becomes the setting for the hero Theseus to defeat the Minotaur, assisted by the princess Ariadne. Ariadne herself might be a later interpretation of an earlier Minoan goddess, symbolizing the intricate cultural and religious links between these two civilizations.

Sacred rituals of the Minoans, like the symbolic bull-leaping, seem to have been integrated into Greek religious rites, potentially underpinning some of their religious festivals. For instance, the Athenian festival of the "Oschophoria," which involved races and a procession, might bear ritualistic similarities with the athletic aspects of Minoan ceremonies. The Minoan rituals may thus have added layers of complexity to Greek religious practices, especially those related to goddess worship.

The snake, a potent symbol in Minoan religion often associated with their goddesses, notably made its way into Greek religious iconography. Goddesses such as Athena are often depicted with snakes, suggesting an assimilation of Minoan religious symbols. As Athena is a goddess of wisdom, the association with the snake—a symbol of rebirth, transformation, and healing—could hint at the transmission of Minoan spiritual concepts.

However, it is crucial to exercise caution while exploring the connections between Minoan and Greek religious practices. While there are clear indications of influence and transmission, it is equally probable that the process of assimilation involved a degree of transformation and reinterpretation of Minoan religious concepts in accordance with the socio-cultural context of ancient Greece.

In summary, the Minoan civilization's influence on Greek goddess worship provides a compelling example of religious syncretism and cultural exchange in the ancient Mediterranean world. The study of this interaction deepens our understanding of the development of Greek religious practices, emphasizing the interconnectedness of these ancient societies. It underscores how the religious concepts of one civilization can echo through time, shaping and being reshaped by the spiritual practices of successive cultures.

The Minoan-Mycenaean Connection: Religious Syncretism

Religious syncretism represents the amalgamation of diverse religious beliefs and practices, often as a result of cultural contact and exchange. A compelling illustration of this process can be observed in the interactions between the Minoan and Mycenaean civilizations, which occupied neighboring geographical spaces in the ancient Aegean. This chapter seeks to explore the multifaceted process of religious syncretism between these two societies, focusing particularly on the assimilation and adaptation of Minoan religious concepts within the Mycenaean context.

The contact between Minoan Crete and the Mycenaean civilization, primarily based on the Greek mainland, is well-documented in the archaeological record. This connection occurred during the Late Bronze Age, a time of significant socio-cultural interaction and exchange across the Mediterranean. Through this contact, a complex process of religious syncretism transpired, with the Mycenaeans seemingly assimilating various aspects of Minoan religion into their own spiritual practices.

One key area of this religious syncretism pertains to sacred iconography. The Minoan civilization produced a rich array of religious symbols and images, many of which appear to have been incorporated into Mycenaean religious practices. For example, the Minoan 'Double Axe', a potent symbol often associated with Minoan religious centers, appears on Mycenaean seals and in the frescoes of Mycenaean palaces. Similarly, the image of the 'Master of Animals', a figure controlling two wild creatures, seen often in Minoan art, also features in Mycenaean iconography.

Another significant aspect of the Minoan-Mycenaean religious syncretism pertains to ritual practice. The Minoan civilization is renowned for its elaborate ceremonies, such as bull-leaping and possibly labyrinth rituals. Elements of these ritual practices seem to have been integrated into Mycenaean religious ceremonies. However, it is worth noting that while the Mycenaeans may have borrowed aspects of Minoan rituals, they likely adapted them to suit their socio-cultural and religious context.

The Minoan influence on Mycenaean religious architecture provides another intriguing avenue of exploration. Minoan palatial complexes such as Knossos were intricate structures likely used for religious rituals. The architectural designs of these structures, notably the 'megaron', a central audience hall, appears to have influenced Mycenaean palace design. The Mycenaeans might have viewed the construction of similar architectural forms as a way to tap into the spiritual power of the Minoans.

It is equally noteworthy that this process of religious syncretism was not merely a one-way transfer. While the Mycenaeans were profoundly influenced by Minoan religious beliefs and practices, they reinterpreted and adapted these elements according to their own religious perceptions and social norms. This reciprocal exchange underscores the dynamism inherent in religious syncretism, a process that involves not merely borrowing but also adapting and transforming.

Although the process of Minoan-Mycenaean religious syncretism is evident, many aspects of it remain shrouded in mystery due to the fragmentary nature of the archaeological record and the complexities involved in interpreting religious practices from physical remains. Nevertheless, this syncretism highlights the fluid nature of ancient Mediterranean religions, demonstrating how religious ideas can cross cultural boundaries, leading to a richer, more multifaceted spiritual landscape.

Understanding the religious syncretism between the Minoans and Mycenaeans provides critical insights into the spiritual life of the Late Bronze Age Aegean. It highlights how ancient societies did not exist in isolation but were interconnected, influencing and being influenced by their neighbors in profound ways. These interactions, particularly in the sphere of religion, led to the development of complex spiritual systems that reflect a rich tapestry of cultural exchange and mutual influence.

Evidence of cultural exchange between the Minoans and Mycenaeans

The Minoan and Mycenaean civilizations, flourishing during the Bronze Age, occupy a crucial position in the annals of ancient Mediterranean history. The cultural exchanges between these two civilizations, manifested particularly in the domains of art, architecture, religion, and language, provide a fascinating area of study. This chapter will dissect these elements of cultural exchange, underlining the depth of interconnectedness and the symbiotic relationship that existed between the Minoans and the Mycenaeans.

Archaeological evidence sheds considerable light on the extent of material and cultural interchange between these two civilizations. The Minoans, hailing from Crete, were renowned for their vibrant frescoes, intricate pottery, and elaborate palatial complexes, and the influence of these elements is evident in the subsequent Mycenaean culture.

One of the most compelling areas of cultural exchange resides in the domain of art. The Minoans are recognized for their naturalistic style of art, encompassing lively frescoes depicting scenes from nature, religious ceremonies, and everyday life. This art style, with its emphasis on dynamism and naturalism, seems to have influenced Mycenaean fresco art, as similar themes and stylistic elements appear in the wall paintings of Mycenaean palaces. Furthermore, Minoan-styled pottery has been unearthed in Mycenaean contexts, indicating not just a trade in goods but also an exchange in aesthetic styles.

In the realm of architecture, the influence of Minoan design on Mycenaean structures is evident. The Minoans are known for their complex palatial centers, such as those found in Knossos and Phaistos, characterized by features like a central courtyard, labyrinthine layout, and advanced drainage systems. Similar architectural elements are found in Mycenaean palaces, such as the palace at Pylos, suggesting a Minoan influence on Mycenaean architectural design.

The area of language provides another lens through which to explore Minoan-Mycenaean cultural exchange. The decipherment of Linear B, a script used by the Mycenaeans, has revealed the presence of loanwords from the Minoan language. This linguistic borrowing suggests a degree of bilingualism or at least familiarity with the Minoan language among the Mycenaeans, hinting at a deeper level of cultural interaction.

The domain of religion, as previously discussed, also exhibits a rich cross-pollination between Minoan and Mycenaean beliefs. The incorporation of Minoan deities into the Mycenaean pantheon, the borrowing of religious symbols, and the adoption of ritual practices exemplify this religious syncretism.

Nevertheless, it is essential to note that this process of cultural exchange was not unidirectional. The Mycenaeans were not mere passive recipients of Minoan culture but actively engaged with and transformed these cultural elements. For instance, while Mycenaean art was heavily influenced by Minoan models, it also displayed distinct characteristics, such as a greater emphasis on martial and hunting scenes.

In conclusion, the Minoan and Mycenaean civilizations were intricately connected, engaging in a dynamic process of cultural exchange and mutual influence. The traces of this interaction, encapsulated in shared artistic styles, architectural designs, linguistic elements, and religious practices, underline the degree of cultural interconnectedness in the ancient Mediterranean. Such interconnectedness underscores the fact that civilizations are not insular entities but part of a broader cultural landscape, continuously shaping and being shaped by their interactions with others. Understanding these cultural exchanges enhances our comprehension of the complexity and diversity of ancient Mediterranean cultures, revealing a dynamic and interconnected world.

The adoption and adaptation of Minoan religious elements by the Mycenaeans

Exploring the juncture between Minoan and Mycenaean civilizations, one observes a fascinating dynamic: the Mycenaeans did not merely absorb the religious elements of the Minoans but adapted them to their own cultural and societal context. The process of adoption and adaptation encapsulates the essence of syncretism, a fundamental phenomenon in the evolution of religious practices.

Unraveling the rich tapestry of Mycenaean religion, one discerns a distinct Minoan thread. The Mycenaeans seem to have incorporated several deities from the Minoan pantheon into their own religious belief system. The "Mistress of Animals," a prominent figure in Minoan religion, appears to have found her way into the Mycenaean pantheon, albeit in a modified form. The Mycenaeans adopted this powerful nature deity but reinterpreted her through their own cultural lens, emphasizing aspects such as dominion over wild animals that were of particular significance in their society.

Moreover, the ritual practices of the Mycenaeans show traces of Minoan influence. The Minoan tradition of peak sanctuaries, for instance, found an echo in Mycenaean practices. These were places of worship, usually located at the summit of mountains, suggesting a veneration of natural features and phenomena. While the Mycenaeans did not emulate the Minoan peak sanctuary tradition exactly, they adapted the concept to their own context, establishing sanctuaries in locations that held natural or symbolic significance.

Another striking example of the Mycenaeans' adaptation of Minoan religious elements can be seen in their treatment of sacred symbols. The double axe, a symbol of potent significance in Minoan religion, was adopted by the Mycenaeans and appears in various Mycenaean contexts. Yet, its meaning and usage were likely altered, reflecting the transformation that often accompanies cultural transfer. Thus, it is essential to view these borrowed symbols not merely as copies of Minoan religious elements but as entities that acquired new layers of meaning and function within the Mycenaean religious context.

The realm of religious art also provides compelling evidence of this adoption and adaptation dynamic. The Mycenaeans appear to have been profoundly influenced by Minoan fresco painting, adopting its vibrant naturalistic style. However, they also imparted their own unique artistic character onto these frescoes. For instance, the themes depicted in Mycenaean frescoes often diverge from those in Minoan ones, reflecting different religious emphases and societal values.

Lastly, the use of the Linear B script, derived from the Minoan Linear A, provides indirect evidence of the Mycenaeans' adoption of certain Minoan religious concepts. The Mycenaeans not only borrowed the script but also incorporated Minoan religious vocabulary, suggesting an adoption of associated religious ideas.

However, it must be emphasized that the process of adoption and adaptation was far from straightforward. As scholars like Jan Driessen have pointed out, the Mycenaeans were selective in what they chose to adopt from the Minoans. Furthermore, the process was not unidirectional: the Minoans too likely adopted and adapted elements from the Mycenaeans, hinting at a reciprocal cultural exchange.

In summary, the religious sphere provides a potent arena to explore the intricate interplay of adoption and adaptation between the Minoans and Mycenaeans. This complex process of cultural exchange underscores the fluidity of ancient religions and the transformative power of intercultural interactions. Understanding this process deepens our knowledge of both Minoan and Mycenaean civilizations, revealing their dynamic nature and their capacity to interact with, learn from, and influence each other in profound ways.

The synthesis of Minoan and Mycenaean religious practices

The confluence of Minoan and Mycenaean civilizations brought about a compelling synthesis of religious practices. This amalgamation provides a compelling example of how religious beliefs and rituals can intermingle and evolve through the process of cultural exchange, reflecting the societies' ability to adapt and assimilate diverse elements in their religious expressions.

At the onset, one must consider the issue of linear progression in the context of Minoan and Mycenaean religious synthesis. It is tempting to envisage this process as a straightforward transmission from Minoan to Mycenaean. However, scholars such as Emily Kearns argue for a more nuanced perspective, suggesting that the process was reciprocal and multifaceted, a veritable give-and-take between the two cultures.

Indeed, the archaeological record illustrates this complex interchange. Minoan elements such as the presence of sacred symbols like the double axe, nature veneration as seen in peak sanctuaries, and the potent religious imagery in frescoes found parallels in Mycenaean practices, albeit often with unique reinterpretations. For instance, the Mycenaeans adopted the Minoan practice of peak sanctuaries but tended to establish them in locations of particular strategic or symbolic importance to their society.

Similarly, the double axe, a sacred symbol for the Minoans, became integrated into the Mycenaean religious iconography. However, its representation and contextual use in Mycenaean culture, especially in frescoes, pottery, and seals, suggest that the symbol might have evolved to encompass new meanings and functions.

Furthermore, the Mycenaeans appeared to have incorporated several Minoan deities into their pantheon, reflecting a significant aspect of religious synthesis. Yet, it was not merely a matter of adopting new gods; rather, it involved a sophisticated process of theological reinterpretation. The Mycenaeans seemed to have taken Minoan deities, such as the 'Mistress of Animals', and melded them into their religious framework, often emphasizing different aspects of these deities that resonated with their socio-cultural context.

However, the synthesis of Minoan and Mycenaean religious practices was not unidirectional. As scholars like Jan Driessen argue, the Minoans too likely incorporated aspects of Mycenaean religious culture. The evidence, although sparse, points towards the possibility of Mycenaean influences in later Minoan religious practices, indicating that the Minoans might have absorbed certain Mycenaean religious ideas and rituals.

The blending of Minoan and Mycenaean religious elements eventually gave rise to unique expressions of spirituality that carried echoes of both cultures. The use of the Linear B script, a derivative of the Minoan Linear A, in the recording of religious rites and offerings attests to this synthesis. The Mycenaeans not only adopted the script but also a significant portion of the Minoan religious lexicon. This interchange of religious language underscores the extent of the religious fusion that occurred between these two civilizations.

In conclusion, the synthesis of Minoan and Mycenaean religious practices is a rich and complex phenomenon, characterized by reciprocal exchanges, adoption, adaptation, and reinterpretation. It underlines the dynamism and fluidity inherent in religious systems and offers valuable insights into how ancient civilizations interacted and influenced each other's spiritual landscapes. The religious fusion between the Minoans and Mycenaeans not only enhanced our understanding of their individual religious cultures but also provided a unique perspective on the broader evolution of religious practices in the ancient Aegean world.

Mycenaean Religion Revisited: Minoan Influences

It is incumbent upon us, as scholars of antiquity, to delve back into the hallowed halls of time and re-examine the multifaceted nature of Mycenaean religion. One can achieve a richer understanding of this complex religious system by scrutinising the notable influence of Minoan culture and practices.

Inherent within the discussion of Minoan influences on Mycenaean religion is the issue of cultural transmission. The relationship between the Minoans and Mycenaeans was not one-sided. As outlined by Anthony Snodgrass, the Mycenaeans demonstrated a propensity for selective adaptation, adopting certain elements of Minoan culture and religion, whilst leaving others untouched, and transforming yet others to suit their socio-cultural milieu.

One of the most potent symbols of Minoan influence on Mycenaean religion is the enigmatic figure of the 'Mistress of Animals', a goddess associated with nature and animals in Minoan belief. Frescoes and sealstones from Mycenaean contexts display this figure, suggesting the transference and possibly the adaptation of this deity into the Mycenaean pantheon.

Moreover, there is substantial evidence of Minoan ritualistic influence. The Minoan practice of peak sanctuaries, sites of worship usually located atop mountains, was adopted and modified by the Mycenaeans. They strategically located their peak sanctuaries near palatial centres or critical trade routes, a divergence from the Minoan practice of siting sanctuaries in more remote, natural locales.

Yet, in this exchange, one must not overlook the issue of reinterpretation. The Mycenaeans did not merely copy Minoan religious elements but recontextualised them to fit their religious framework. An illustrative case is the double axe, a sacred symbol in Minoan Crete. While the Mycenaeans adopted the symbol, they often placed it within different contexts, hinting at an evolution of its symbolic significance within their religious system.

Minoan influence also extended to ritualistic practices. Archaeological evidence points towards the use of Minoan-style libation vessels and the adoption of ritualistic practices such as bull leaping, attesting to a level of religious interaction between these two Aegean civilizations.

Importantly, the question of decipherment and translation of Linear B tablets, which record Mycenaean administrative activities, offers further insights. The presence of deities with names possibly derived from the Minoan pantheon underlines the adoption and modification of Minoan religious elements. However, as Emily Kearns cautions, we must be careful not to overstate the case for Minoan influence given the linguistic and cultural barriers to perfect translation.

On a concluding note, while there is substantial evidence of Minoan influence on Mycenaean religion, one must acknowledge that the process was complex and multifaceted. It was not a simple case of adoption but rather a sophisticated process of selective borrowing, adaptation, and reinterpretation, a testament to the Mycenaeans' creative engagement with Minoan culture. The discussion warrants a more profound exploration, encouraging students to critically engage with the existing archaeological and textual evidence, and to consider the broader implications for the study of cultural interactions in the ancient world.

Traces of Minoan religious practices in Mycenaean artifacts and inscriptions

The complexity and richness of the Mycenaean religious landscape is inextricably entwined with Minoan influences, a connection manifested conspicuously in archaeological findings and epigraphical records. The discernible imprints of Minoan religious practices in Mycenaean artifacts and inscriptions engender a nuanced understanding of the trans-cultural interplay of these ancient civilizations.

A salient example of such imprints is evident in the religious iconography on Mycenaean frescoes and sealstones, a form of miniature carving that originated in the Minoan civilization. Prominent among these is the image of the 'Mistress of Animals', a central deity in the Minoan pantheon associated with nature and animal life. The diffusion of this icon into Mycenaean art is indicative of the assimilation of Minoan goddesses into the Mycenaean religious cosmos.

Another example of Minoan influence is found in the appearance of sacred symbols on Mycenaean artifacts. The double axe or "labrys", a paramount Minoan religious symbol, is recurrently depicted in Mycenaean contexts, demonstrating the borrowing and possible transformation of its symbolic meanings by the Mycenaeans. Furthermore, Minoan-style libation vessels found in Mycenaean sites suggest the adoption of Minoan ritualistic practices, highlighting the transference of religious behaviour between these cultures.

Evidence of Minoan religious practices also permeates the Mycenaean epigraphical records. In particular, the Linear B tablets, the earliest form of Greek, offer profound insights into the spiritual interchange between the Minoans and Mycenaeans. Names of gods that potentially originate from the Minoan pantheon have been identified in these tablets, though the interpretation of these deities remains subject to scholarly debate due to the complex nature of deciphering ancient languages. For instance, the name "Diwia", possibly related to the later Greek goddess Dione, and "Potnia", the term often used in Minoan Crete for 'Lady' or 'Mistress', are frequently encountered in these tablets, suggesting a degree of religious confluence.

However, as Jan N. Bremmer rightly advises, we must approach this evidence with measured caution. The Mycenaean adoption of Minoan religious elements was not a mere mimicry but a selective and creative process. Elements were taken, adapted, and recontextualised to fit the Mycenaean religious and societal structure, a testament to the dynamic and evolving nature of religious syncretism.

To delve deeper, it is recommended that students critically engage with the archaeological and epigraphic evidence. Examine the artifacts and inscriptions, contemplate their original context, consider their symbolism, and question their function. Further, consider the challenges inherent in the interpretation of these artifacts and inscriptions. Such a study will stimulate not only a richer understanding of the Mycenaean and Minoan religions but also a greater appreciation of the intricate process of cultural exchange and adaptation in ancient civilizations.

The potential significance of Minoan rituals in Mycenaean religious life

The integration of Minoan rituals into Mycenaean religious life suggests an intercultural influence that extends beyond the realm of deities and iconography, providing compelling insights into the dynamic religiosity of the Bronze Age Aegean world.

The influence of Minoan ritualistic practices on Mycenaean religious life is most discernible in the realm of sacred architecture. Minoan peak sanctuaries, for instance, are believed to have played a significant role in shaping Mycenaean open-air cults. These hilltop sanctuaries, uniquely Minoan in their architectural conception, served as communal religious spaces where rituals were performed, including animal sacrifices, votive offerings, and feasts. Mycenaean adoption of such open-air ritual spaces suggests a possible emulation of Minoan ritualistic practices.

Another noteworthy influence is observed in the ceremonial function of Minoan libation vessels, which were frequently used in religious ceremonies for pouring liquid offerings to the gods. Mycenaean artifacts and frescoes depict similar ritual practices, suggesting an appropriation of this Minoan religious custom. The importance of this shared ritual practice is underscored by its continuity in later Greek religion.

The significance of Minoan ritualistic dance in Mycenaean religious life is another area of intriguing speculation. Dance played a central role in Minoan religious ceremonies, serving as a means of communication with the divine. Several Mycenaean frescoes exhibit scenes of dancing figures, leading some scholars to propose that Minoan ritualistic dance was adopted and transformed in the Mycenaean religious context.

The influence of Minoan bull-leaping rituals on Mycenaean religious life is another subject of scholarly interest. This ritual, depicted extensively in Minoan frescoes, involved acrobats leaping over a bull's horns in a dangerous and highly choreographed performance. While not directly represented in Mycenaean iconography, the prominence of bovine symbols in Mycenaean artifacts may suggest an adoption of Minoan bull-related rituals, albeit in an altered form.

However, as Anthony Snodgrass advises, we must caution against simplistic interpretations of these influences. Minoan rituals, like all religious practices, were embedded in a specific social, cultural, and historical context. Their transplantation into the Mycenaean world would necessitate adaptation to the local religious landscape, possibly leading to substantial transformations in their significance and execution.

As an exercise, students might critically evaluate the primary archaeological and iconographic evidence for Minoan ritual practices in the Mycenaean religious context. It may be useful to consider the potential challenges and limitations inherent in such an analysis, including issues of interpretation, the problem of archaeological context, and the possible evolution of ritual practices over time. This critical approach will cultivate an understanding of not only the tangible aspects of ancient religious practices but also the intangible elements, such as belief systems, religious experiences, and societal structures.

Identifying Minoan religious symbols and their integration into Mycenaean religious iconography

Identifying the religious symbols of an ancient civilization and tracing their integration into the religious practices of a succeeding culture is a complex and nuanced task. This is especially true for the Minoan civilization and its influence on the Mycenaeans. The challenge lies not only in the decipherment of the symbols themselves but also in discerning their evolving significance in different cultural contexts.

The ritualistic practices of the Minoans, as reflected in the archaeological record, offer an insightful lens through which to examine the integration of Minoan religious symbols into the Mycenaean religious iconography. The Minoans were a society characterized by a rich symbolic language, the substance of which profoundly influenced the Mycenaeans.

One salient symbol in Minoan ritualistic practice is the 'Horns of Consecration.' This symbol, frequently represented in Minoan sacred architecture and artifacts, is believed to have been derived from the horns of the sacred bull. Minoan bull-leaping rituals offer compelling evidence for the bull's sacred status. This symbol, initially a tangible reference to Minoan ritual, was subsequently incorporated into Mycenaean religious iconography, where it often appears on frescoes and seals, albeit in a stylized form, emphasizing the continuity and adaptation of Minoan symbols in Mycenaean culture.

Another potent Minoan symbol is the double axe, or Labrys. Frequently found in Minoan sanctuaries and shrines, it is hypothesized to have had a significant ritualistic function, possibly associated with animal sacrifice. In the Mycenaean context, the double axe appears in various settings, notably in the Mycenaean palace of Pylos, suggesting a continuing sacred significance, likely shaped by its Minoan antecedents.

The role of Minoan ritualistic dance in the religious life of the Minoans offers further symbolism for examination. The dynamic images of dancing figures in Minoan frescoes provide a glimpse into the kinetic aspect of Minoan religious practice. The subsequent appearance of similar dancing scenes in Mycenaean iconography may suggest an assimilation of this symbolic expression of divine communion.

Snake symbolism, deriving from the Minoan 'Snake Goddess' figurines, represents another potent element incorporated into Mycenaean religious iconography. Although the exact symbolic meaning of these figures remains a matter of academic debate, the frequency of serpentine motifs in Mycenaean artifacts, especially on signet rings, reflects the continued significance of this Minoan symbol.

While tracing these symbol integrations, one should heed Emily Kearns' counsel about the multivalence of ancient symbols. These symbols likely held multiple, overlapping meanings, shaped by their specific religious, social, and cultural contexts. As such, the adoption of Minoan symbols by the Mycenaeans does not necessarily imply an exact replication of their original Minoan meanings. Instead, it signals a dynamic process of cultural borrowing and adaptation, demonstrating the inherent fluidity of religious symbols and practices.

Students are encouraged to study Minoan and Mycenaean religious iconography closely, examining the visual language of symbols as an integral component of religious practices. This exploration should ideally incorporate a critical evaluation of the methodological challenges inherent in this area of study, including issues of subjective interpretation, the contextual complexity of symbols, and the potential for change in symbolic meanings over time. Such an analysis would offer not only an understanding of the symbols themselves but also a window into the dynamic nature of ancient religiosity, where symbols served as vital components in the negotiation of sacred meanings.

The Transition to Greek Religion: Merging of Cultures

The development of religious practices and beliefs in ancient Greece is a rich and complex narrative, woven from the threads of diverse cultural influences. Central to this narrative is the interaction between the Minoan and Mycenaean civilizations, and the subsequent emergence of classical Greek religion. The synthesis of Minoan and Mycenaean religious elements, coupled with their adaptation to local contexts, marked a significant phase in the genesis of Greek religion.

The Mycenaean civilization, flourishing on the mainland of Greece from circa 1600-1100 BCE, was deeply influenced by the preceding Minoan civilization of Crete. As evident from archaeological and textual evidence, the Mycenaeans adopted and adapted a significant amount of Minoan religious practices, symbols, and deities. This interaction marked the first substantial cultural merging that contributed to the formation of Greek religion.

An important caveat, articulated by Anthony Snodgrass, is the need to avoid simplistic cultural categorizations. The incorporation of Minoan elements into Mycenaean religion was not a one-directional, homogeneous process. It was a complex interaction marked by selectivity, localization, and synthesis, reflecting the dynamic and nuanced nature of cultural exchanges.

Religious practices and beliefs, in particular, are deeply ingrained in a society's worldview and are often characterized by a high degree of flexibility and syncretism. The Minoan-Mycenaean interaction exemplifies this flexibility. For example, some Minoan deities, discernible through iconographic and epigraphic evidence, seem to have been integrated into the Mycenaean pantheon, sometimes under Mycenaean names. This is indicative of a process of syncretism, wherein deities from different cultures merge and evolve in a complex matrix of cultural interaction.

Following the fall of the Mycenaean civilization, Greece entered a period known as the 'Dark Ages' (c. 1100–800 BCE). The religious practices during this period are shrouded in obscurity due to the paucity of archaeological and literary evidence. However, it is generally accepted that the religious practices and beliefs of this period, influenced by the preceding Minoan and Mycenaean religious traditions, played a significant role in shaping the religious landscape of the ensuing Archaic period (800-480 BCE). This period witnessed the consolidation of the Greek pantheon and the establishment of the religious practices that characterized classical Greek religion.

A quintessential example of this process is the goddess Athena. Scholars like Emily Kearns have noted possible Minoan antecedents to Athena, primarily in the

form of the Minoan 'Snake Goddess'. The synthesis of this Minoan influence, coupled with Mycenaean and other influences, resulted in the formation of the complex figure of Athena, who emerged as a key deity in the classical Greek pantheon.

The transition to Greek religion was not an abrupt change but rather a gradual evolution characterized by continuity and transformation. The cultural merging between Minoan and Mycenaean civilizations played a crucial role in this evolution, contributing significant elements to the rich tapestry of Greek religion.

Students are encouraged to approach the study of Greek religion as a dynamic continuum, focusing not just on the religious practices themselves but also on their cultural and historical contexts. This perspective underscores the necessity to view ancient religions as integral components of their respective cultures, deeply intertwined with broader societal, political, and economic systems. Additionally, the study should be an exploration of the complex processes of cultural interaction, adaptation, and synthesis that have shaped religious traditions throughout history.

The gradual transformation from Minoan and Mycenaean religions to early Greek religion

The transition from Minoan and Mycenaean religious traditions to early Greek religion is a topic of significant interest and complexity in the realm of ancient history. This transformation involved intricate processes of cultural assimilation, adaptation, and innovation, all woven into the evolving fabric of societal norms and structures. This evolutionary progression from the prehistoric religions of the Minoan and Mycenaean civilizations to the polytheistic systems of early Greek religion offers profound insights into the continuity and change in religious practices over time.

Minoan civilization (c. 2700-1420 BCE), which flourished on the island of Crete, is characterized by an apparent emphasis on nature worship, as evidenced by its various religious symbols and iconography. A preponderance of the sacred symbols of the Minoans pertained to natural elements, such as trees, mountains, animals, and the sea, indicative of an ecospiritual focus.

The succeeding Mycenaean civilization (c. 1600-1100 BCE) on the mainland of Greece, while significantly influenced by Minoan religion, began to display a more formalized religious system with a structured pantheon of gods and goddesses. Mycenaean religion also demonstrated a heightened emphasis on ritual practices, notably those associated with the burial of the dead and propitiatory offerings to the gods.

From Mycenae to Olympus: Tracing the Evolution of Greek Religion

In the period of transition between these Bronze Age cultures and the advent of the Greek Dark Ages (c. 1100-800 BCE), significant transformations began to occur in the religious landscape. There is substantial archaeological and textual evidence indicating a continuity of religious practices and beliefs, particularly in terms of the reverence for certain deities and sacred symbols.

The onset of the Archaic period (c. 800-480 BCE) marked a period of extensive religious, political, and societal changes in Greece. As Jan N. Bremmer elucidates, the Archaic period witnessed the solidification of the Greek pantheon and the formalization of religious practices. During this period, the gods and goddesses of the Greek pantheon, many of whom can be traced back to Minoan and Mycenaean precursors, began to acquire the characteristics they are known for in Classical Greek religion.

This transformation was not an abrupt shift but a gradual evolution marked by continuity and adaptation. While many of the old religious symbols and deities were preserved, they were also reinterpreted and redefined to fit the evolving societal and cultural norms of the Greek mainland.

For instance, Zeus, the chief deity in the Mycenaean pantheon, retained his position of prominence in Greek religion, but his persona and attributes underwent significant changes. Similarly, the Minoan 'Mistress of Animals,' a potent symbol of nature worship, was assimilated into the figure of Artemis, the Greek goddess of the hunt.

This period also marked a distinct shift towards anthropomorphism in the portrayal of gods, a key characteristic of Greek religion. The deities, instead of being represented by symbols or animal forms, began to be depicted in human forms, complete with human emotions and characteristics.

From a pedagogical perspective, understanding this transition involves discerning patterns of continuity and change, adaptation, and innovation. By studying the gradual transformation from Minoan and Mycenaean religions to early Greek religion, one can gain profound insights into the dynamic nature of religious evolution and its deep interconnection with the broader societal and cultural contexts.

In analyzing this process, it is beneficial to draw parallels with analogous transitions in other cultures and periods. For instance, the transformation from prehistoric pagan practices to organized religions in other parts of the world offers interesting comparative perspectives. These comparative studies can engender a broader and deeper understanding of the complex processes that shape the evolution of religious practices and beliefs over time.

The impact of Minoan and Mycenaean religious elements on the development of Greek mythology

The profound impact of Minoan and Mycenaean religious elements on the development of Greek mythology is palpable in the continuation, reinterpretation, and embellishment of ancient themes, figures, and narratives. Indeed, as in other fields, it is in mythology that the process of cultural synthesis—whereby aspects of the Minoan and Mycenaean religious tradition are melded into a new, distinctively Greek system of belief—becomes particularly evident. The interplay of continuity and change in this transformation reflects the complex dynamics of cultural transmission and adaptation.

The Minoan civilization, being one of the earliest in the Aegean world, had a substantial influence on the mythology that developed subsequently. The symbolic elements from Minoan religious practices, such as the bull, the double axe (labrys), and the snake goddess, among others, found their way into Greek myths. For instance, the Minoan bull-leaping ritual is often connected to the Greek myth of Theseus and the Minotaur, where the bull, labyrinth, and the ruler of Knossos form integral elements of the narrative.

The Minoan 'Mistress of Animals', a prominent figure in Minoan iconography who holds sway over animals, particularly birds and snakes, can be traced in the Greek pantheon to goddesses like Artemis and Athena. Such transferences illustrate the assimilation of Minoan divinities and their iconography into the evolving corpus of Greek mythology.

The Mycenaean civilization, which succeeded the Minoan, also left indelible marks on Greek mythology. Mycenaean deities, including Zeus, Hera, Poseidon, and Athena, among others, found their way into the classical Greek pantheon and mythology. However, these deities, while maintaining their names and some aspects of their character, underwent transformations to fit the evolving cultural and religious landscape of ancient Greece.

Linear B tablets from the Mycenaean period provide valuable insights into the early forms of these deities and their roles, offering a tangible connection to the classical Greek gods. For instance, the Mycenaean 'di-wi-ja', believed to be an early form of the goddess Hera, or 'Diwo', thought to be Zeus, can be seen as predecessors to the deities known in later Greek mythology.

The transition from the Bronze Age cultures to the Greek world involved not only the continuation of older deities and symbols but also the creation of new narratives around these figures. The re-contextualization of older figures in new narratives, such as the heroic adventures of Heracles, the exploits of Odysseus, or the trials of Perseus, demonstrates the innovative aspect of this cultural transformation.

By integrating these pre-existing religious elements, early Greek mythology bridged the gap between the older Bronze Age civilizations and the new socio-political reality of the Greek city-states. This synthesis reflects the dynamic interplay between continuity and change in the cultural evolution, where ancient religious symbols and deities were not discarded but rather redefined and incorporated into a new, complex system of mythology and belief.

As an exercise, students are encouraged to delve into a specific Greek myth, such as the Labours of Heracles, and attempt to trace the potential Minoan and Mycenaean influences within it. By doing so, students will gain an understanding of the complexity of cultural transmission and the creative reinterpretation that characterizes the development of Greek mythology.

An understanding of this transformation is also valuable when considering parallel phenomena in other religious systems. The adaptation and evolution of religious elements, seen in the transition from Minoan and Mycenaean religions to early Greek religion, offer valuable comparative perspectives on similar processes in other cultures. Such comparative analysis can broaden our understanding of the mechanisms of cultural adaptation and the complex interplay between continuity and change in the evolution of religious beliefs and practices.

The emergence of iconic Greek deities and their connections to earlier Minoan and Mycenaean divinities

The development of the iconic Greek pantheon is a fascinating amalgamation of continuity, adaptation, and innovation, a narrative woven from the diverse threads of Minoan and Mycenaean divinities. This evolution is demonstrative of the mechanisms of cultural synthesis, whereby disparate elements coalesce into a coherent and interconnected system of belief.

Minoan religion, flourishing during the Bronze Age in Crete, is renowned for its vibrant iconography and variety of divine figures, with a particular emphasis on nature, fertility, and female divinities. One such divinity is the 'Snake Goddess' or 'Priestess', often depicted in Minoan frescoes and figurines with open arms, clutching snakes, and wearing a flounced skirt and exposed bodice. This figure is considered by some scholars as a precursor to later Greek goddesses, such as Hera, Demeter, and possibly Athena, given their shared emphasis on fertility, protection, and domestic spaces.

Moreover, the emphasis on bulls in Minoan religion—demonstrated in their iconography and potentially in the ritual practice of bull-leaping—also found resonances in the Greek religious imagination, most notably in the myths of the Minotaur and Europa, where the bull is a central figure. These continuities suggest a significant degree of influence from Minoan divinities on the formation of early Greek mythology and religious practice.

Mycenaean religious elements, as preserved in Linear B tablets, also reveal early formations of the later Greek pantheon. Names recognisable in the Homeric and Hesiodic traditions appear on these tablets, including Zeus (Di-we), Hera (E-ra), Poseidon (Po-se-da-o), Athena (A-ta-na), and Dionysus (Di-wo-nu-so). This lends weight to the argument that the Mycenaean pantheon became an integral part of the Greek pantheon.

It is important to note, however, that these divine figures underwent significant transformation as they transitioned from the Minoan and Mycenaean world to that of the Greeks. The divine figures of the Bronze Age Aegean may have shared names and certain characteristics with their Greek counterparts, but they also possessed unique features that reflected the specific religious, cultural, and social contexts of these early civilisations. The Greek divinities, while maintaining links with their Bronze Age predecessors, were redefined to suit the values, needs, and understandings of the emerging Greek culture.

The goddess Athena provides an instructive example of this transformation. The Mycenaean 'A-ta-na' may represent an early form of Athena, yet the goddess revered in Classical Athens differs in key aspects. While the Bronze Age deity may have been associated with the palace and potentially warfare, the Athena of classical Greece is a complex figure embodying wisdom, warfare, weaving, and the protective deity of the polis. This evolution reflects the adaptation and reinterpretation of older religious elements in response to changing cultural contexts.

To facilitate an in-depth understanding of these processes, students are encouraged to select an iconic Greek deity, trace their potential origins in Minoan and Mycenaean religious elements, and examine how their characteristics evolved over time. Consider not only the continuities but also the changes that occurred in these divine figures' transition from the Bronze Age cultures to the Greek world. This exercise will help students understand the complex interplay of continuity, adaptation, and innovation in cultural and religious evolution.

The emergence of the iconic Greek pantheon from the rich tapestry of Minoan and Mycenaean religious beliefs offers a case study in the mechanisms of cultural synthesis. It demonstrates how older religious elements are not merely discarded with the advent of a new culture, but instead redefined, integrated, and recontextualised to form an evolving system of belief that continues to resonate through the ages.

Conclusion

The ancient cultures of Minoan Crete and the Mycenaean world left an indelible imprint on the religious landscape of Ancient Greece, both in terms of the pantheon of gods and goddesses and the ritual practices that suffused daily life. An amalgamation of Minoan and Mycenaean religious elements, synthesised with indigenous practices and beliefs, led to the emergence of a distinctively Greek religious system.

The Minoan civilization, with its notable emphasis on nature and fertility, significantly shaped the perception of divinity in the Greek mind. Elements such as the snake goddess, bull symbolism, and other ritually significant iconography found in Minoan religion, contributed to the early formation of Greek mythology. Mycenaean religious elements, on the other hand, most strikingly captured in Linear B tablets, provided names and epithets that would eventually become integral to the Greek pantheon.

However, as these elements transitioned into the Greek context, they were subject to adaptation and transformation, attesting to the dynamic nature of religious evolution. Divine figures that traced their origins to the Minoan and Mycenaean period were redefined to align with the specific socio-cultural demands of the Greeks. The example of Athena is a testament to this transformative process.

Reflection on the Enduring Impact of Ancient Mediterranean Civilizations on Modern Understanding of Religious History

Ancient Mediterranean civilizations, particularly the Minoan and Mycenaean cultures, have profoundly shaped our modern understanding of religious history. They remind us that religions do not develop in isolation; rather, they emerge from intricate patterns of cultural interaction, adaptation, and reinterpretation.

These civilizations elucidate how older religious elements can be retained, altered, and repurposed to fit the contours of new cultural landscapes. In doing so, they contribute to a historical continuity that links the religious imaginations of different epochs, allowing us to trace the threads of religious evolution over time.

Furthermore, these ancient civilizations underscore the importance of iconography, myth-making, and ritual practice in defining the sacred and constructing meaningful religious experiences. These aspects continue to influence our interpretation of religious phenomena and our broader understanding of the sacred, the divine, and the role of religion in society.

The Value of Studying Cultural Syncretism in Enriching Our Knowledge of Ancient Civilizations and Their Interconnectedness

Studying the synthesis of Minoan, Mycenaean, and Greek religious cultures underscores the value of understanding ancient civilizations as interconnected entities rather than isolated phenomena. Cultural syncretism is not merely a process of addition but a dynamic interplay of retention, rejection, adaptation, and innovation.

By examining the intercultural exchanges between these Bronze Age civilizations and early Greece, we can better comprehend the mechanisms of cultural and religious transformation. This enhances our understanding of how societies assimilate foreign elements, adjust them to align with their cultural framework, and create a hybrid system that possesses its unique character while reflecting its multifaceted heritage.

In essence, the exploration of cultural syncretism in the ancient Mediterranean enriches our understanding of the dynamism of human cultures. It invites us to view cultural evolution as a dialogue, an intricate process of negotiation, wherein elements of different origins coalesce to forge a distinct identity.

Therefore, the study of Minoan and Mycenaean influences on Greek religion not only unveils the intricacies of ancient religious systems but also offers broader insights into the nature of cultural exchange and evolution. It urges us to recognize the persistent threads of human ingenuity that weave together disparate cultural elements, crafting a rich tapestry of religious belief that continues to inform and fascinate us in the present.